# NNAT

Naglieri Nonverbal Ability Test®

# SERIAL

# REASONING

## A step by step STUDY GUIDE

# GRADE 3

## by MindMine

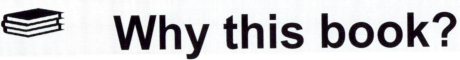

# Why this book?

Cognitive abilities are brain-based skills related with the mechanisms of learning, memorizing, and paying attention rather than actual knowledge that was learned. **The more you practice, the more you develop** your cognitive flexibility.

- This book is designed to teach concepts and skills in a way kids understand with ease.

- Concepts are taught step by step and introduced incrementally.

- The focus of this book is to provide a solid foundation to fundamental skills. All the skills taught in the book will collectively increase the knowledge and will help kids to prepare and take the test confidently.

- Practice tests that are available in the market may not provide all the concepts needed. This book is aimed to give both concepts and practice.

# Who should buy this book?

- 3rd graders taking NNAT test (NNAT2)

- 2nd graders planning to take NNAT (Any Form)

- 1st, 2nd and 3rd graders seeking to enrich their Nonverbal reasoning and Problem-solving skills

# 📚 What is covered?

This book extensively covers **SERIAL REASONING** section of **NNAT Test** with 300 unique questions and 500 secondary questions.

📚 **2 FULL LENGTH PRACTICE TESTS with Answers**

| | |
|---|---|
| Full Length Practice Test#1 | 15 Questions |
| Full Length Practice Test#2 | 15 Questions |

📚 **FUNDAMENTAL CONCEPTS**

📚 **SERIAL REASONING QUESTIONS**      250 Questions

📚 **FULLY SOLVED ANSWERS**

# 📚 Table of Contents

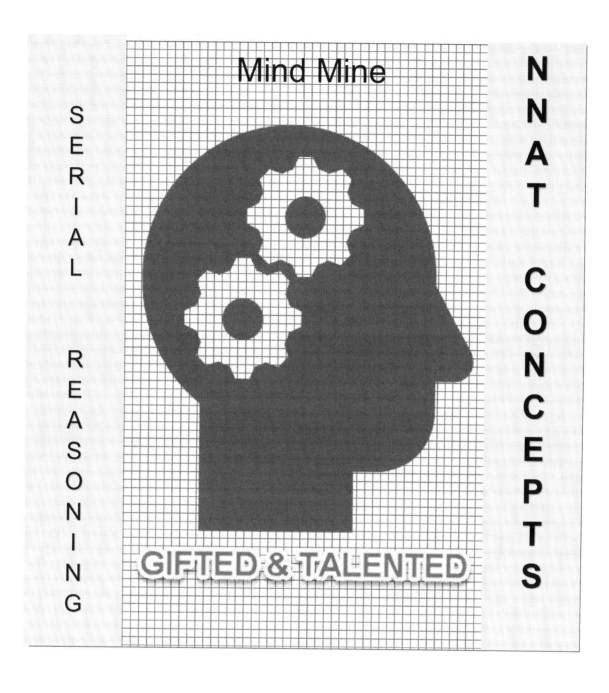

# SERIAL REASONING

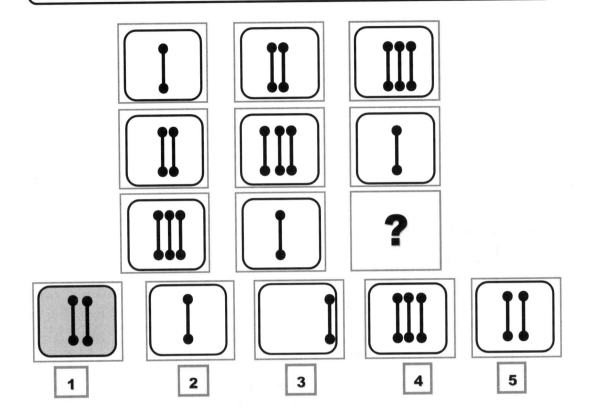

ANSWER: 5

1

# SERIAL REASONING

## How to solve?

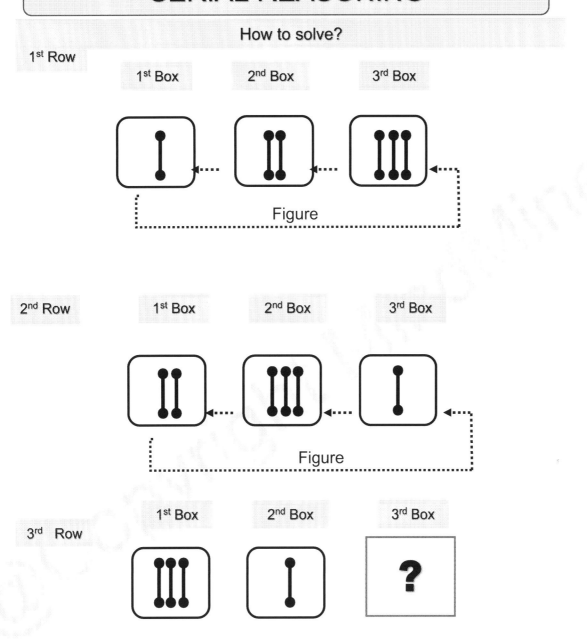

### STEP-1: Understand the Reasoning from 1st row

Figure in first box is moving all the way to the right. As a result, Figures in 2nd and 3rd boxes are shifting to the left.

**Result of the move is shown in 2nd row**

### STEP-2: Apply the same Reasoning to 2nd row

Move Figure in the first box all the way to the right. As a result, Figures in 2nd and 3rd boxes shift to the left.

### STEP-3: Find the answer

Answer is: 5

**STEP-1:** Analyze figures given in all 3 boxes to find their **CLASSIFICATION**

CLASSIFICATION is "**NUMBER OF VERTICAL LINES**"

**Number of Vertical lines are 1, 2, 3**

**STEP-2:** FIND the missing one

**Missing Figure is**

**Number of vertical lines is "2"**

**Answer is 5**

4

# SERIAL REASONING

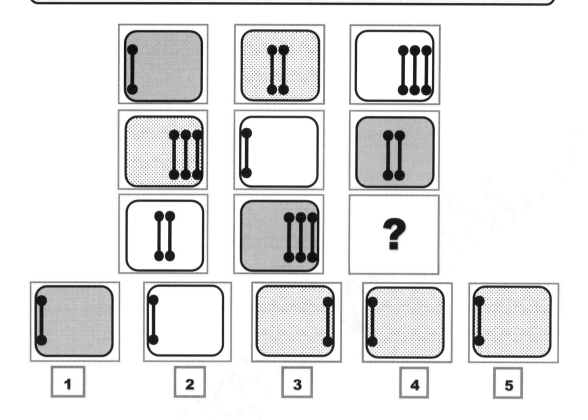

## ANSWER: 4

5

# SERIAL REASONING

## How to solve?

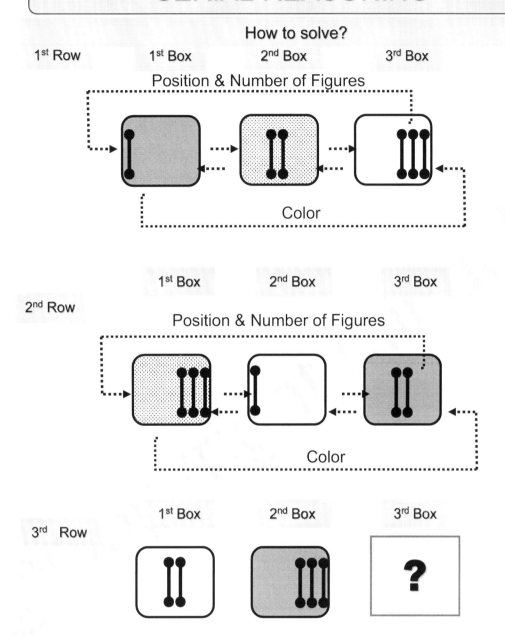

Figures in boxes may come with different characteristics such as "Shape", "Position", "Color", "Number", "Size" etc.,

When figures are moved either to the left or right, sometimes entire figure moves as is. However, sometimes a characteristic move to the left and other characteristic moves to the right. As a result, "**Solve by Reasoning**" becomes much harder and Technique (**Find the missing one**) becomes handy.

### STEP-1:  Understand the Reasoning from 1st row

"**POSITION**" of lines in third box is moving all the way to the left. As a result, POSITION of lines in 1st and 2nd boxes are shifting to the right.

"**NUMBER of figures**" in third box is moving all the way to the left. As a result, NUMBER of figures in 1st and 2nd boxes are shifting to the right.

"**COLOR**" of first box is moving all the way to the right. As a result, COLOR of 2nd and 3rd boxes is shifting to the left.

**Result of the move is shown in 2nd row**

### STEP-2:  Apply the same Reasoning to 2nd row

Move "**POSITION**" of lines in third box all the way to the left. As a result, 1st and 2nd boxes shift to the right.

Move "**NUMBER of figures**" in third box all the way to the left. As a result, "**NUMBER of figures**" in 1st and 2nd boxes shift to the right.

Move "**COLOR**" of first box all the way to the right. As a result, "**COLOR**" of 1st and 2nd boxes shift to the left.

### STEP-3:  Find the answer

Answer is:  4

Position of line is "**LEFT**"

Number of Vertical lines is "**1**"

Pattern is "**DOTS**"

**STEP-1: Analyze figures given in all 3 boxes to find their CLASSIFICATION**

FIRST CLASSIFICATION is "**COLOR**"

**Color of three outside boxes is**

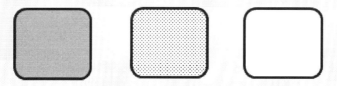

SECOND CLASSIFICATION is "**NUMBER OF VERTICAL LINES**"

**Numbers of Vertical lines are 1, 2, 3**

THIRD CLASSIFICATION is "**POSITION**"

**Vertical lines are positioned at "LEFT, MIDDLE, RIGHT"**

**STEP-2: FIND the missing one**

**Missing Background Color or Pattern is "DOTS"**

**Missing POSITION is "LEFT"**

**Missing "Number of vertical lines is 1"**

**Answer is 4**

9

Problems can be solved either by **Reasoning** or **Technique**

All Answers in **this book** are explained by using the Technique, **"find the missing one"**

This technique helps to solve problems in a timely manner

# FUNDAMENTAL CONCEPTS
## (using one classification)

# Classifications

for "**Serial Reasoning Problems**"

Figures can be classified

By SHAPE

By SIZE

By COLOR

By PATTERN

By OUTLINE

By POSITION

By NUMBER OF SHAPES

By NUMBER OF SIDES

By FRACTIONAL VALUE

By LETTERS

By NUMBERS

12

## SHAPES

13

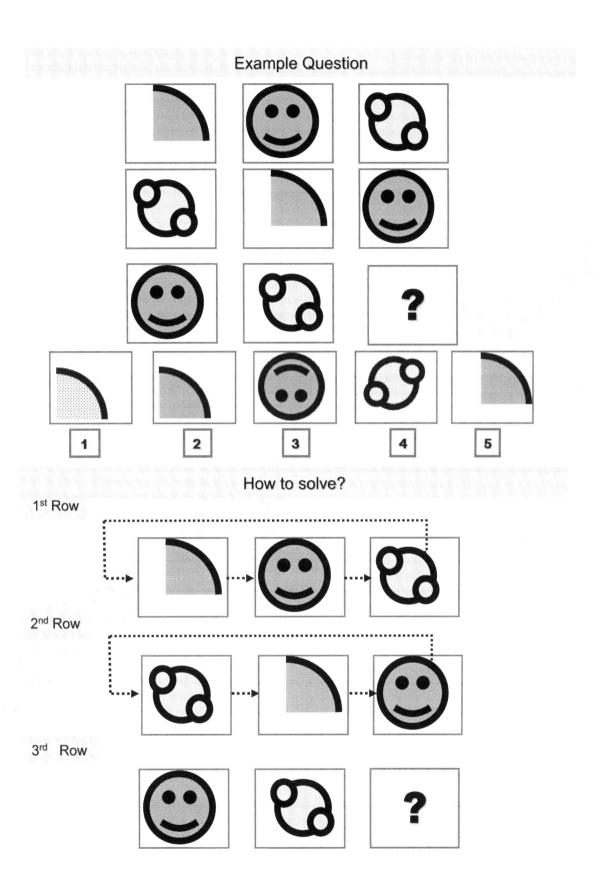

Example Question

How to solve?

1st Row

2nd Row

3rd Row

14

## Solve by **REASONING**

**STEP-1: Understand the Reasoning from 1st row**

SHAPE in third box is moving all the way to the left. As a result, shapes in 1st and 2nd boxes are shifting to the right.

Result of the move is shown in 2nd row

**STEP-2: Apply the same Reasoning to 2nd row**

Move SHAPE in third box all the way to the left. As a result, shapes in 1st and 2nd boxes shift to the right.

**STEP-3: Find the answer**

**SHAPE** in the 3rd box moves to the 1st box

Answer is: 5

## Solve by **TECHNIQUE (Find the Missing one)**

**STEP-1: Analyze figures given in all 3 boxes to find their CLASSIFICATION**

CLASSIFICATION is "**SHAPES**"

Three Shapes are

**STEP-2: FIND the missing one**

**Missing SHAPE is**

15

# Example Question

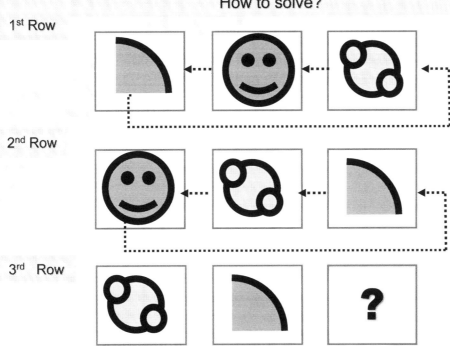

## How to solve?

**1st Row**

**2nd Row**

**3rd Row**

16

## Solve by **REASONING**

### STEP-1:  Understand the Reasoning from 1st row

SHAPE in first box is moving all the way to the Right. As a result, shapes in 2nd and 3rd boxes are shifting to the left.

Result of the move is shown in 2nd row

### STEP-2:  Apply the same Reasoning to 2nd row

Move SHAPE in first box all the way to the right. As a result, shapes in 2nd and 3rd boxes shift to the left.

### STEP-3:  Find the answer

SHAPE in the 1st box moves to the 3rd box

Answer is:  1


## Solve by **TECHNIQUE (Find the Missing one)**

### STEP-1:  Analyze figures given in all 3 boxes to find their CLASSIFICATION

CLASSIFICATION is "**SHAPES**"

Three Shapes are

### STEP-2:  FIND the missing one

**Missing SHAPE is**

17

## Classification by "Number of Sides"

### Figures with NO (Zero) Sides

### Figures with ONE Side

### Figures with TWO Sides

   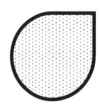

18

## Classification by "Number of Sides"

### Figures with THREE Sides

3-sides of
Equal Length

2-sides of
Equal Length

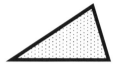

NO-sides of
Equal Length

### Figures with THREE Sides

RIGHT Angle
Triangle

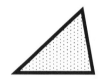

ACUTE Angle
Triangle

OBTUSE Angle
Triangle

### Figures with FOUR Sides

   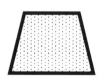

19

## Figures with FOUR Sides

 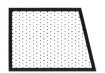  

## Figures with FIVE Sides

  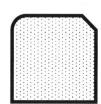 

## Figures with SIX Sides

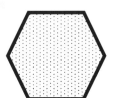 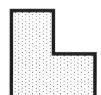  

### Figures with SEVEN Sides

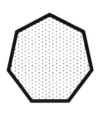 

### Figures with EIGHT Sides

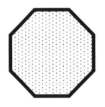 

### Figures with NINE Sides

## Example Question

|   1   |   2   |   3   |   4   |   5   |

## How to solve?

**1st Row**

**2nd Row**

**3rd Row**

22

## Solve by REASONING

**STEP-1:  Understand the Reasoning from 1st row**

Figure in third box is moving all the way to the Left. As a result, figures in 1st and 2nd boxes are shifting to the Right.

Result of the move is shown in 2nd row

**STEP-2:  Apply the same Reasoning to 2nd row**

Move Figure in third box all the way to the Left. As a result, figures in 1st and 2nd boxes shift to the Right.

**STEP-3:  Find the answer**

**Figure** in the 3rd box moves to the 1st box

Answer is:  5

## Solve by TECHNIQUE (Find the Missing one)

**STEP-1:  Analyze figures given in all 3 boxes to find their CLASSIFICATION**

CLASSIFICATION is "**Number of sides**"

Three Figures are

**STEP-2:  FIND the missing one**

**Missing Figure is**

**Number of  sides is "5"**

23

# Classification by "**Position**"

## POSITION

**White Shape is in the Front**

White Shape is in the Back

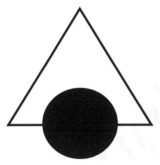

Triangle is in the Front

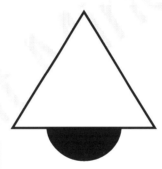

Triangle is in the Back

**Rectangle is on the Bottom**

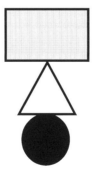

**Rectangle is on the Top**

# POSITION

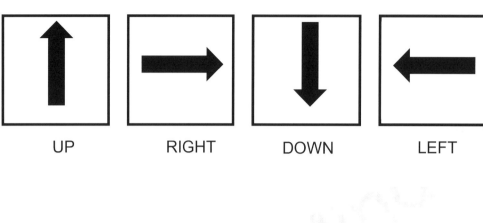

UP          RIGHT          DOWN          LEFT

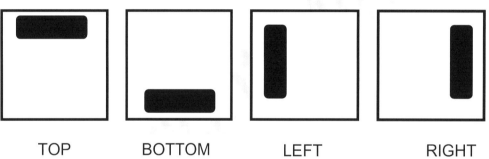

TOP          BOTTOM          LEFT          RIGHT

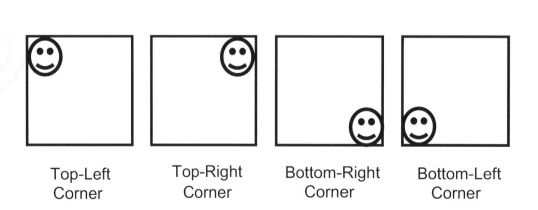

Top-Left
Corner

Top-Right
Corner

Bottom-Right
Corner

Bottom-Left
Corner

# Classification by "**Position**"

Points to the
**Bottom-Right
Corner**

Points to the
**Bottom-Left
Corner**

Points to the
**Top-Left
Corner**

Points to the
**Bottom-Left
Corner**

## Example Question

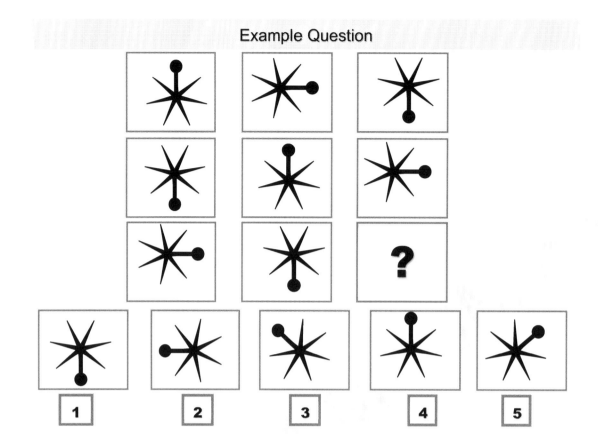

## How to solve?

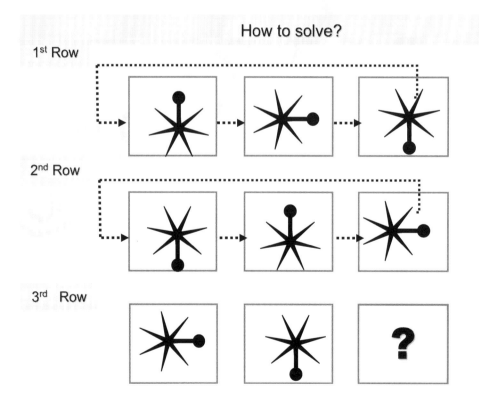

27

## Solve by **REASONING**

### STEP-1: Understand the Reasoning from 1st row

Figure in third box is moving all the way to the Left. As a result, figures in 1st and 2nd boxes are shifting to the Right.

Result of the move is shown in 2nd row

### STEP-2: Apply the same Reasoning to 2nd row

Move Figure in third box all the way to the Left. As a result, figures in 1st and 2nd boxes shift to the Right.

### STEP-3: Find the answer

Figure in the 3rd box moves to the 1st box

Answer is: 4

## Solve by **TECHNIQUE (Find the Missing one)**

### STEP-1: Analyze figures given in all 3 boxes to find their CLASSIFICATION

CLASSIFICATION is "**POSITION**"

Three Figures are

### STEP-2: FIND the missing one

**Missing Figure is**

**Figure is pointing "Up"**

28

# Example Question

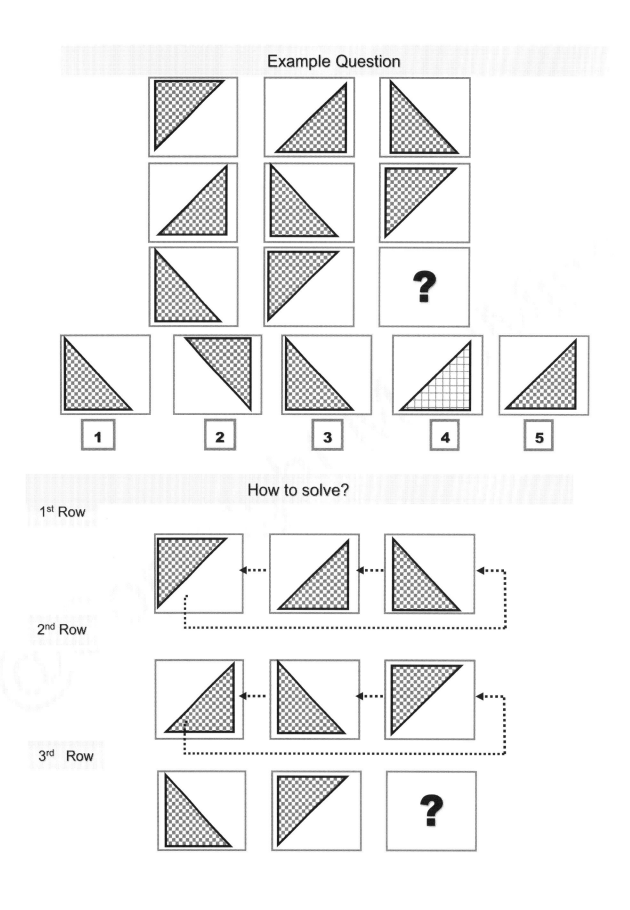

## How to solve?

1st Row

2nd Row

3rd Row

29

## Solve by **REASONING**

**STEP-1: Understand the Reasoning from 1st row**

Figure in first box is moving all the way to the Right. As a result, figures in 2<sup>nd</sup> and 3<sup>rd</sup> boxes are shifting to the left.

Result of the move is shown in 2<sup>nd</sup> row

**STEP-2: Apply the same Reasoning to 2nd row**

Move Figure in first box all the way to the right. As a result, figures in 2<sup>nd</sup> and 3<sup>rd</sup> boxes shift to the left.

**STEP-3: Find the answer**

**SHAPE** in the 1<sup>st</sup> box moves to the 3<sup>rd</sup> box

Answer is: 5

## Solve by **TECHNIQUE (Find the Missing one)**

**STEP-1: Analyze figures given in all 3 boxes to find their CLASSIFICATION**

CLASSIFICATION is "**POSITION**"

Three Figures are

**STEP-2: FIND the missing one**

**Missing SHAPE is**

**Position is "Bottom-Right corner"**

# Classification by "**Rotation**"

## Rotation

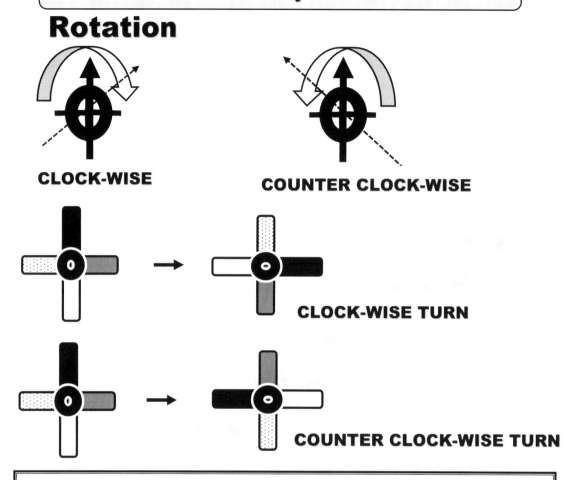

**CLOCK-WISE**

**COUNTER CLOCK-WISE**

**CLOCK-WISE TURN**

**COUNTER CLOCK-WISE TURN**

Pay Attention to the order of colors. When a Figure is turned, ORDER of COLORS remains the same.

Example: For the figure given above, order of colors remains the same when figure is turned clock-wise or counter clock-wise.

**Order of Colors:**
Black
Gray
White
Dotted Pattern

## Classification by Color
### "Fill/Pattern/Outline"

**COLOR**

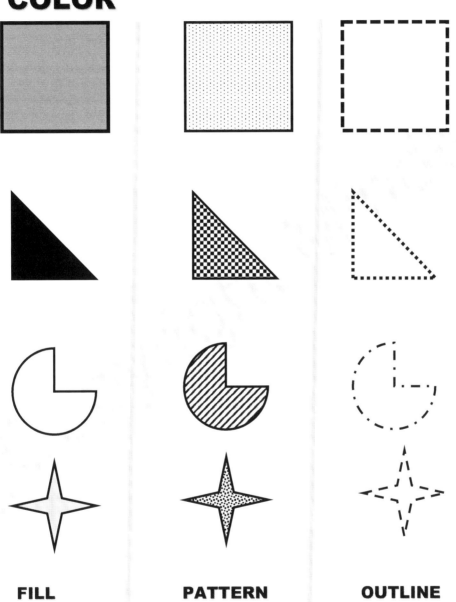

FILL        PATTERN        OUTLINE

32

## Example Question

|   1   |   2   |   3   |   4   |   5   |

## How to solve?

1st Row

2nd Row

3rd Row

33

## Solve by REASONING

**STEP-1: Understand the Reasoning from 1st row**

Figure in first box is moving all the way to the Right. As a result, figures in 2nd and 3rd boxes are shifting to the left.

Result of the move is shown in 2nd row

**STEP-2: Apply the same Reasoning to 2nd row**

Move Figure in the first box all the way to the right. As a result, figures in 2nd and 3rd boxes shift to the left.

**STEP-3: Find the answer**

**Figure** in the 1st box moves to the 3rd box

Answer is: 5

## Solve by TECHNIQUE (Find the Missing one)

**STEP-1: Analyze figures given in all 3 boxes to find their CLASSIFICATION**

CLASSIFICATION is "**Color(or) Pattern(or) Outline**"

Three Figures are

**STEP-2: FIND the missing one**

**Missing Figure is**

Outline is "dotted line", Pattern is "dots"

## Classification by "Number of Parts (Fractional Value)"

**PARTS**

**4 -PARTS, NONE SHADED**

**4 -PARTS, ONE PART SHADED**

**FRACTIONAL VALUE: 1 OUT OF 4**

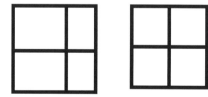

**4 -PARTS. BUT NOT ALL ARE OF EQUAL SIZE**

35

## Classification by "**Number of Parts (Fractional Value)**"

**PARTS**

**4 -PARTS. 2 PARTS NEXT TO EACH OTHER ARE SHADED (FARCTIONAL VALUE: 2 OUT OF 4)**

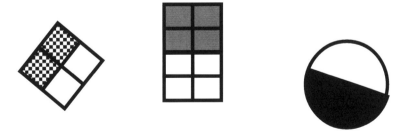

**4 -PARTS. 2 PARTS DIAGONALLY ACROSS ARE SHADED (FARCTIONAL VALUE: 2 OUT OF 4)**

**HALF OF THE FIGURE IS SHADED (FARCTIONAL VALUE: HALF (OR) 1 OUT OF 2)**

**PARTS**

  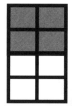

**PARTS BY CUTTING SIDES**

**PARTS BY CUTTING CORNERS**

37

## Example Question

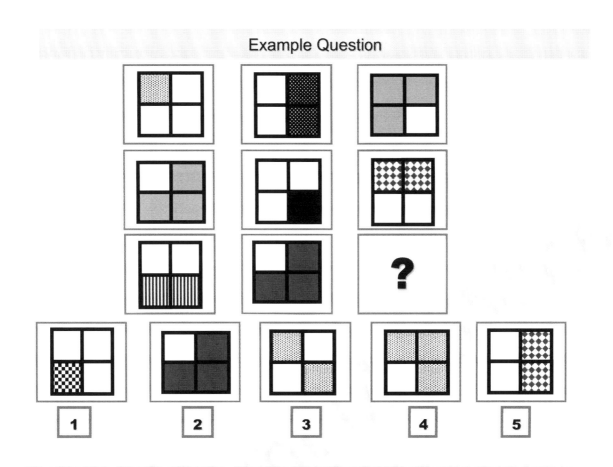

## How to solve?

1st Row

2nd Row

3rd Row

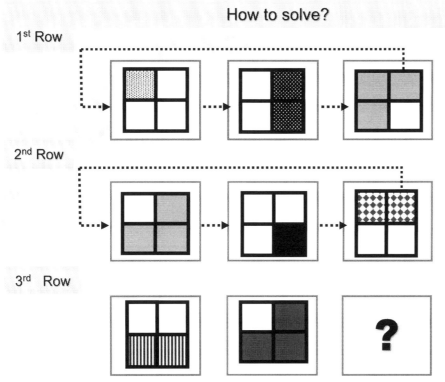

38

# Solve by REASONING

**STEP-1: Understand the Reasoning from 1st row**

Figure in third box is moving all the way to the Left. As a result, figures in 1st and 2nd boxes are shifting to the Right.

Result of the move is shown in 2nd row

**STEP-2: Apply the same Reasoning to 2nd row**

Move Figure in third box all the way to the Left. As a result, figures in 1st and 2nd boxes shift to the Right.

**STEP-3: Find the answer**

**Figure** in the 3rd box moves to the 1st box

Answer is: 1

---

# Solve by TECHNIQUE (Find the Missing one)

**STEP-1: Analyze figures given in all 3 boxes to find their CLASSIFICATION**

CLASSIFICATION is "**FRACTIONAL VALUE**"

Three Figures are

**STEP-2: FIND the missing one**

**Missing Figure is**

**Fractional value is "1 out of 4"**

# Classification by "Size"

**SIZE**

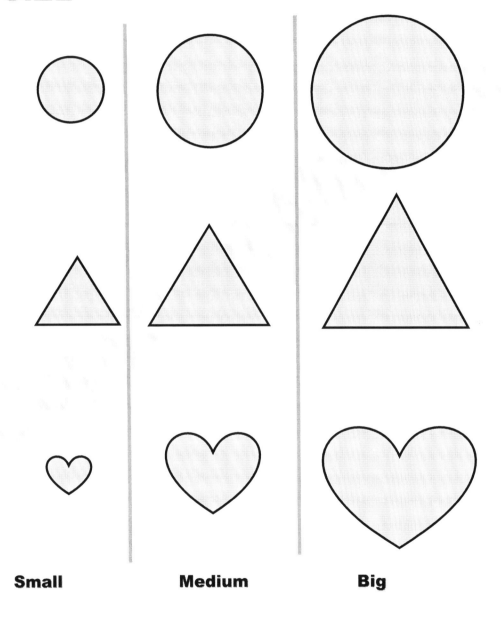

| Small | Medium | Big |

# Example Question

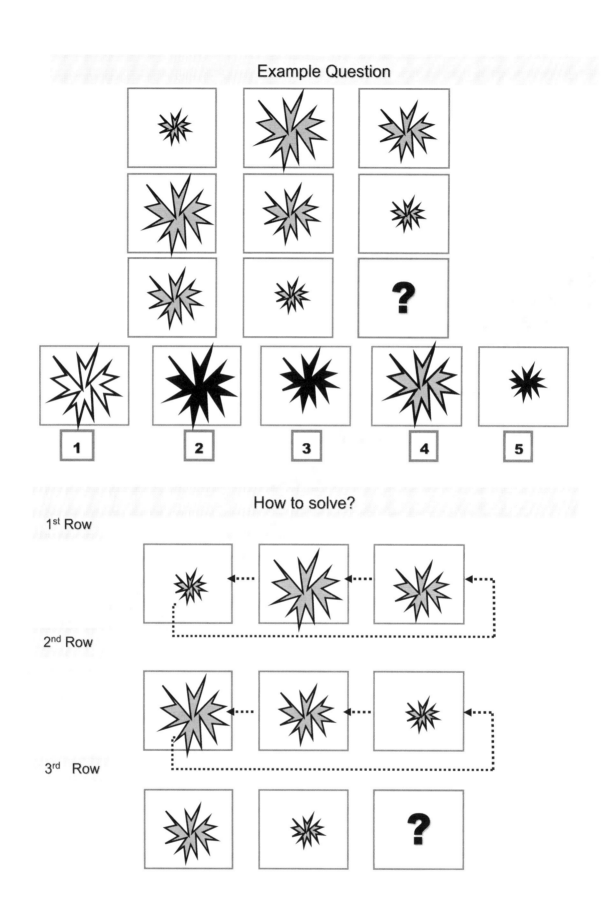

## How to solve?

1st Row

2nd Row

3rd Row

41

# Solve by **REASONING**

## STEP-1:  Understand the Reasoning from 1st row

Figure in first box is moving all the way to the Right. As a result, figures in 2$^{nd}$ and 3$^{rd}$ boxes are shifting to the left.

Result of the move is shown in 2$^{nd}$ row

## STEP-2:  Apply the same Reasoning to 2nd row

Move Figure in the first box all the way to the right. As a result, figures in 2$^{nd}$ and 3$^{rd}$ boxes shift to the left.

## STEP-3:  Find the answer

**Figure** in the 1$^{st}$ box moves to the 3$^{rd}$ box

Answer is:  4

# Solve by **TECHNIQUE (Find the Missing one)**

## STEP-1:  Analyze figures given in all 3 boxes to find their CLASSIFICATION

CLASSIFICATION is "**SIZE**"

Three Figures are

## STEP-2:  FIND the missing one

**Missing Figure is**

**Figure is "Big"**

42

## Classification by "**NUMBER OF SHAPES**"

## Number of Shapes

**1 Shape**

**2 Shapes**

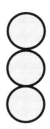

**3 Shapes**

**1 Shape**

**2 Shapes**

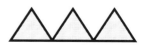

**3 Shapes**

**1 Row**

**2 Rows**

**3 Rows**

43

## Example Question

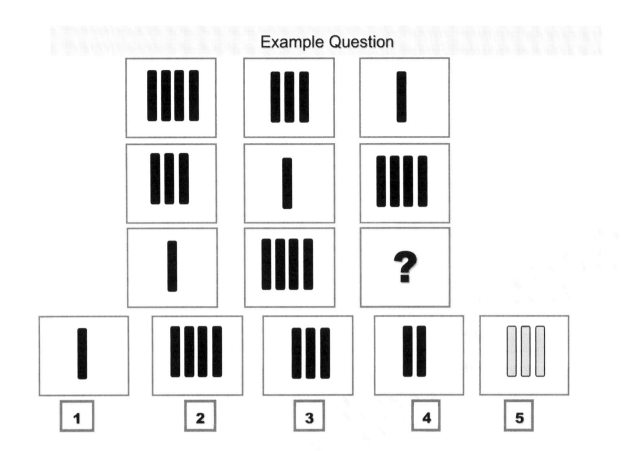

| 1 | 2 | 3 | 4 | 5 |

## How to solve?

1st Row

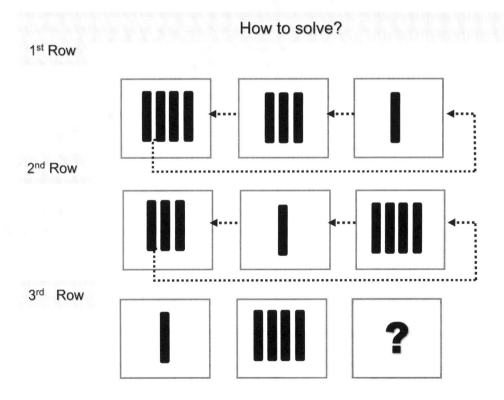

2nd Row

3rd Row

44

**STEP-1: Understand the Reasoning from 1st row**

Figure in first box is moving all the way to the Right. As a result, figures in 2nd and 3rd boxes are shifting to the left.

Result of the move is shown in 2nd row

**STEP-2: Apply the same Reasoning to 2nd row**

Move Figures in the first box all the way to the right. As a result, figures in 2nd and 3rd boxes shift to the left.

**STEP-3: Find the answer**

**Figure** in the 1st box moves to the 3rd box

Answer is: 3

Solve by **TECHNIQUE (Find the Missing one)**

**STEP-1: Analyze figures given in all 3 boxes to find their CLASSIFICATION**

CLASSIFICATION is "**NUMBER OF SHAPES**"

Three Figures are

**STEP-2: FIND the missing one**

**Missing Figure is**

**Number of vertical stripes is "3"**

45

## CONGRUENT SHAPES

**Same Shape (Figure) and same size
Figures are called congruent.**

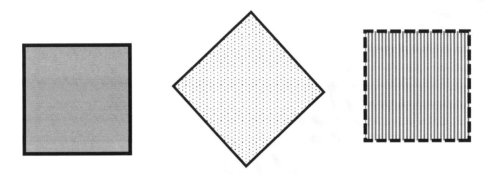

**3 squares above are congruent.**

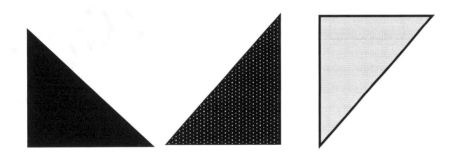

**3 Right angled Triangles above are
congruent.**

## Classification by "Types of Arrows"

## ARROWS / LINES

**ONE HEADED**
**ARROW**

**TWO HEADED**
**ARROW**

**THREE**

**ONE HEADED**

**ARROW**

**FOUR HEADED**

**ARROW**

**LINE**

**LINE WITH**

**ONE END**

**POINT**

**LINE WITH**

**TWO END**

**POINTS**

**(Line Segment)**

## Classification by "Letters/Numbers"

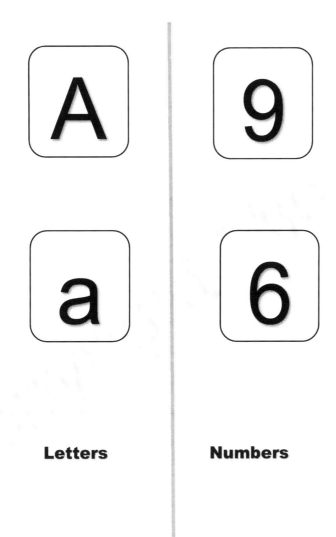

**Letters**          **Numbers**

# FUNDAMENTAL CONCEPTS

(using more than one Classification)

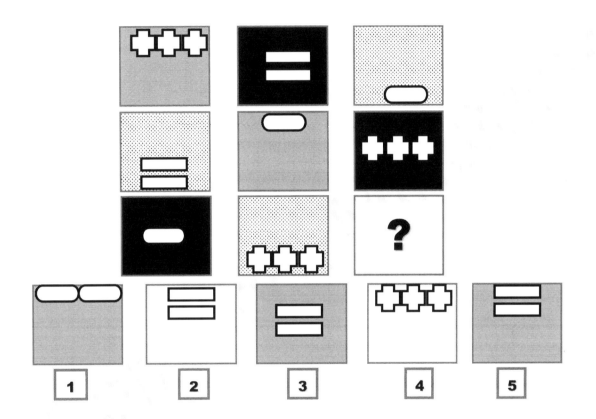

50

Solve by **TECHNIQUE (Find the Missing one)**

**STEP-1: Analyze figures given in all 3 boxes to find their CLASSIFICATION**

FIRST CLASSIFICATION is "**COLOR**"

**Color of three outside boxes is**

SECOND CLASSIFICATION is "**SHAPES**"

**Three Shapes are**

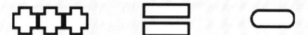

THIRD CLASSIFICATION is "**POSITION**"

**Positions are Top, Bottom, Center**

**STEP-2: FIND the missing one**

**Missing Background Color is "GRAY"**

**Missing Shape is**

**Missing Position is "TOP"**

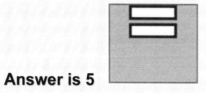

**Answer is 5**

51

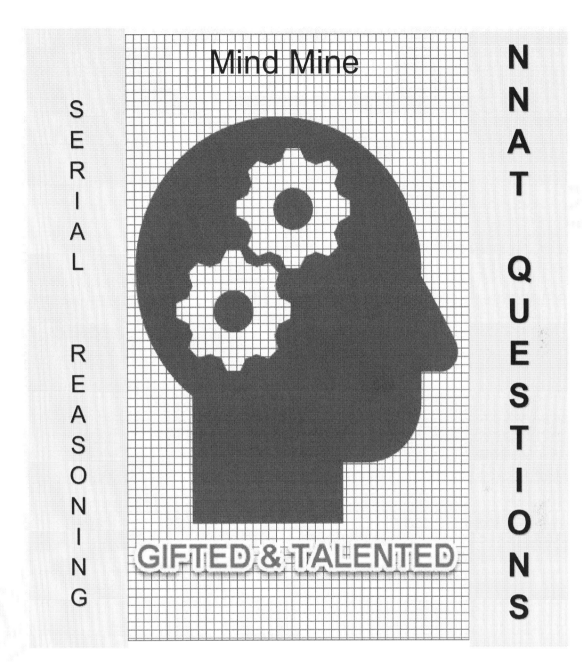

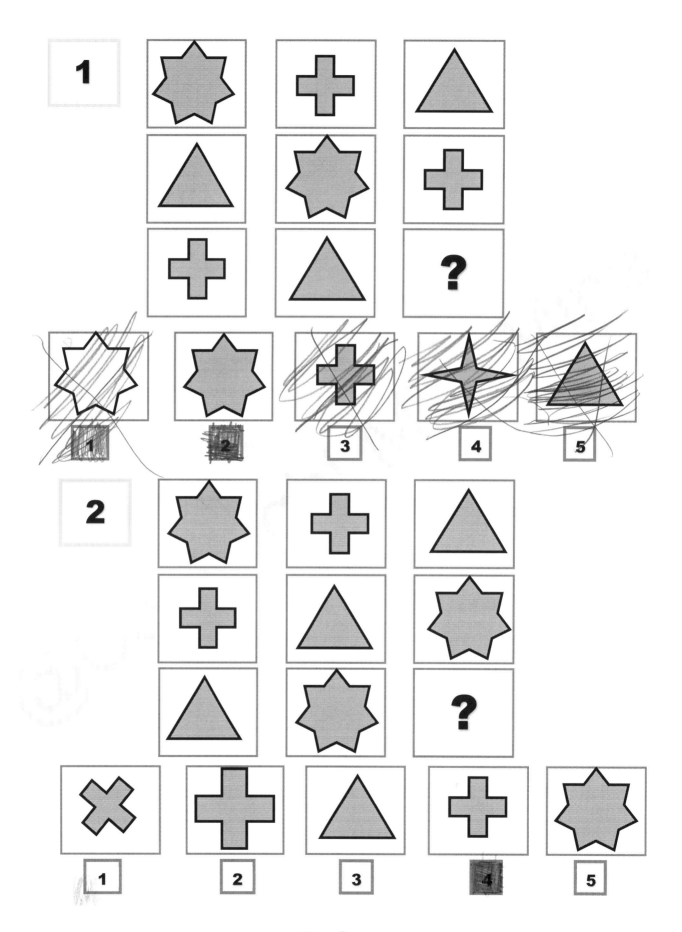

53

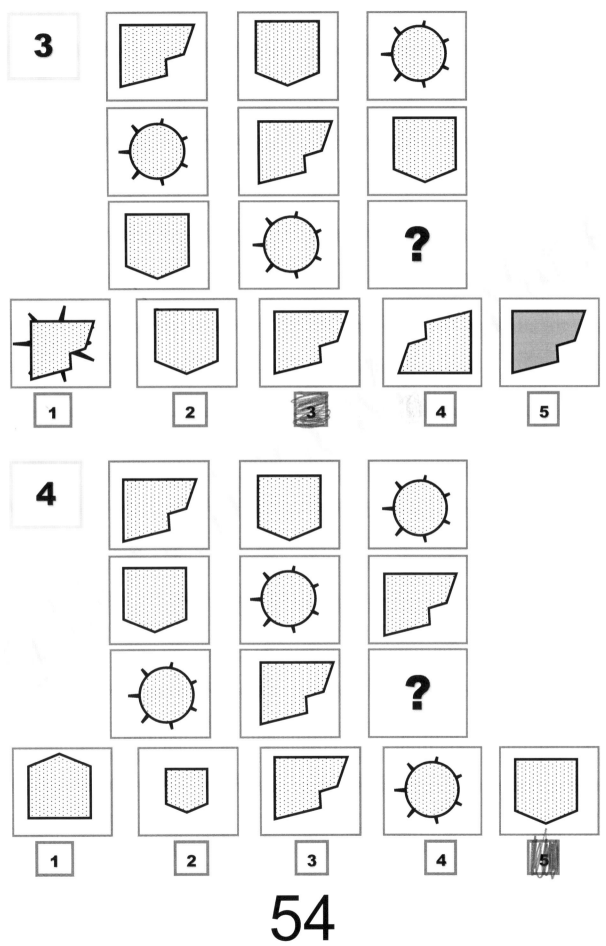

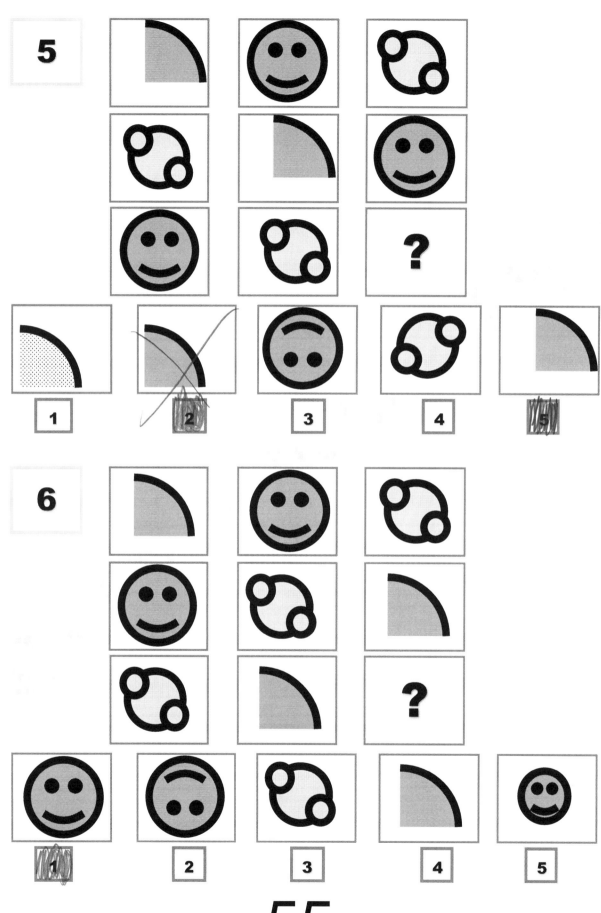

55

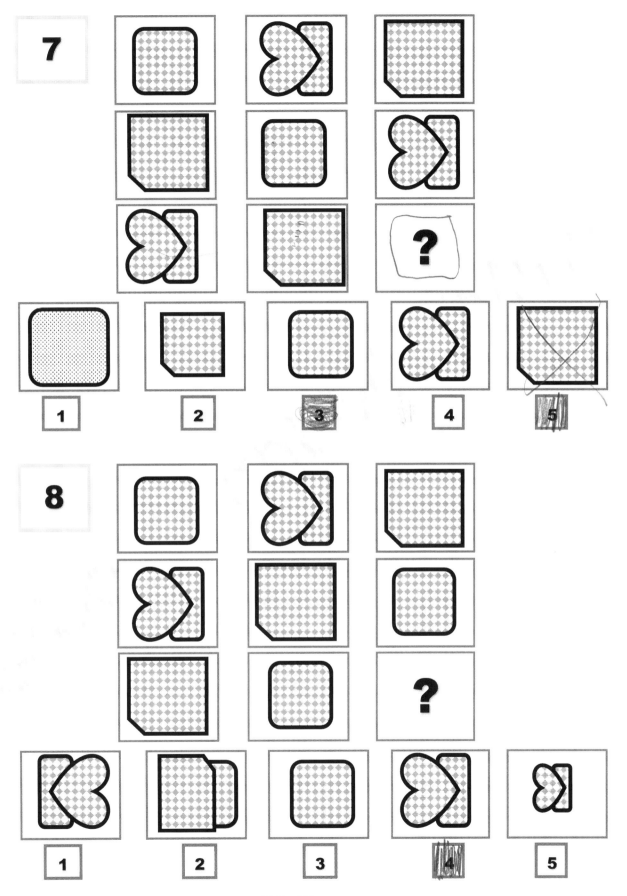

56

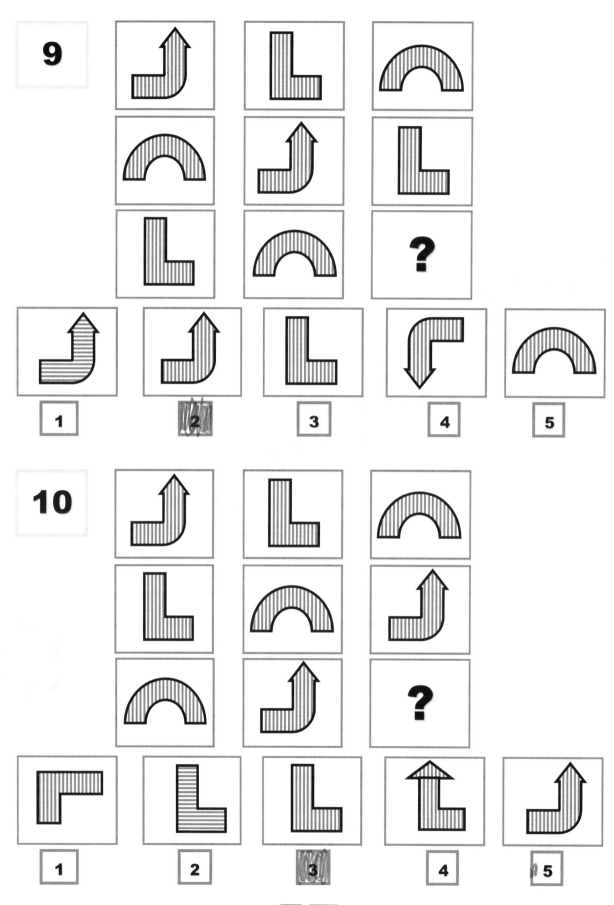

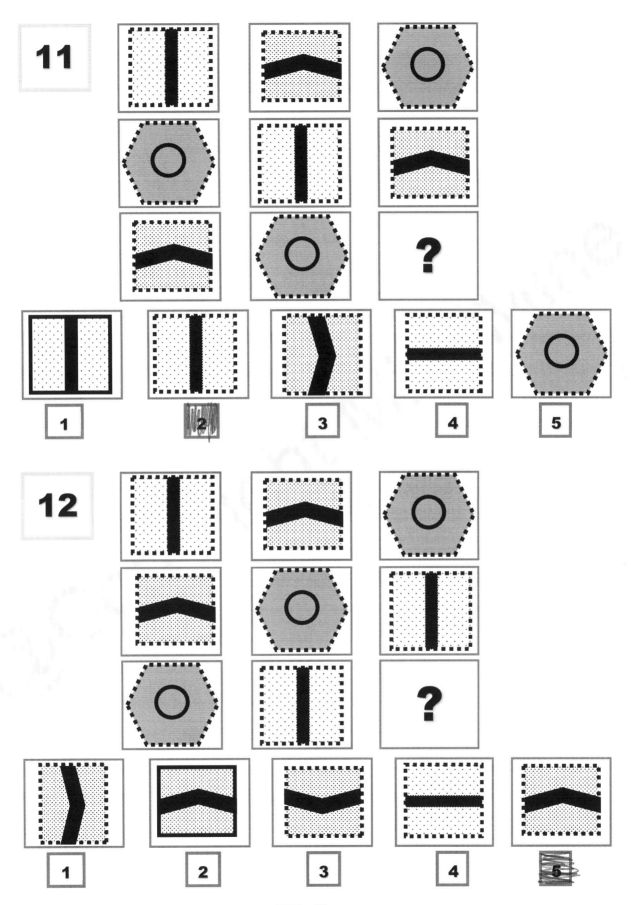

58

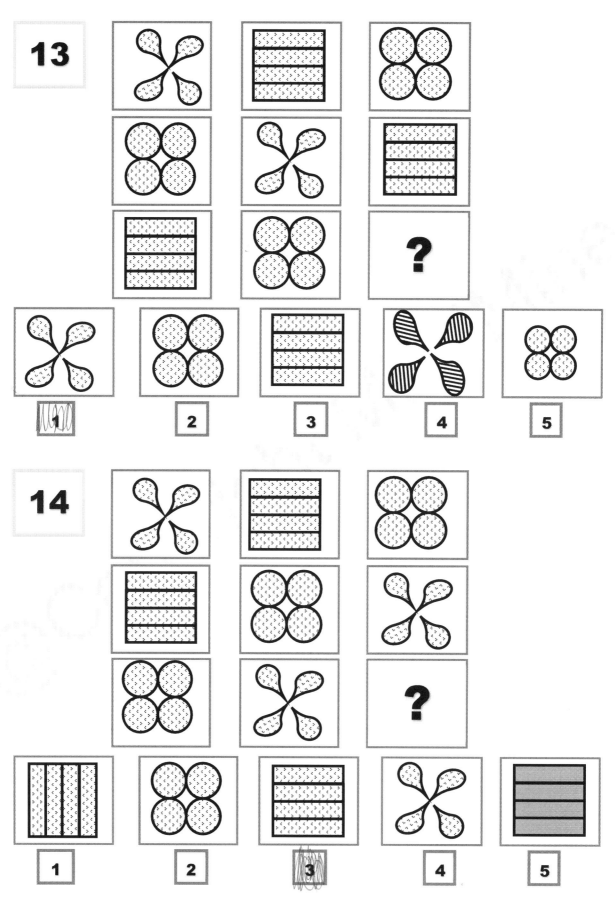

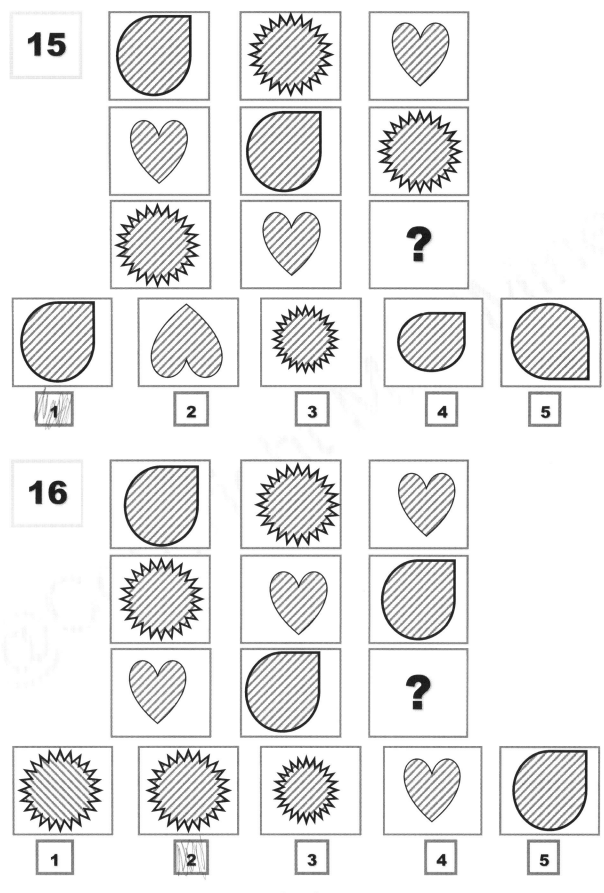

60

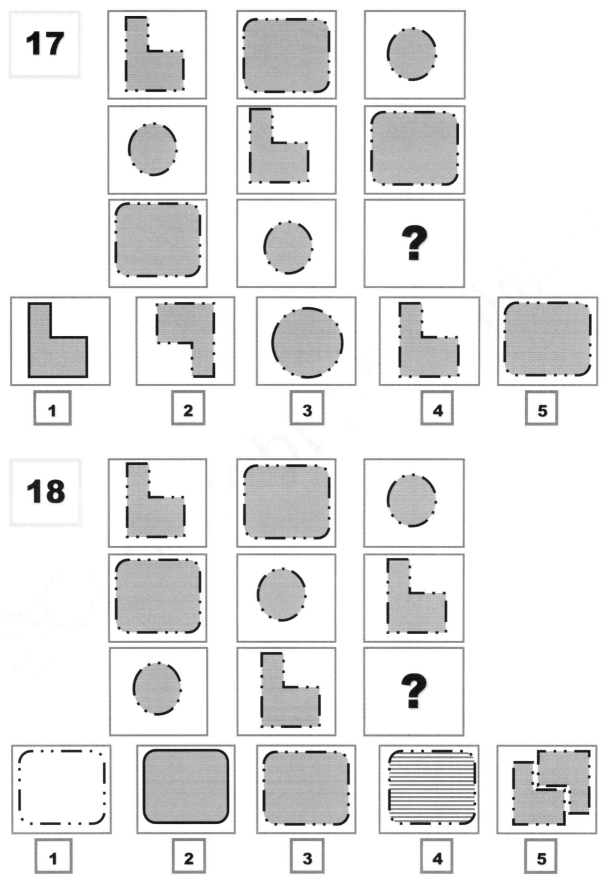

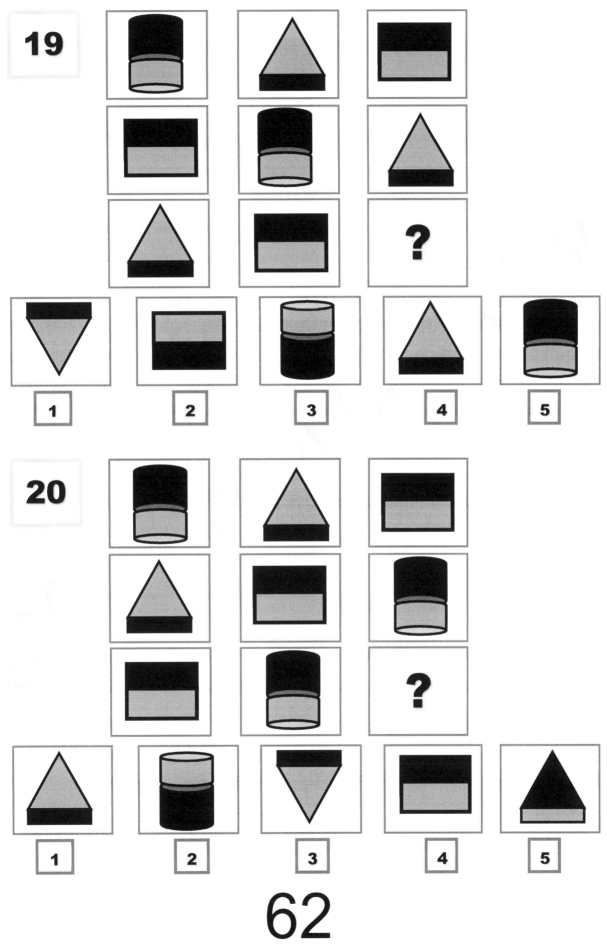

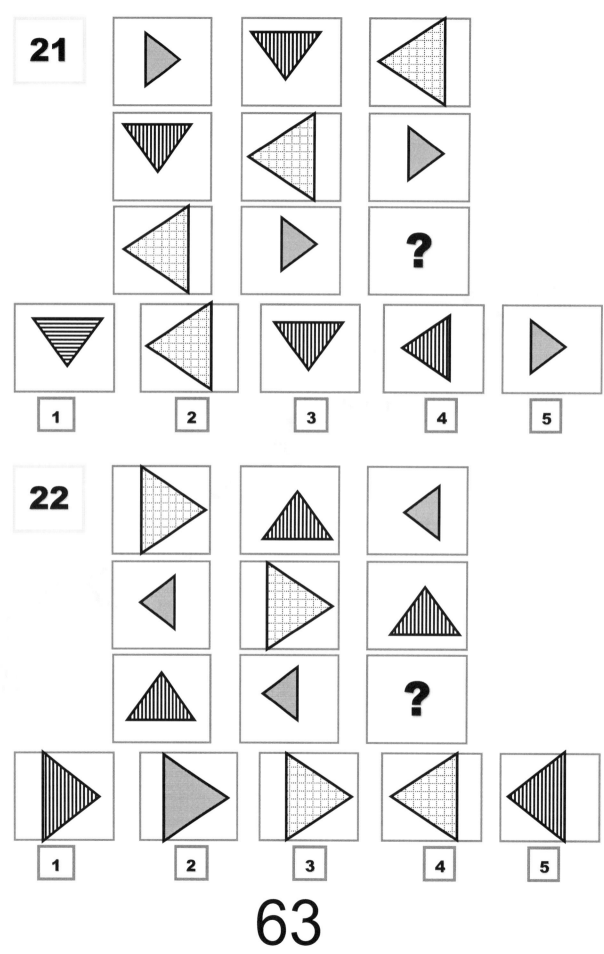

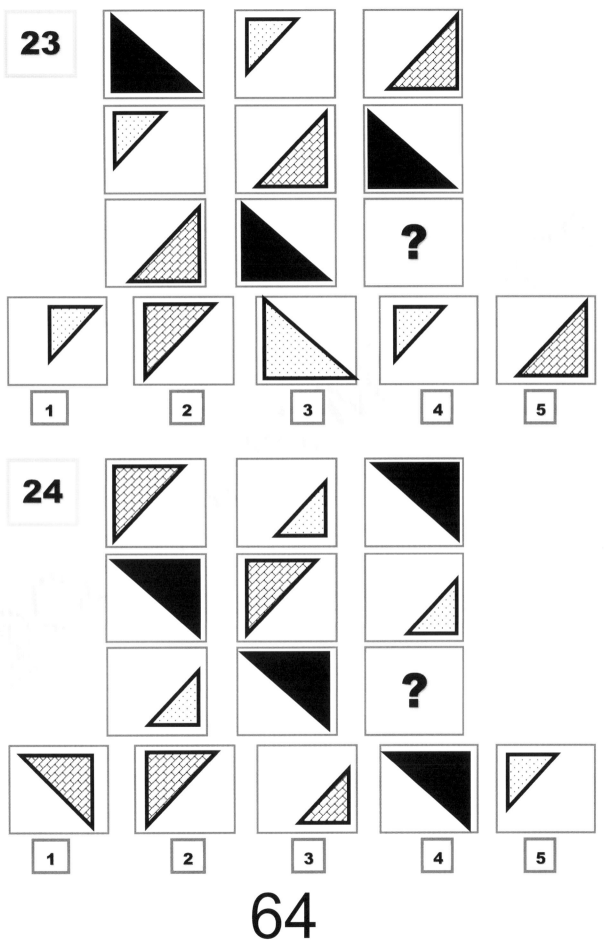

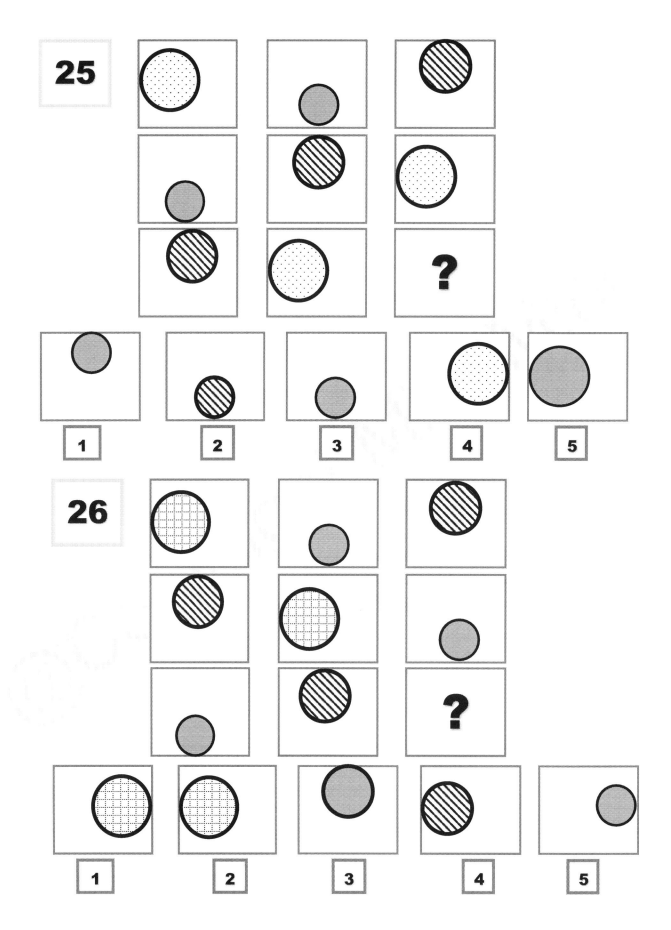

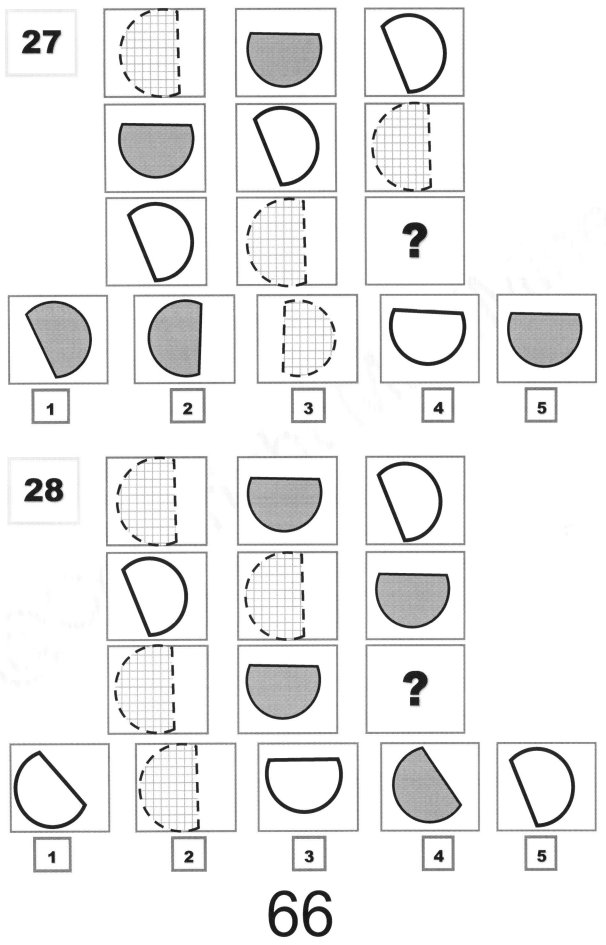

27

28

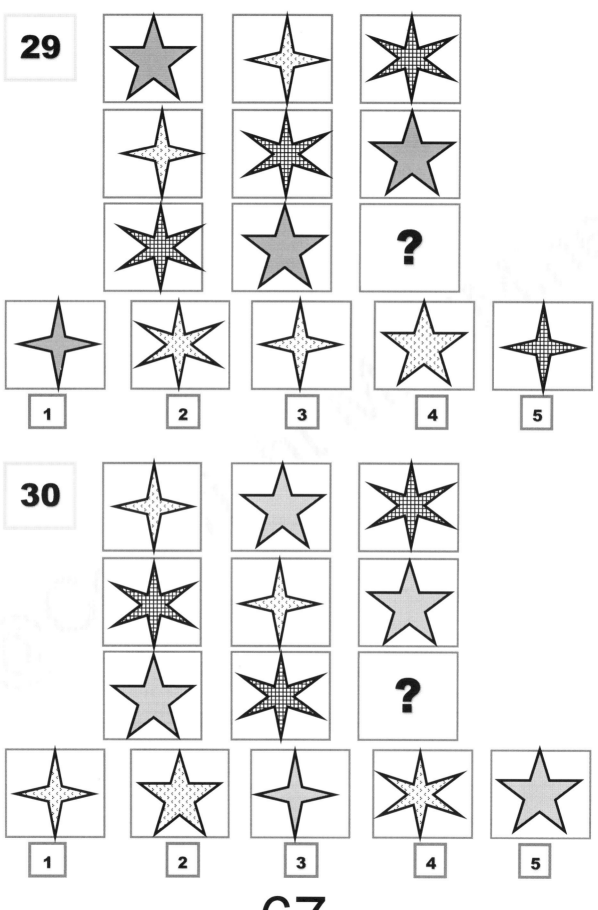

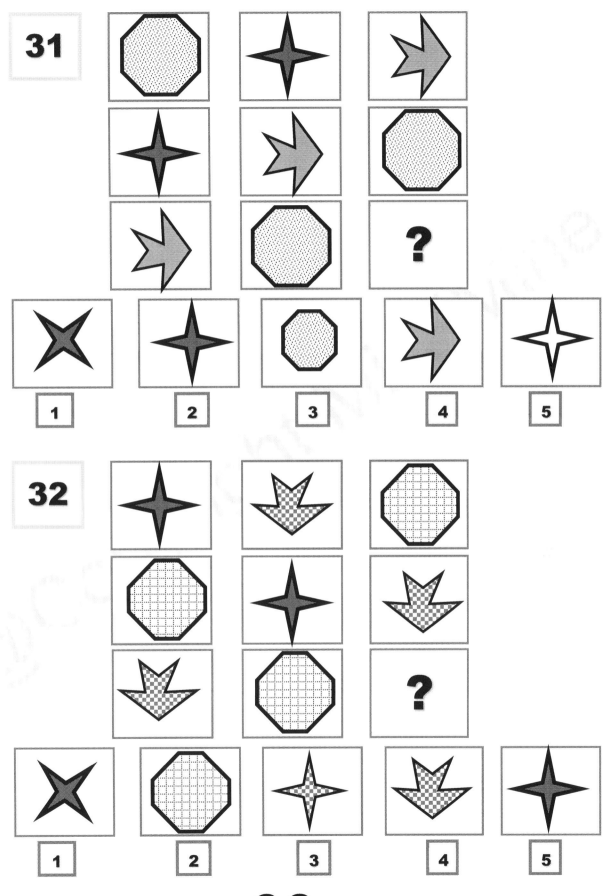

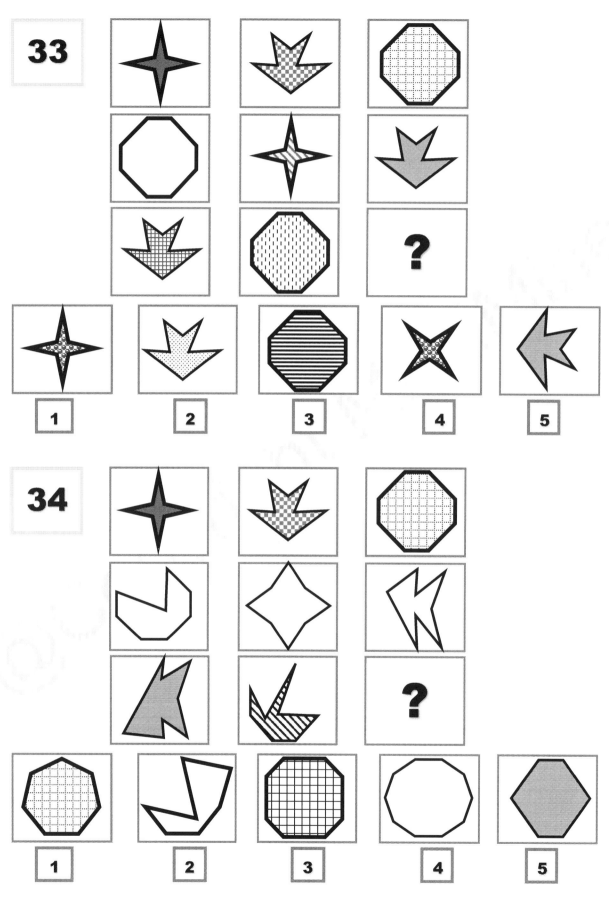

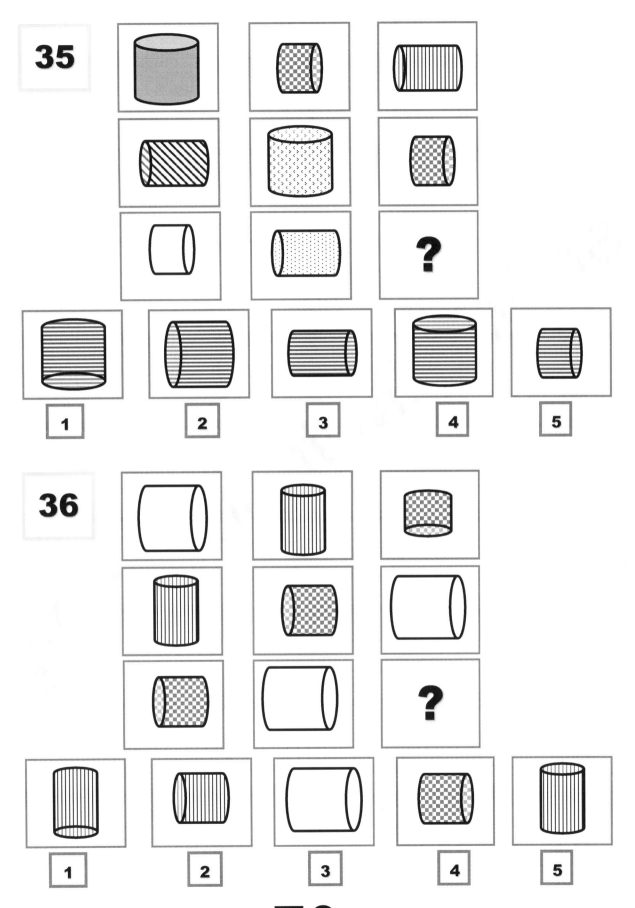

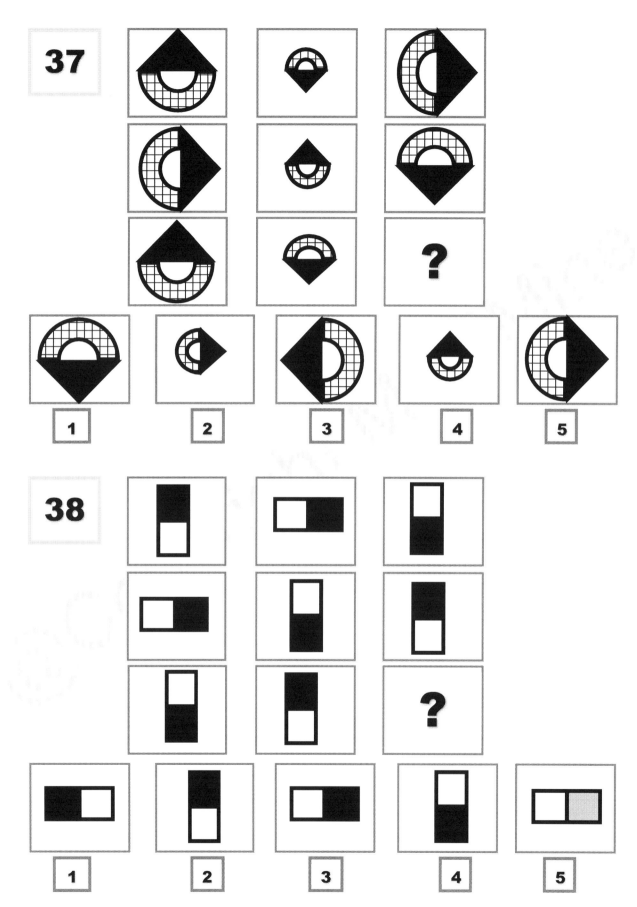

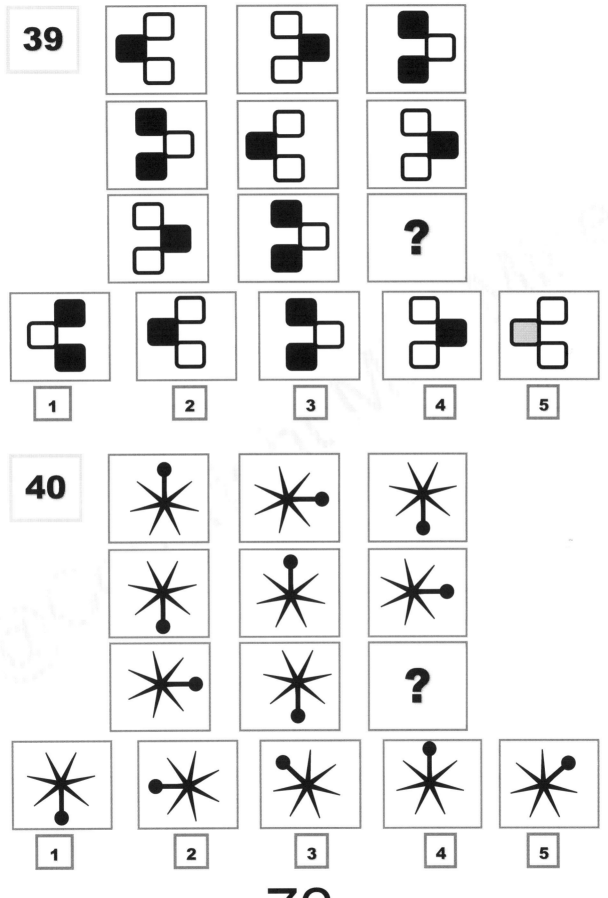

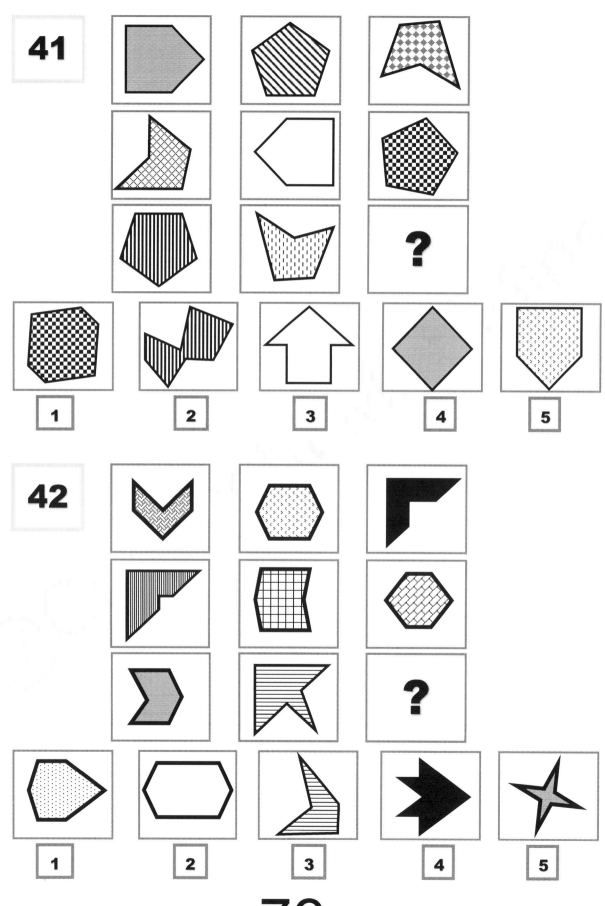

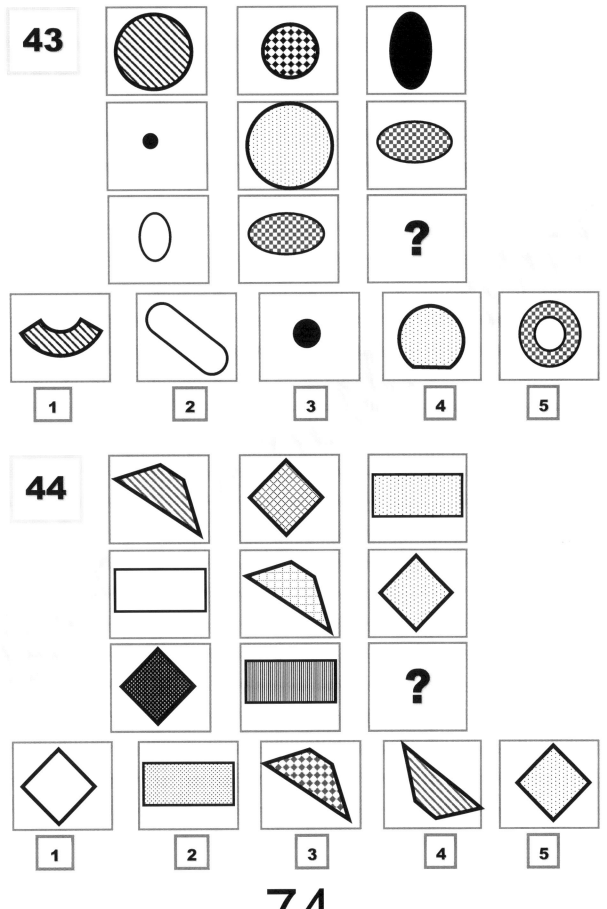

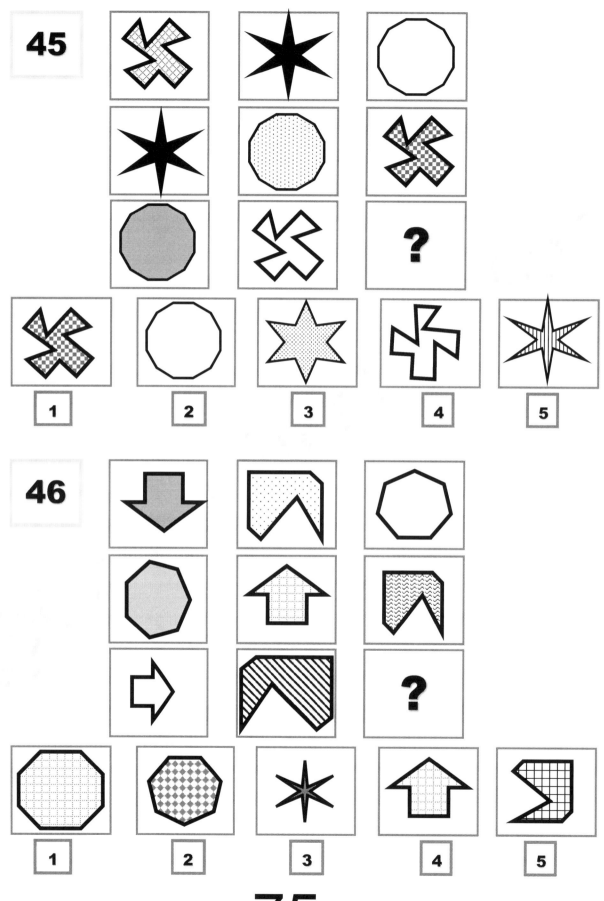

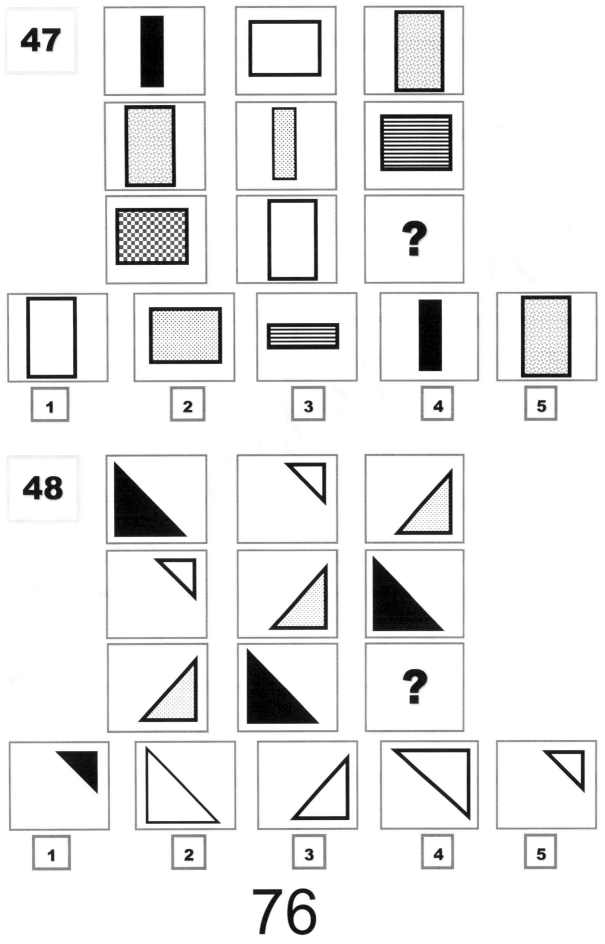

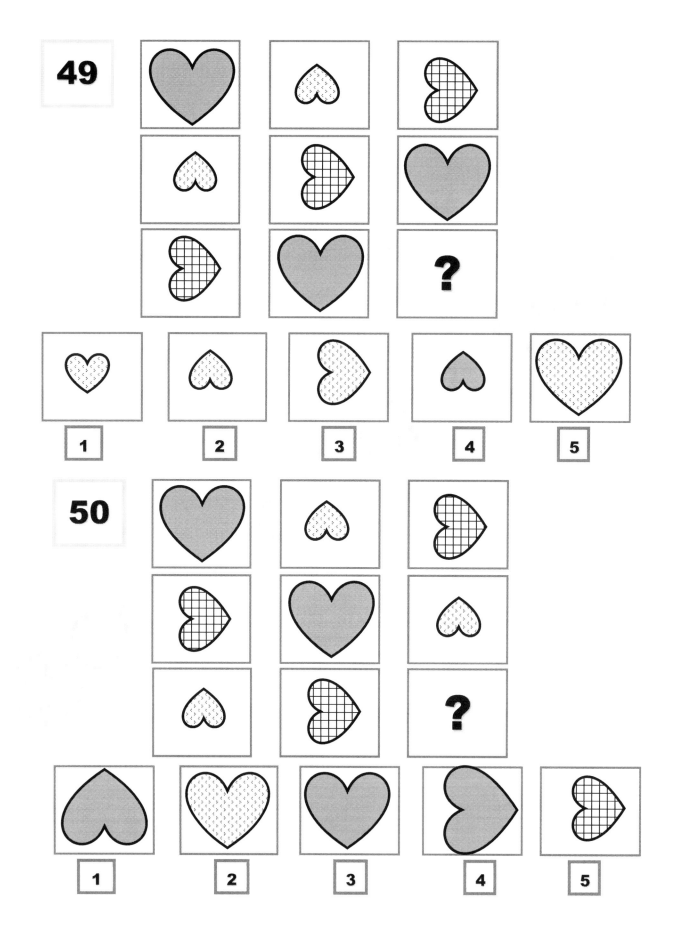

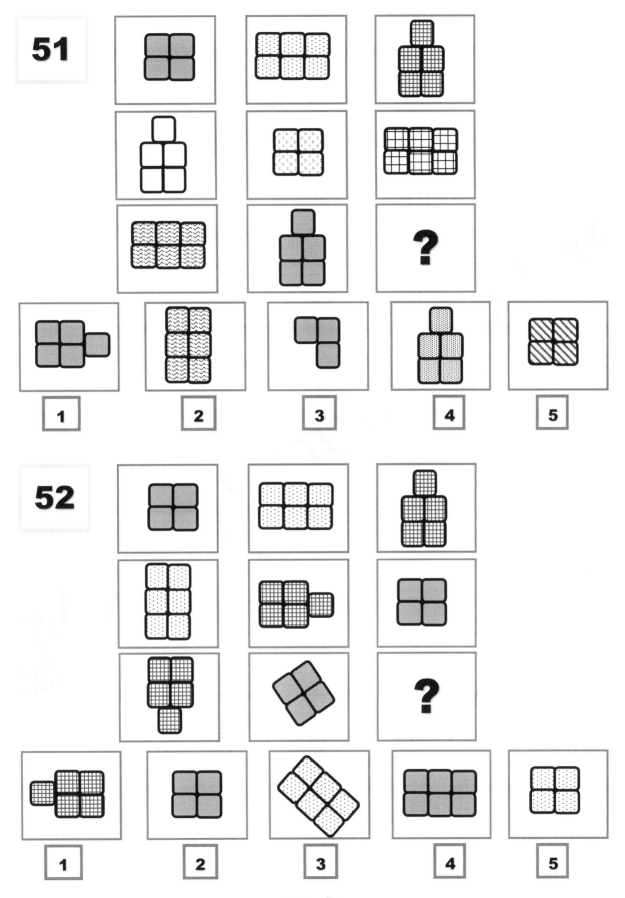

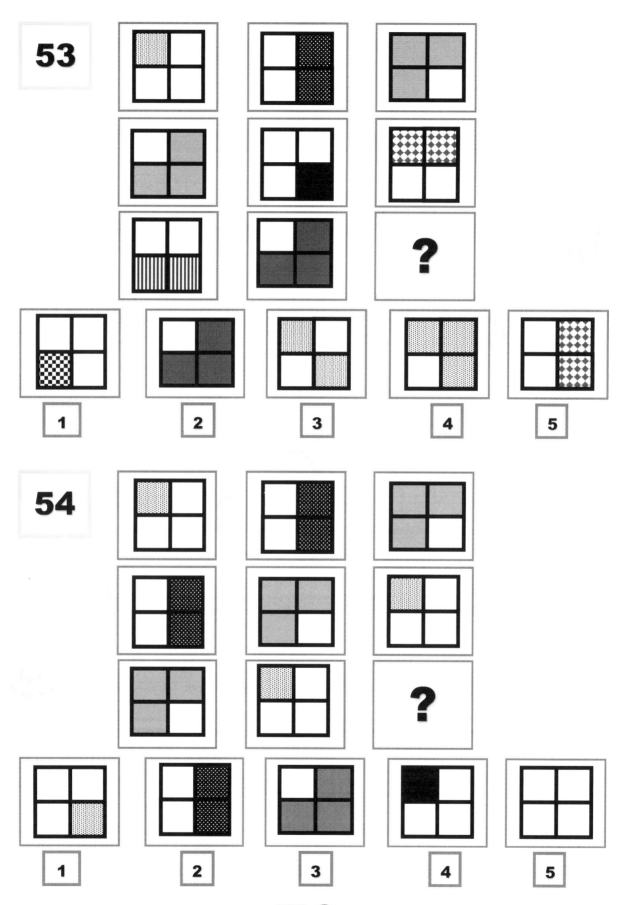

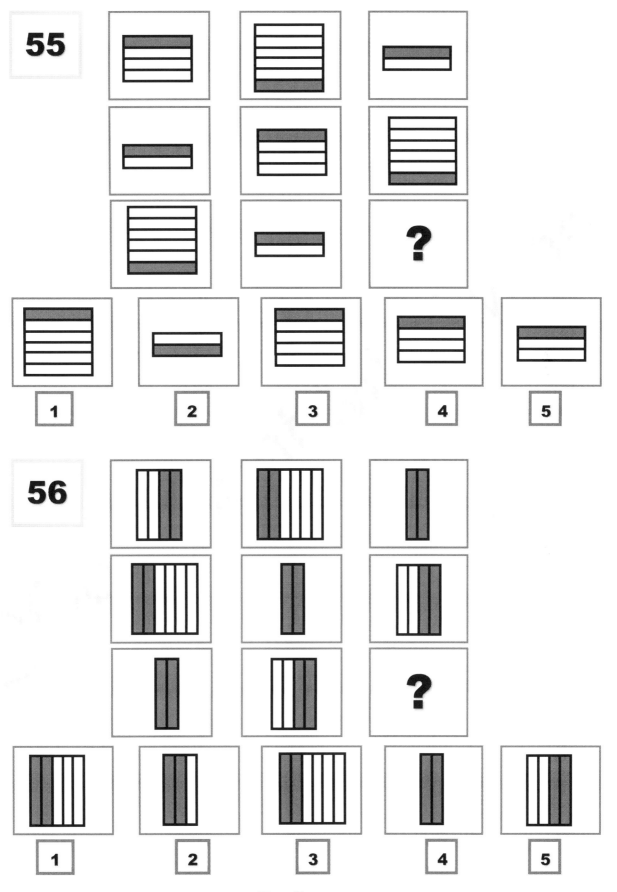

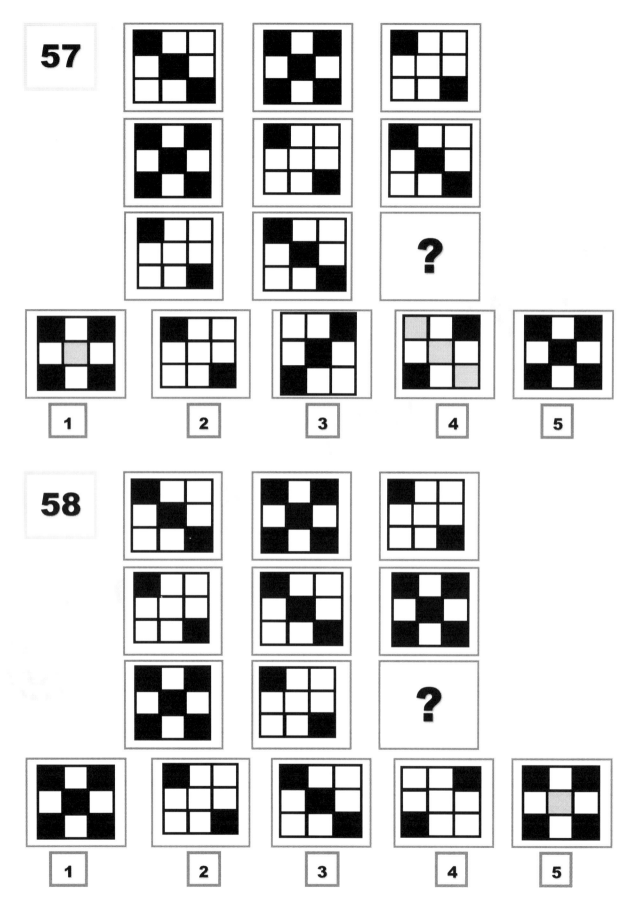

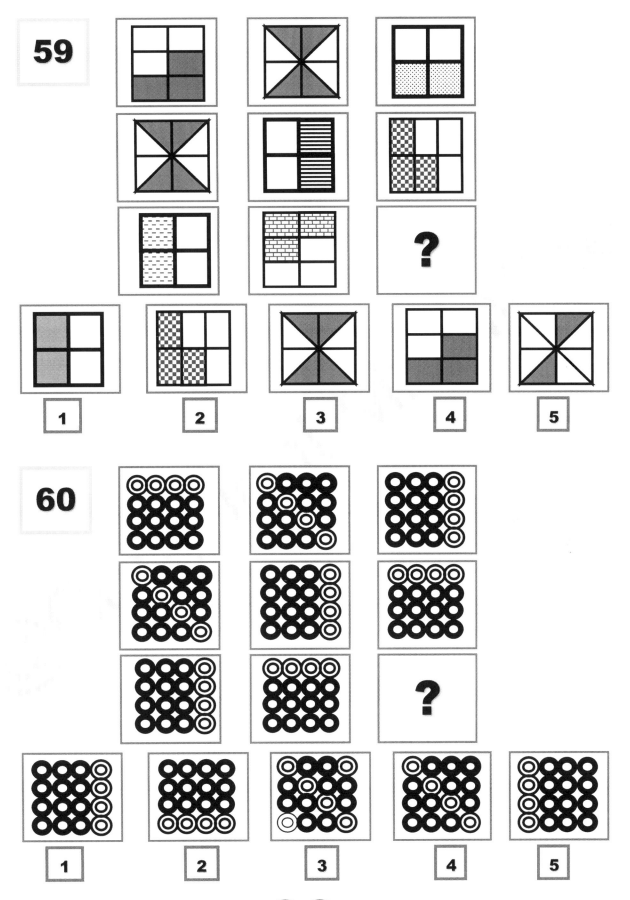

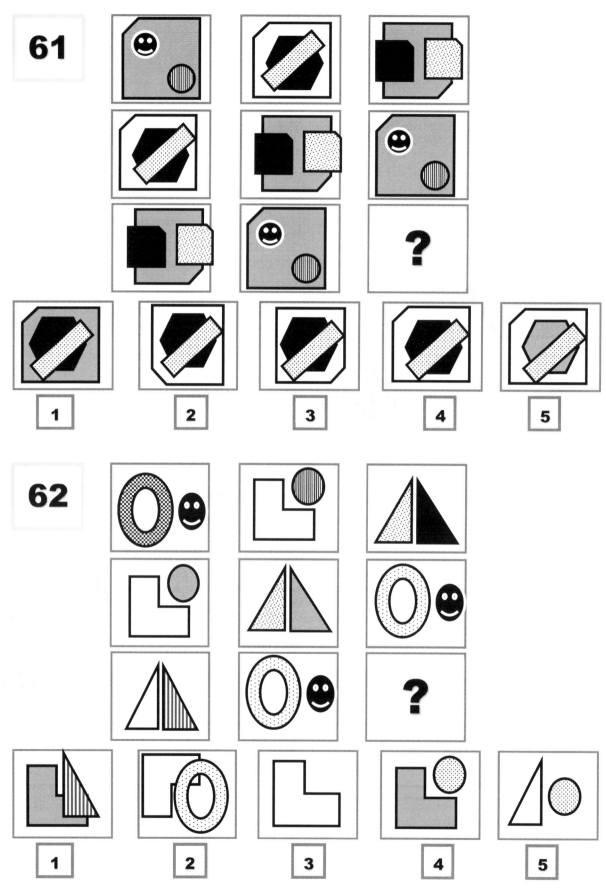

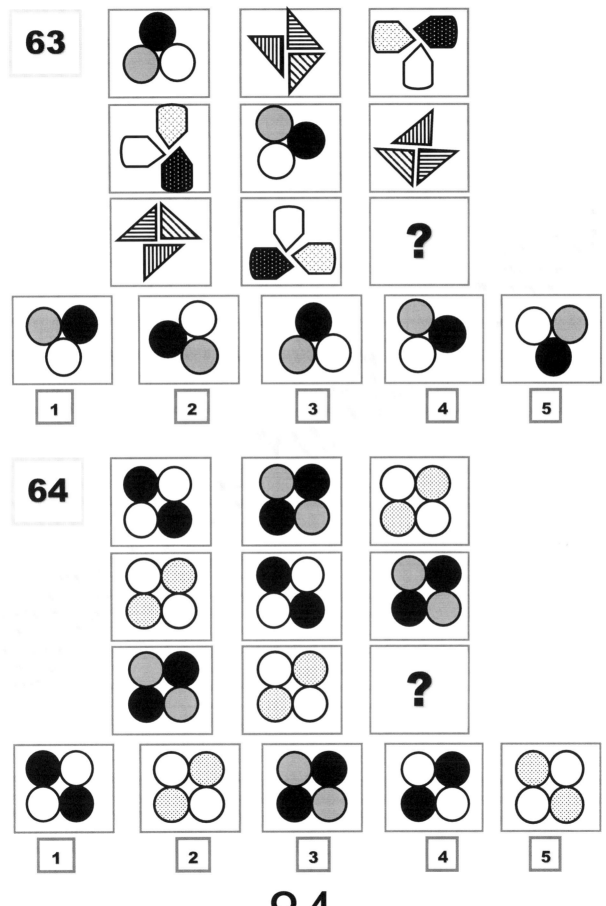

84

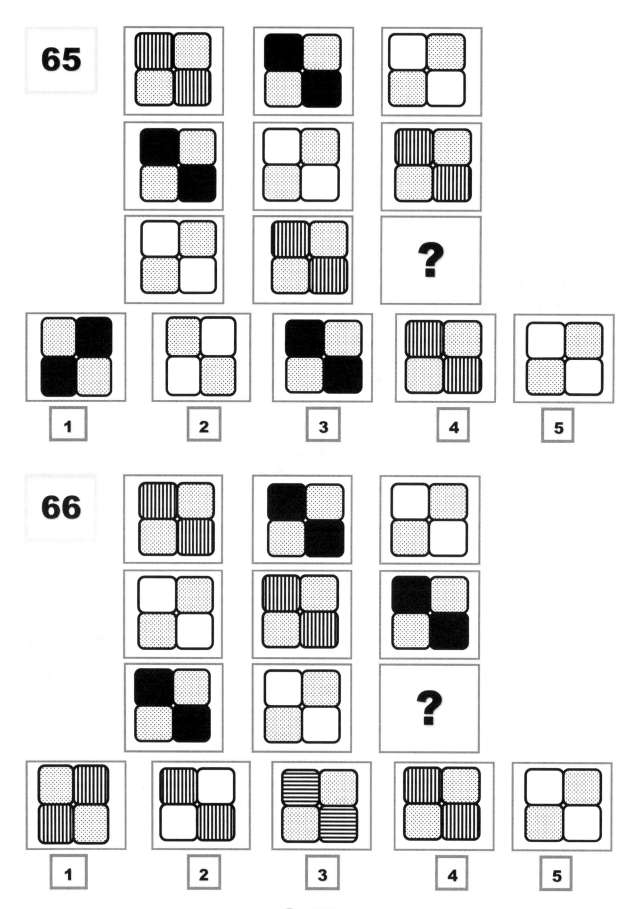

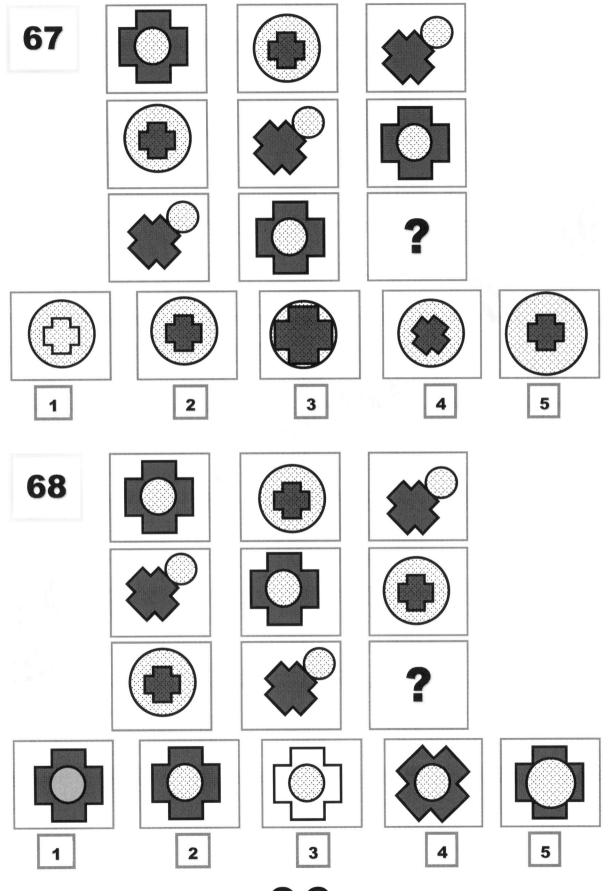

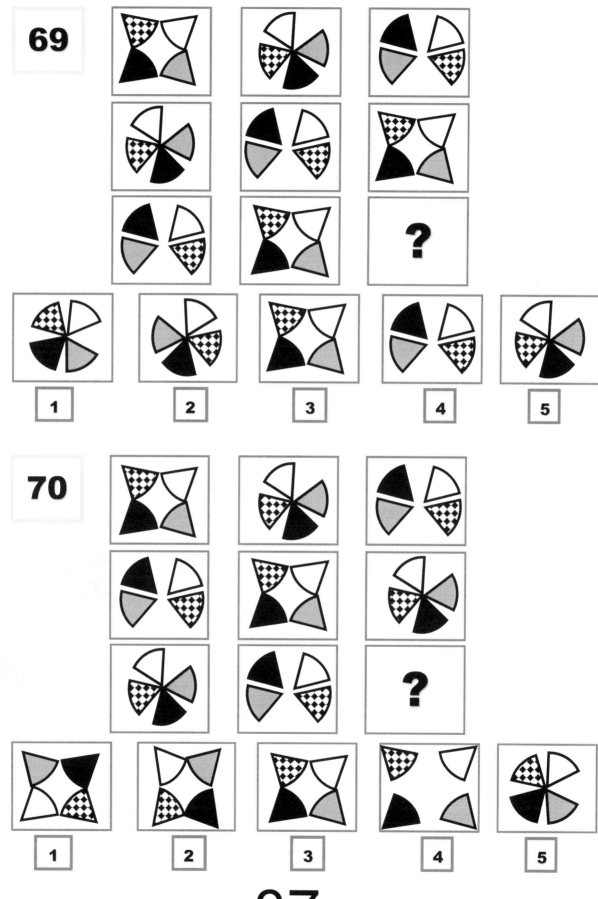

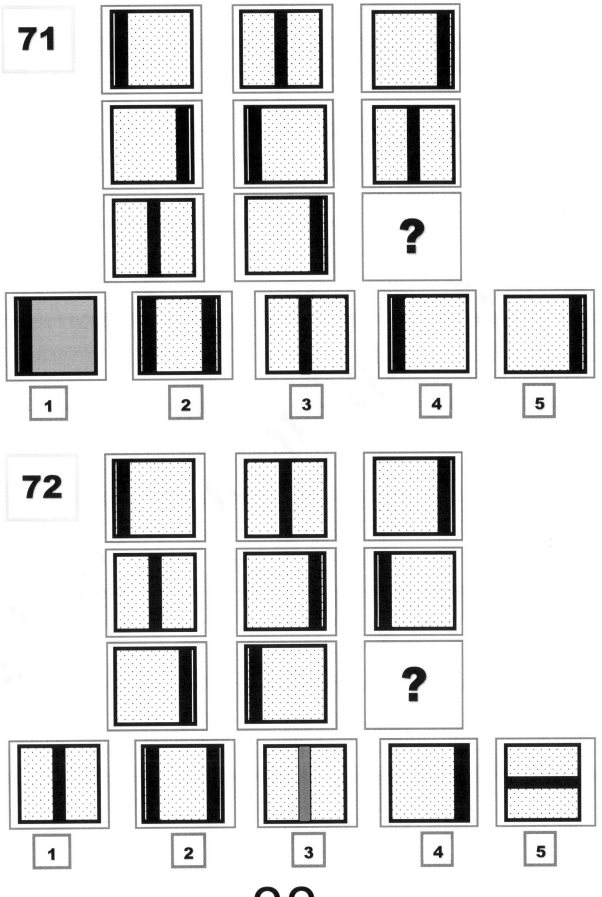

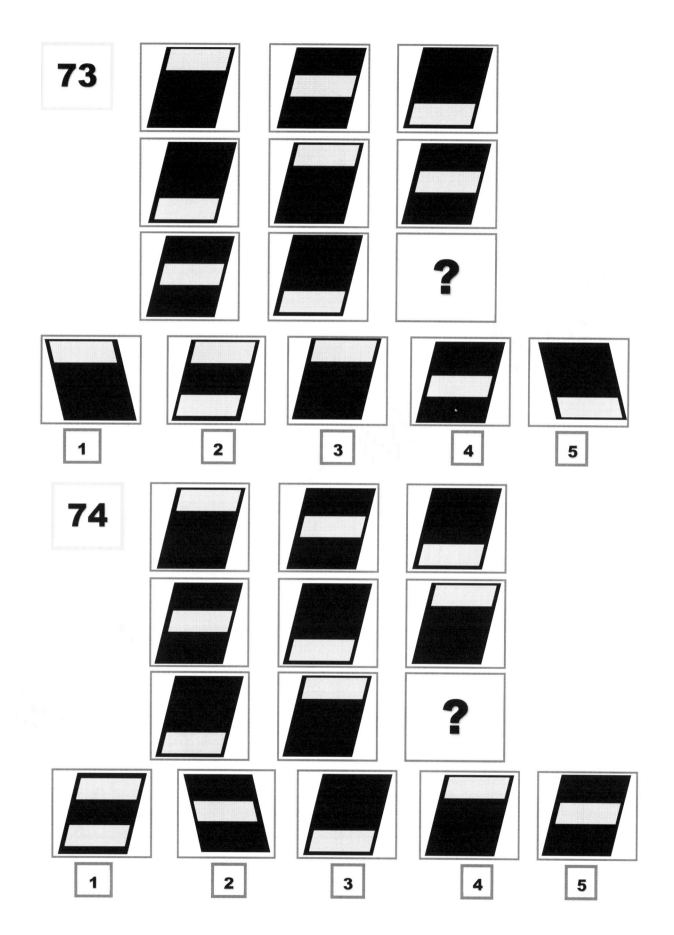

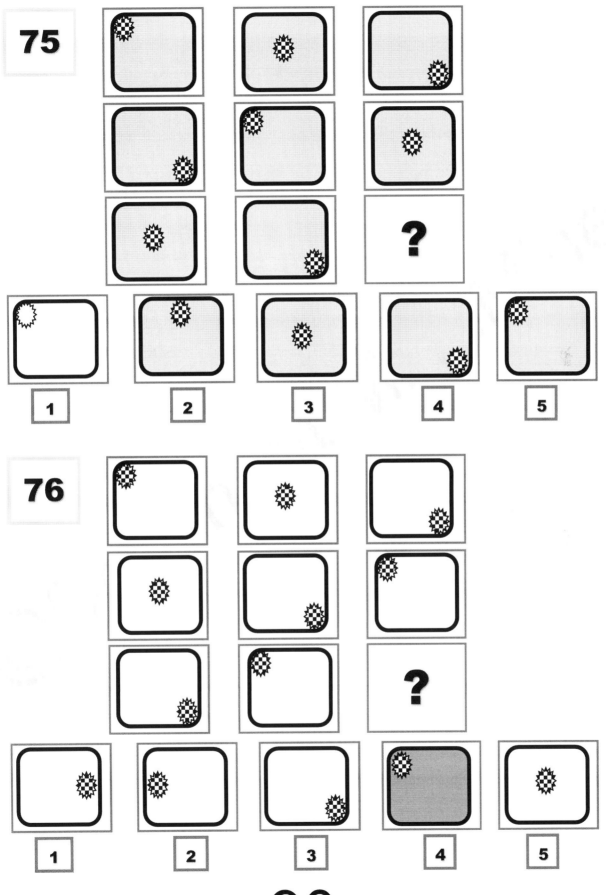

75

76

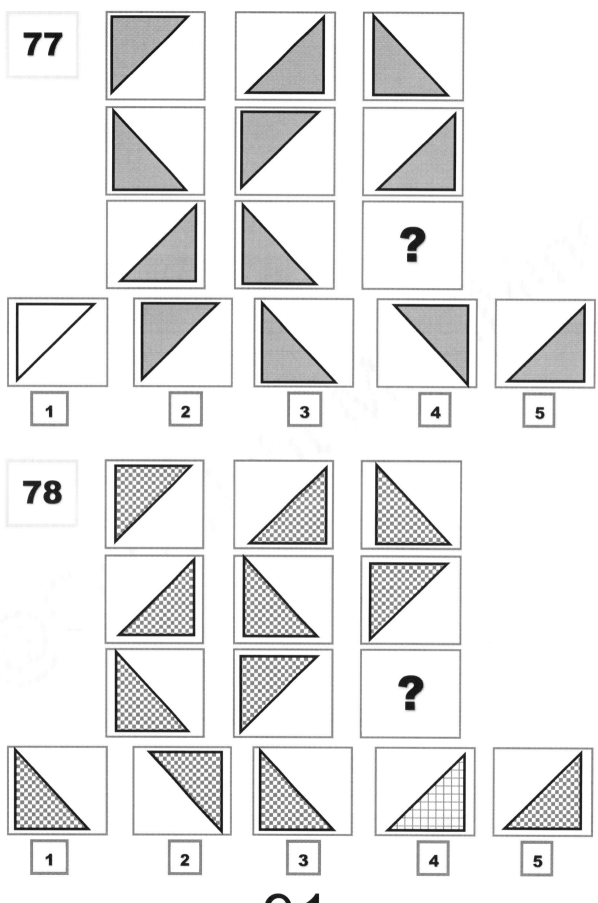

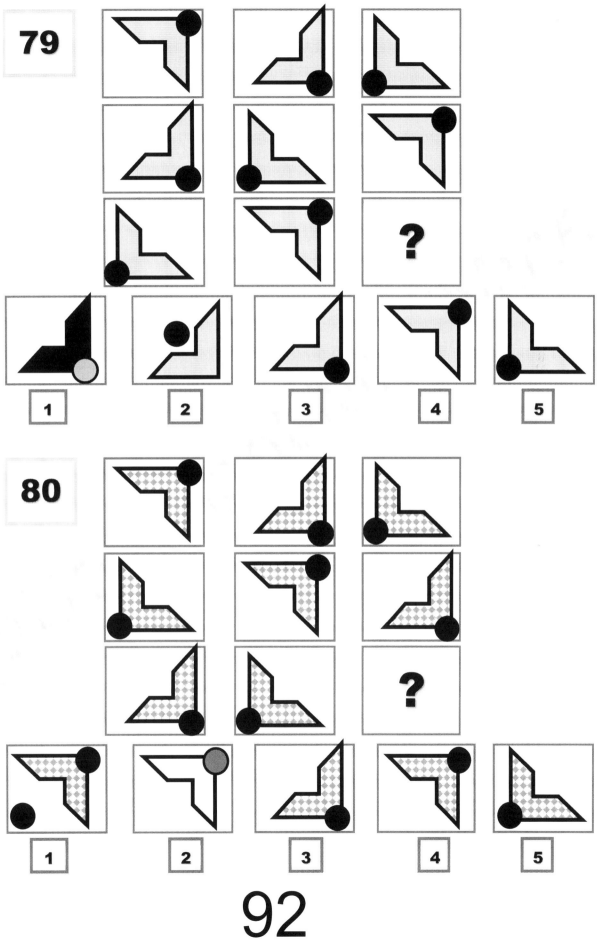

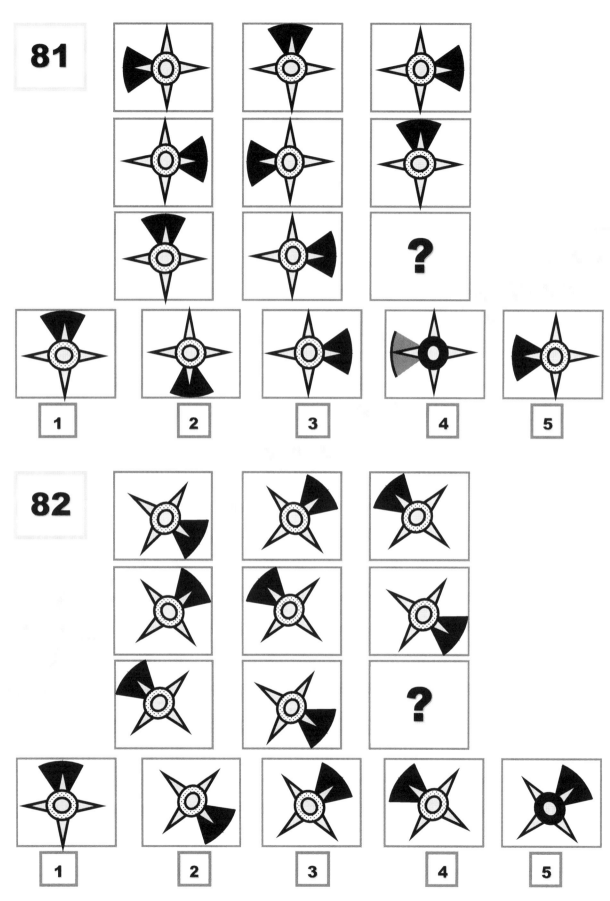

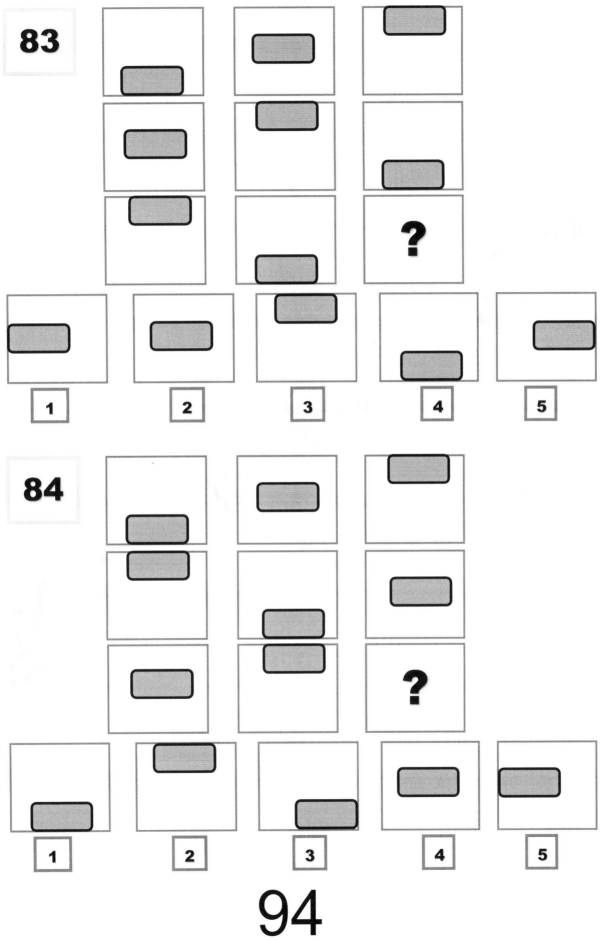

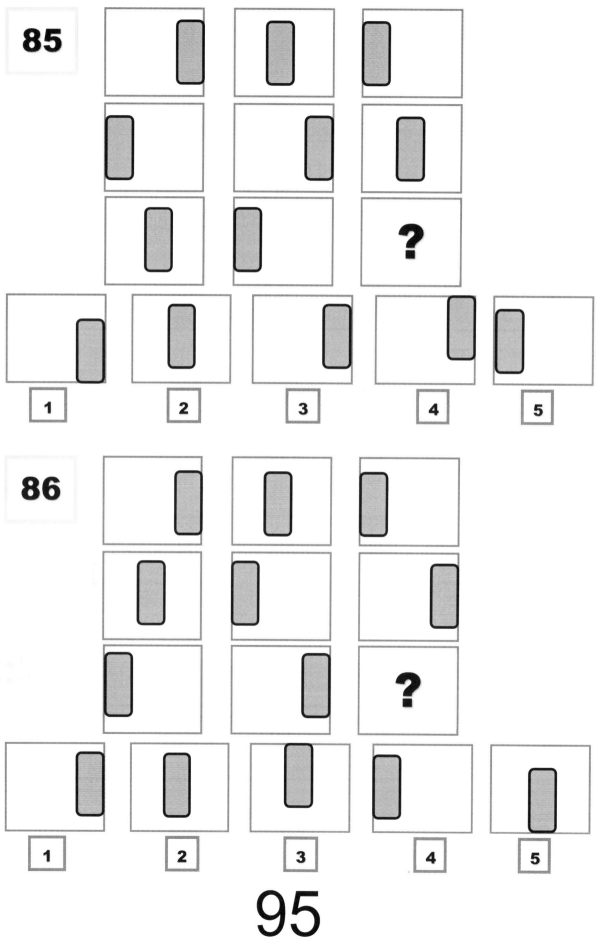

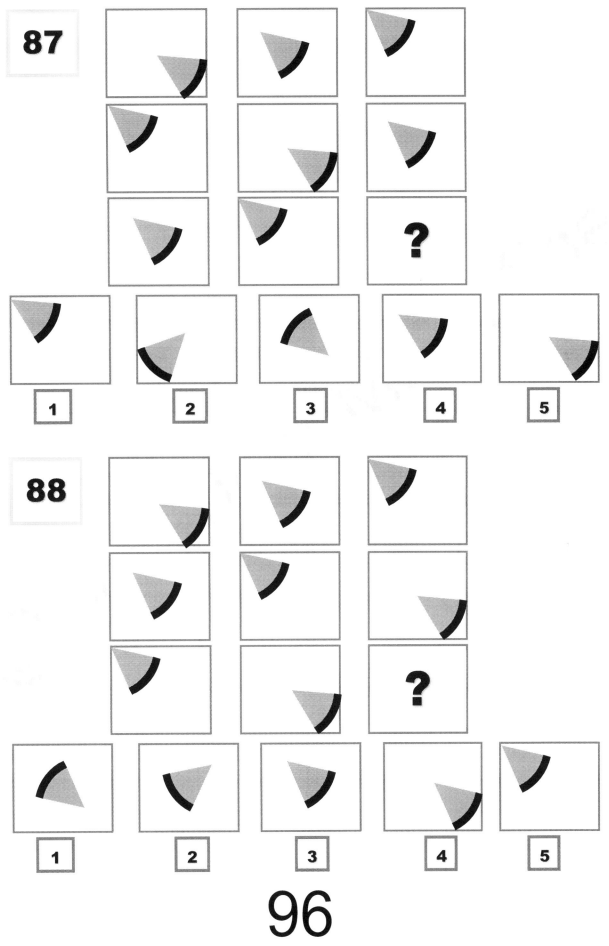

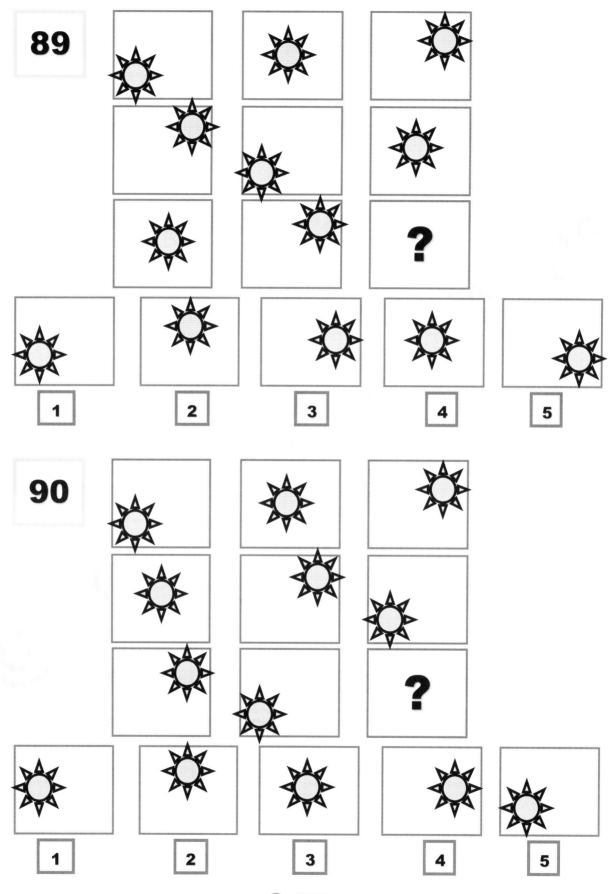

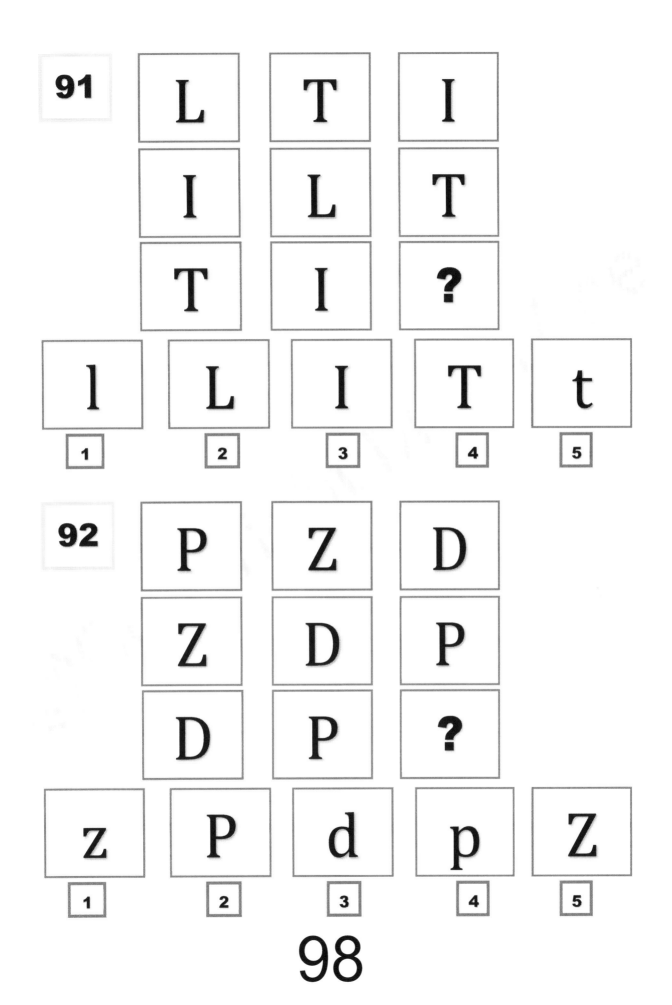

**93**

| p | d | q |
|---|---|---|
| q | p | d |
| d | q | ? |

| p | q | d | P | r |
|---|---|---|---|---|
| 1 | 2 | 3 | 4 | 5 |

**94**

| p | d | q |
|---|---|---|
| d | q | p |
| q | p | ? |

| q | d | D | p | r |
|---|---|---|---|---|
| 1 | 2 | 3 | 4 | 5 |

99

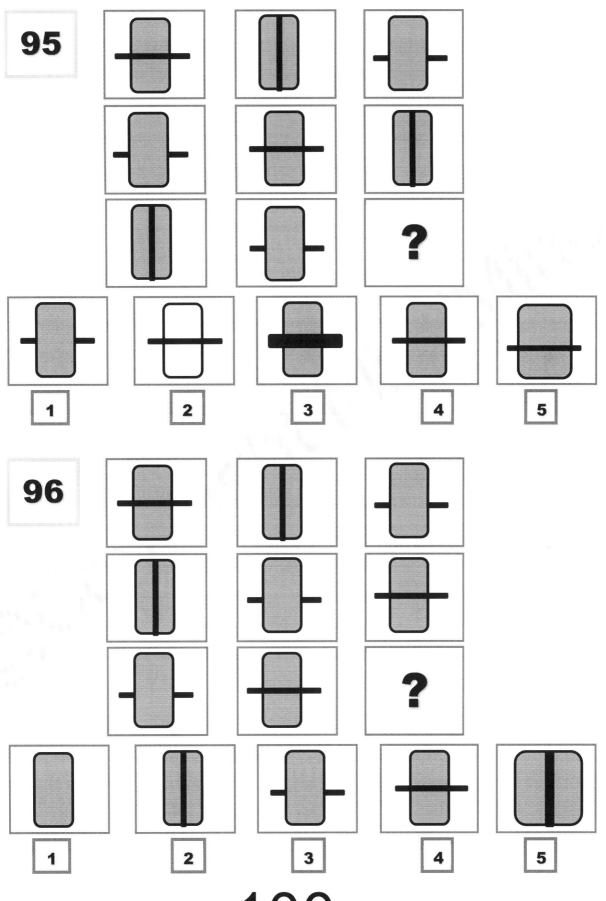

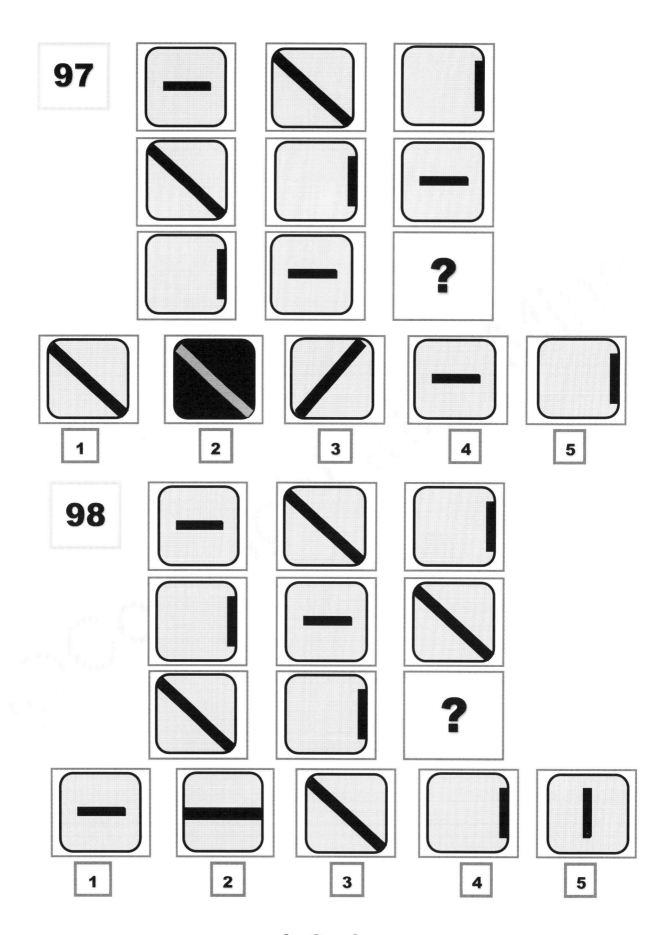

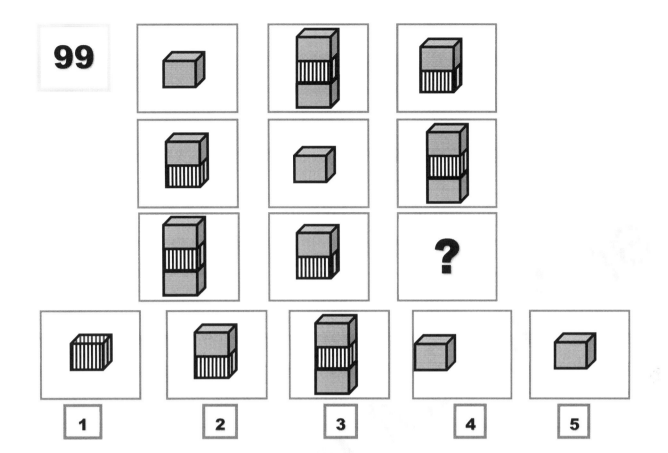

1 2 3 4 5

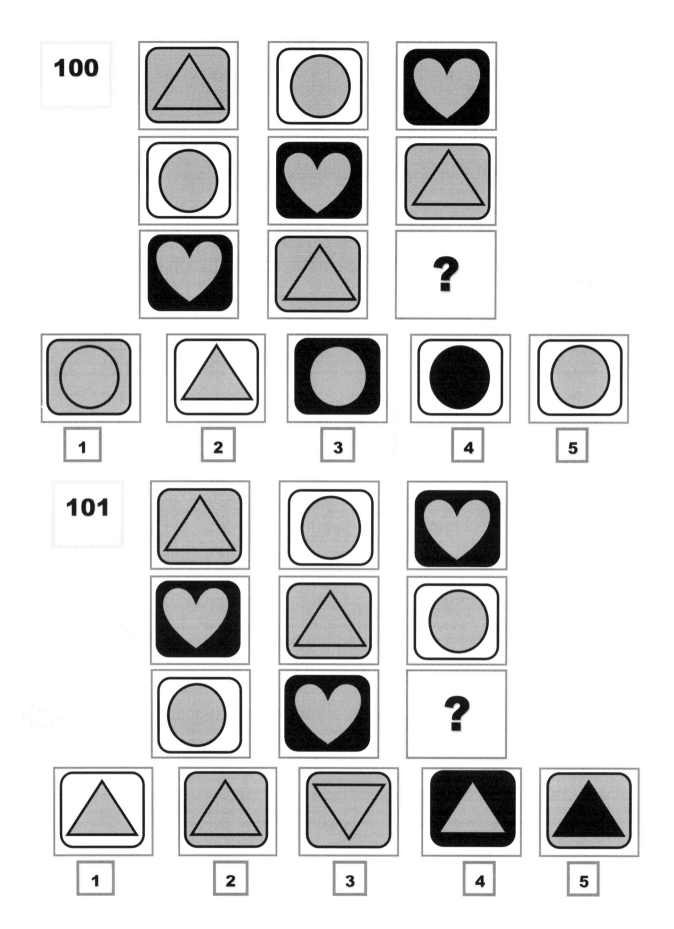

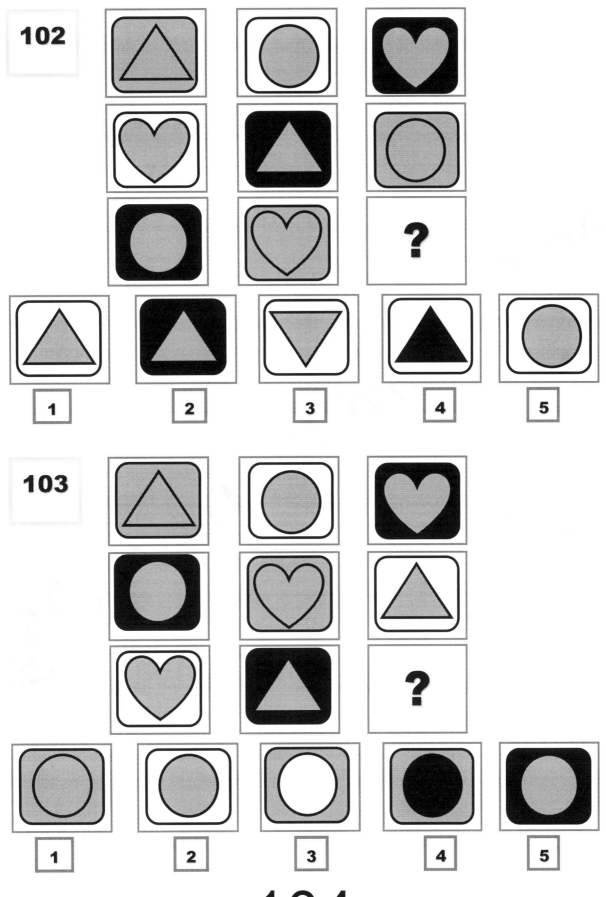

104

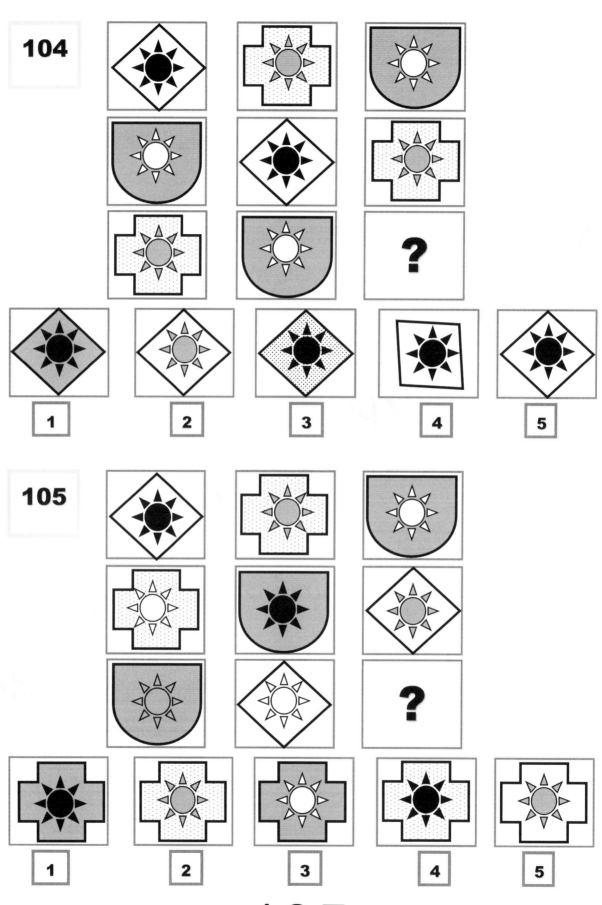

104

105

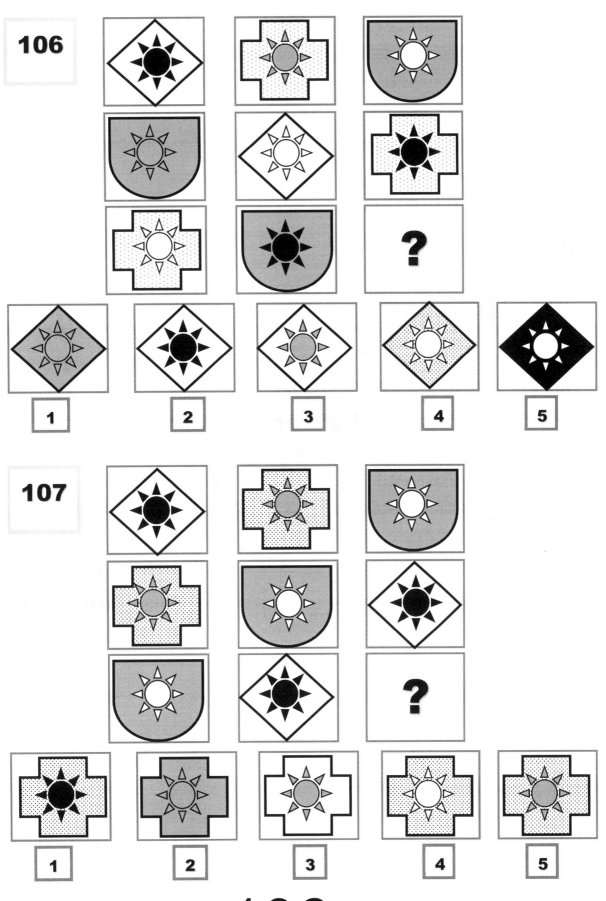

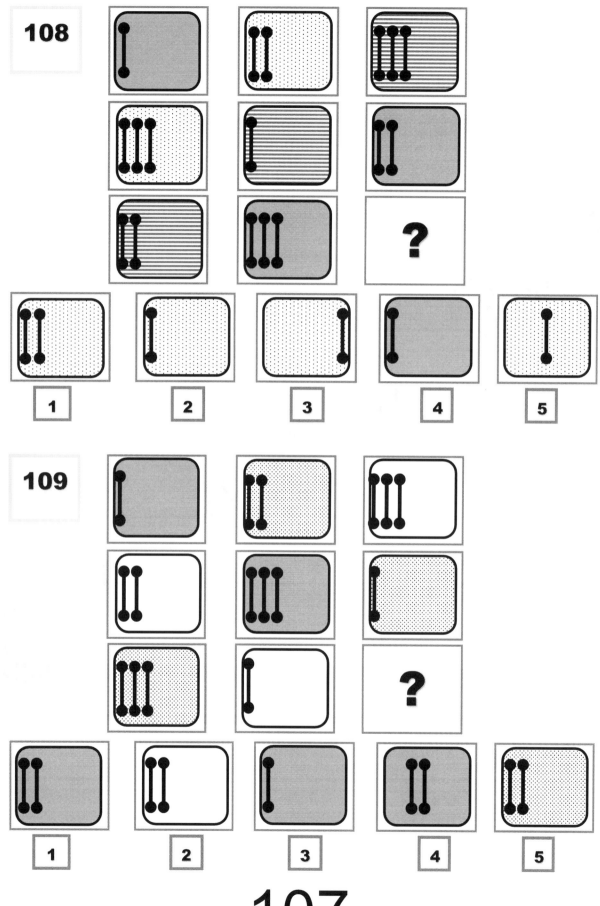

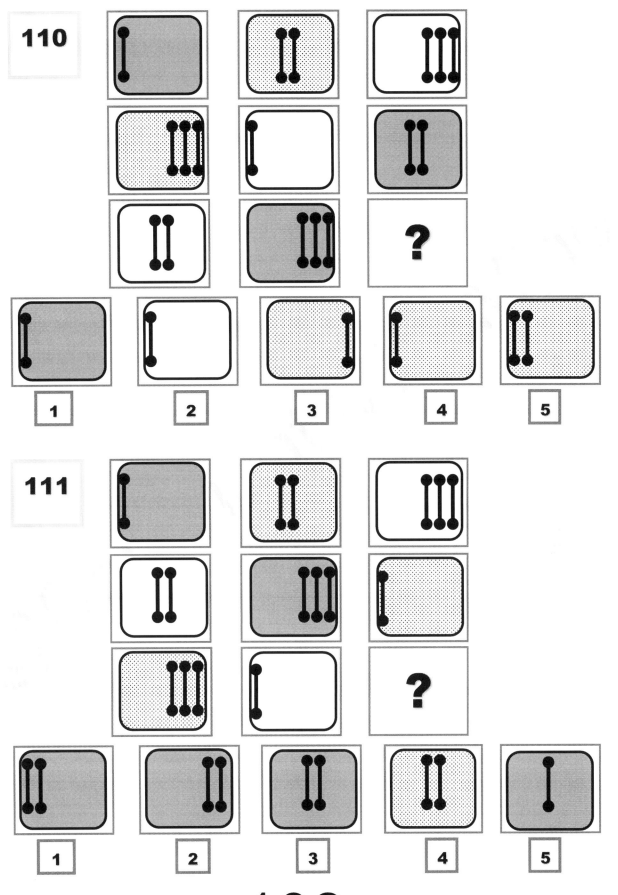

108

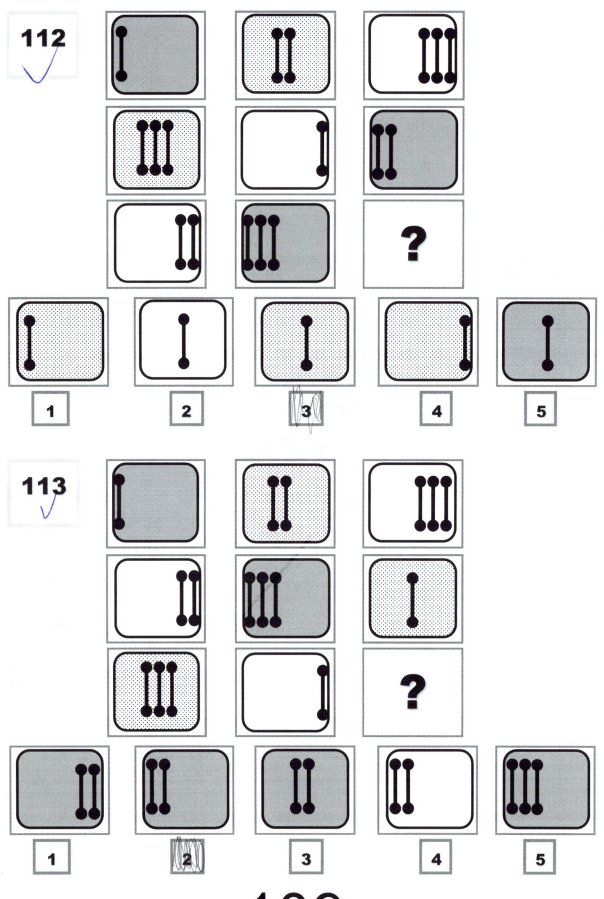

109

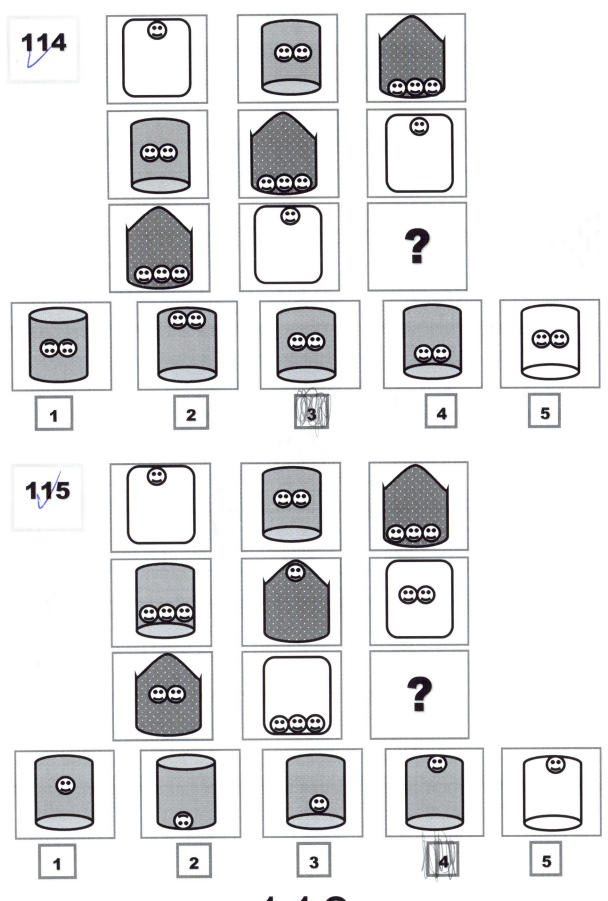

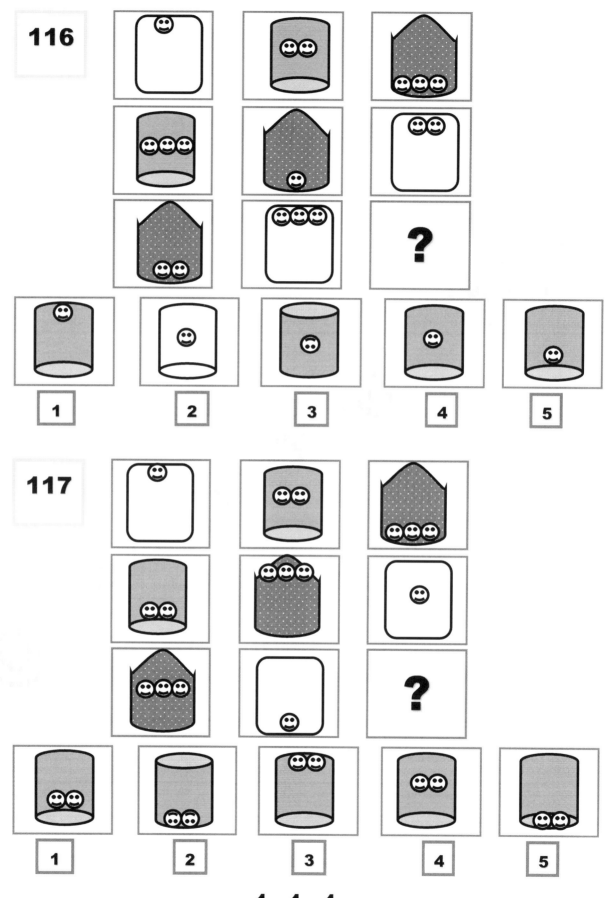

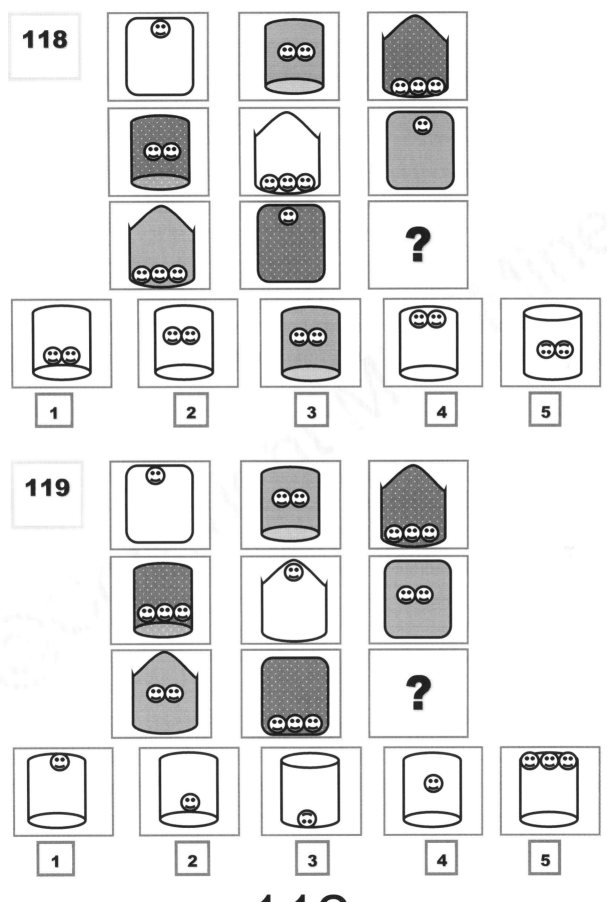

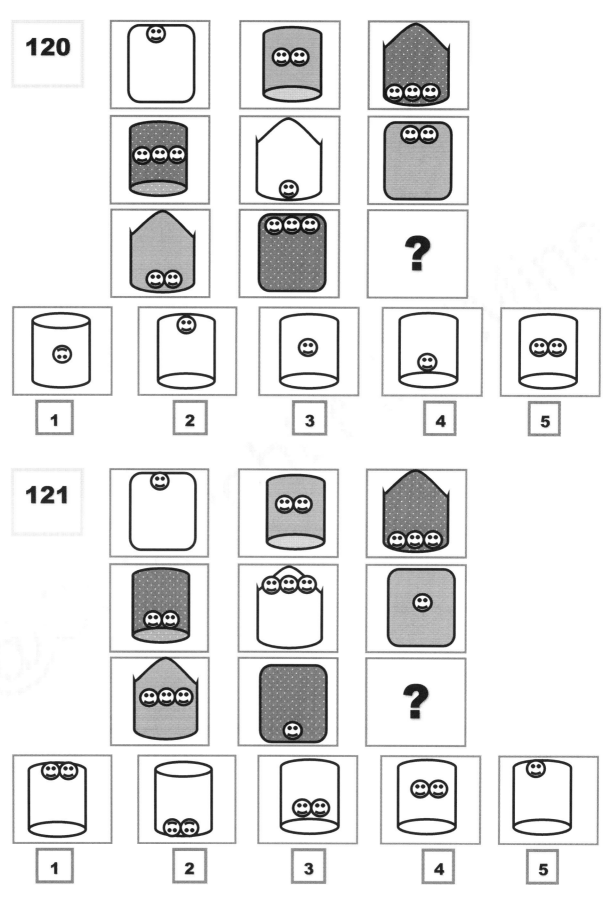

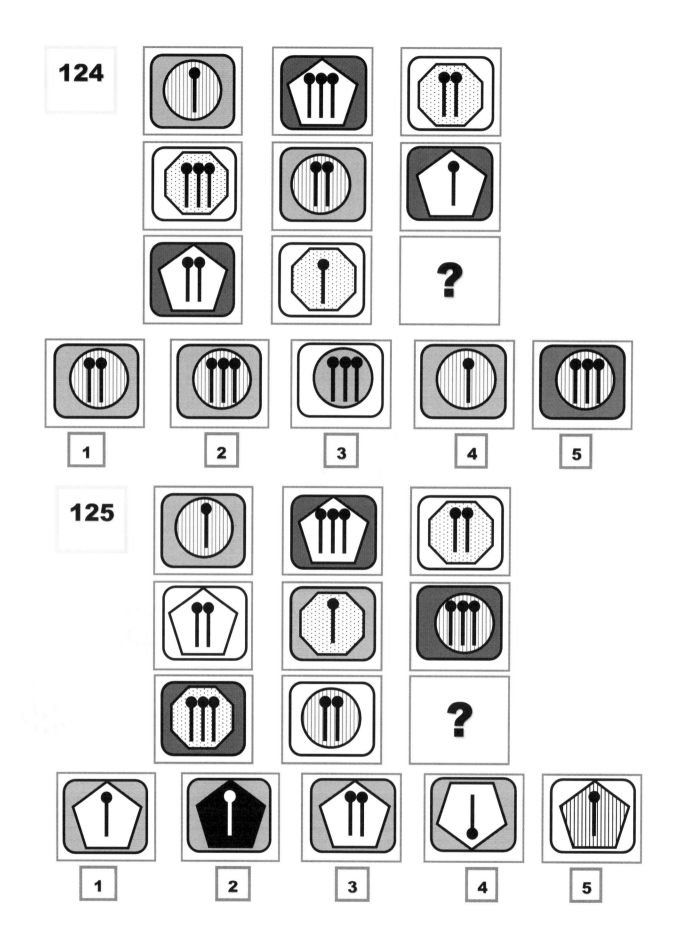

124

1  2  3  4  5

125

1  2  3  4  5

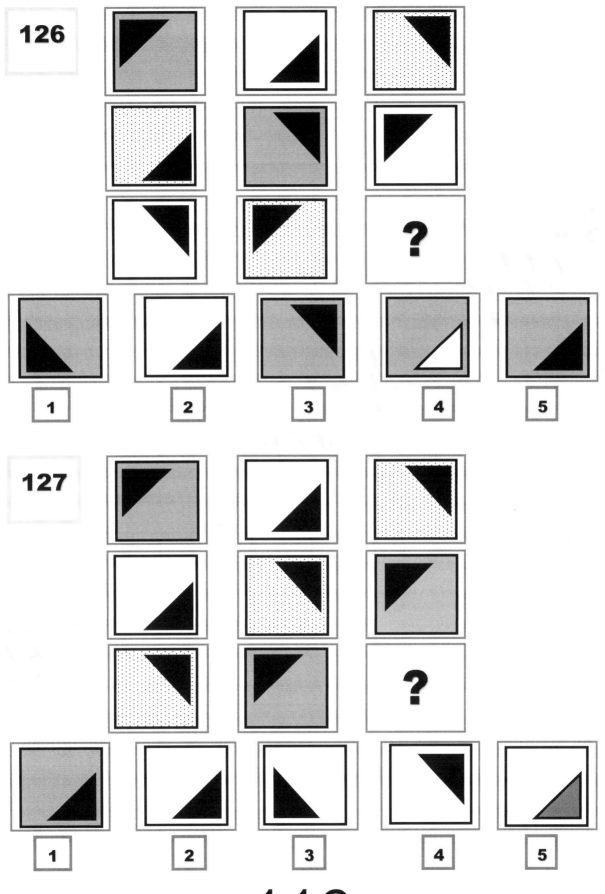

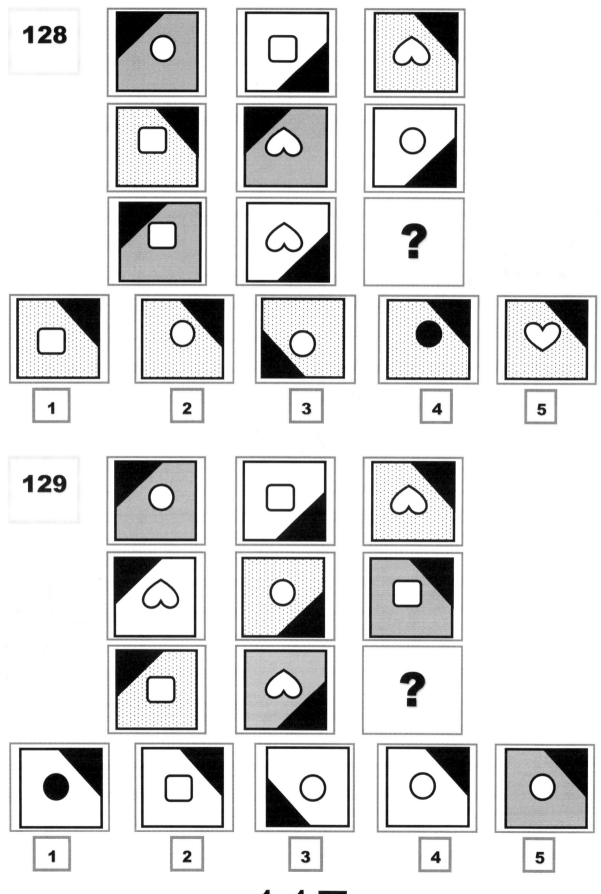

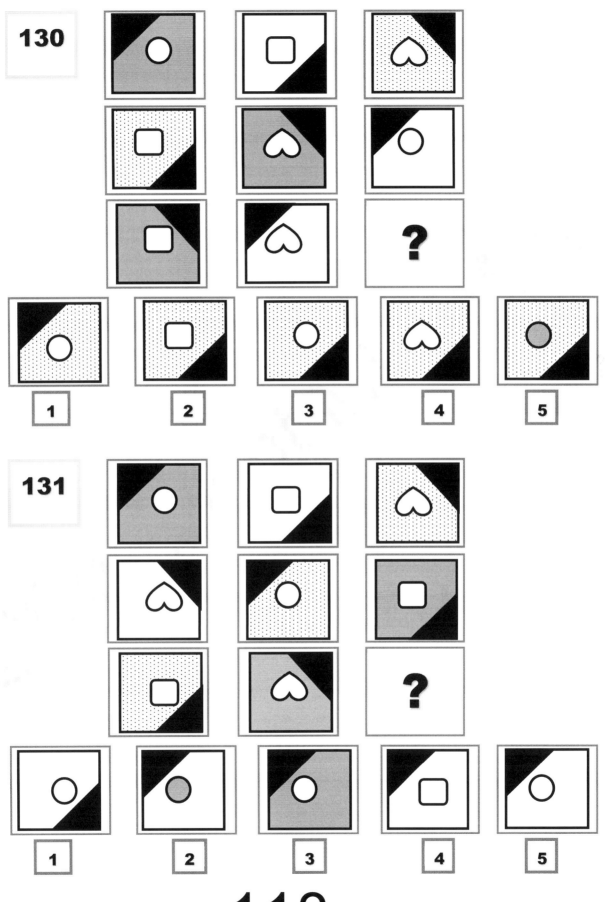

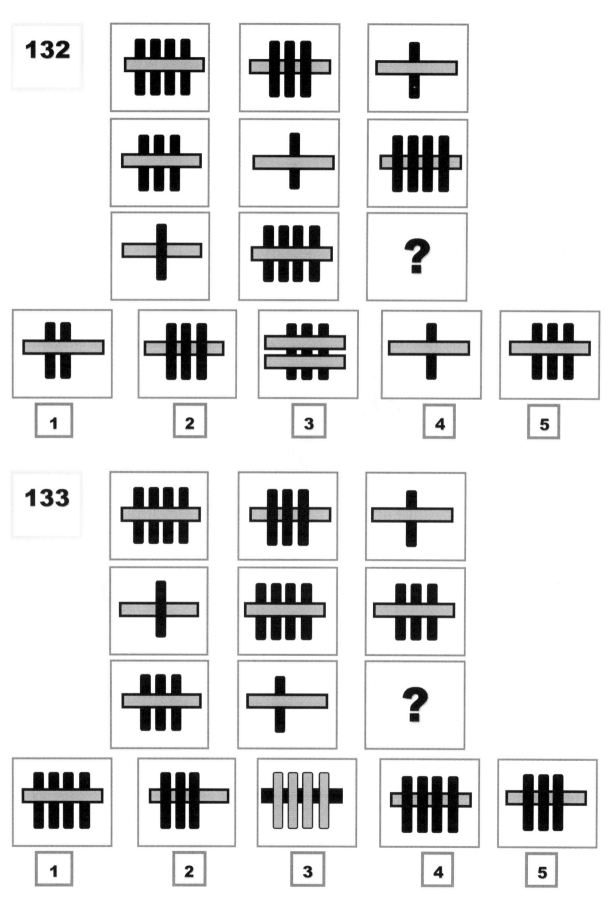

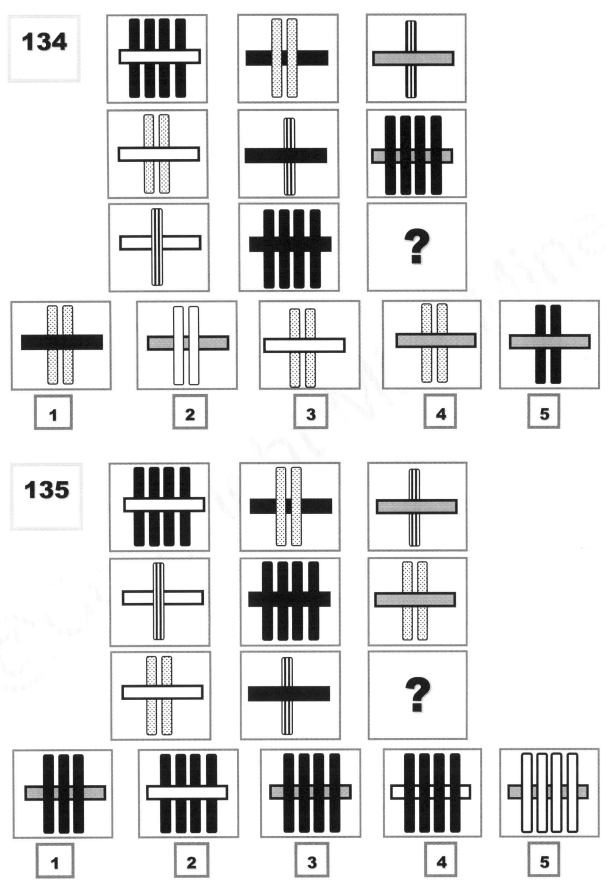

134

135

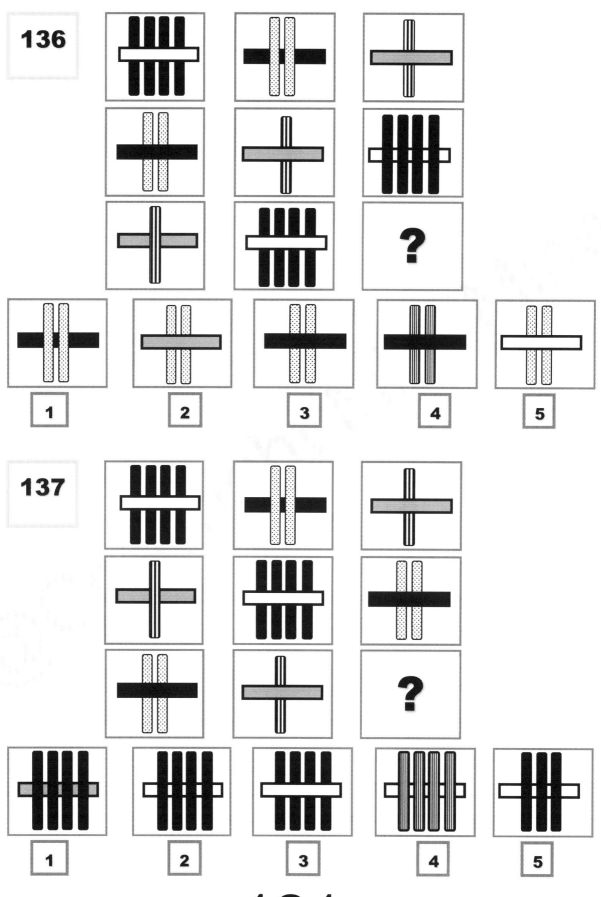

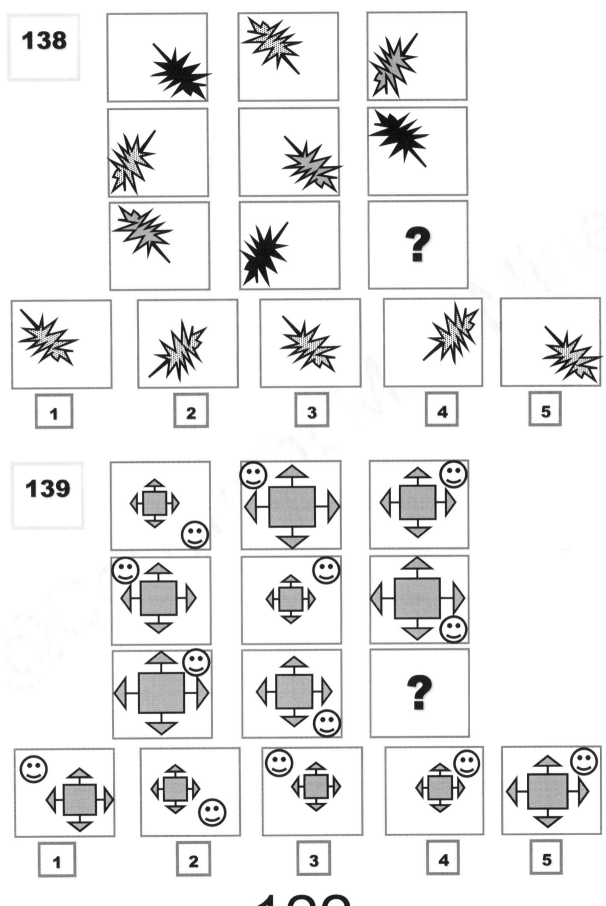

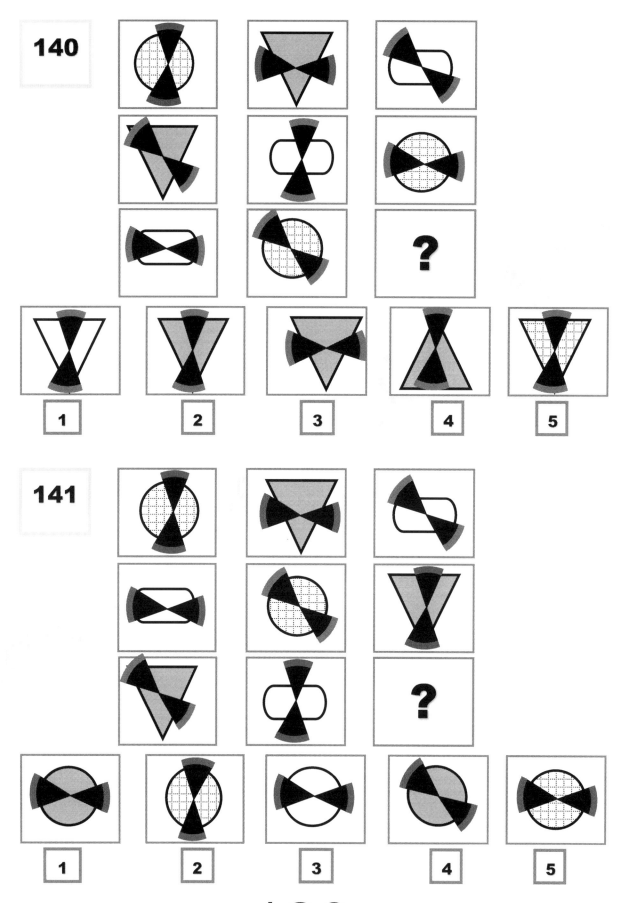

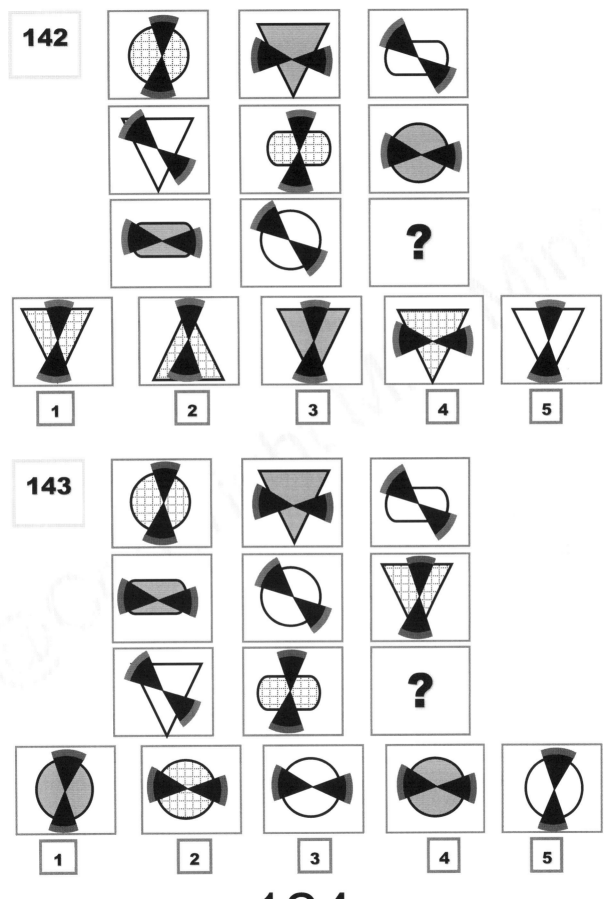

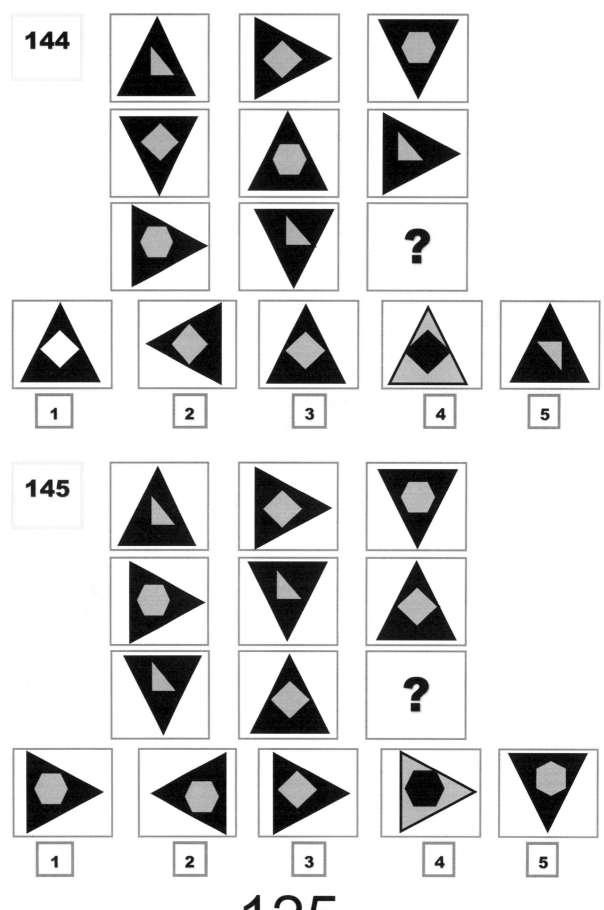

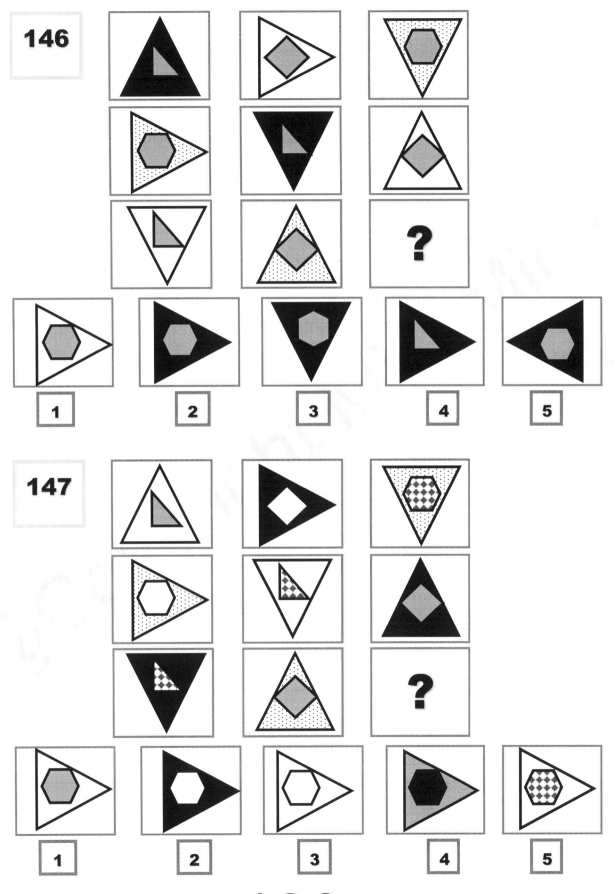

146

147

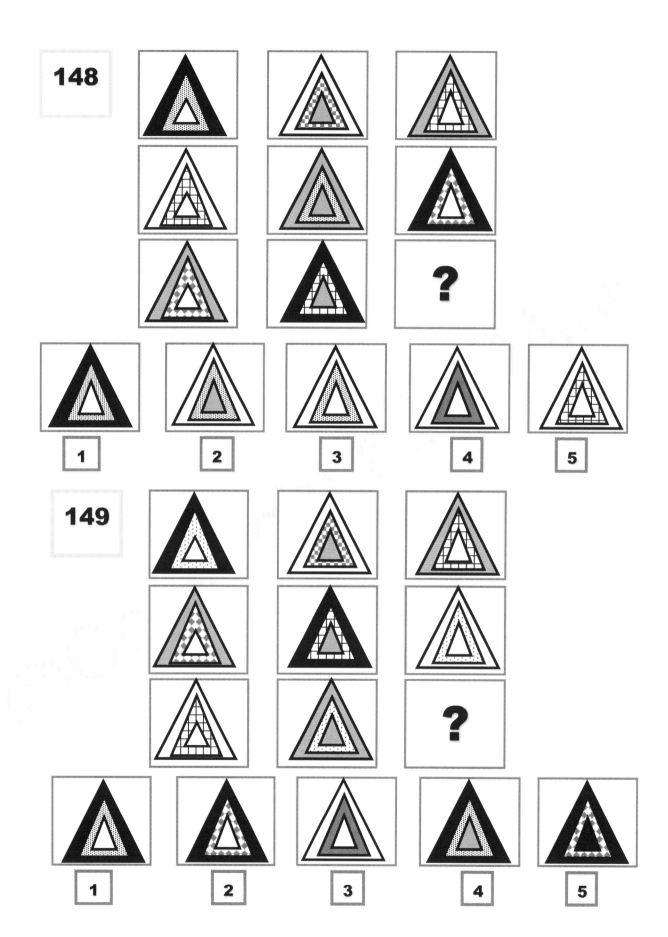

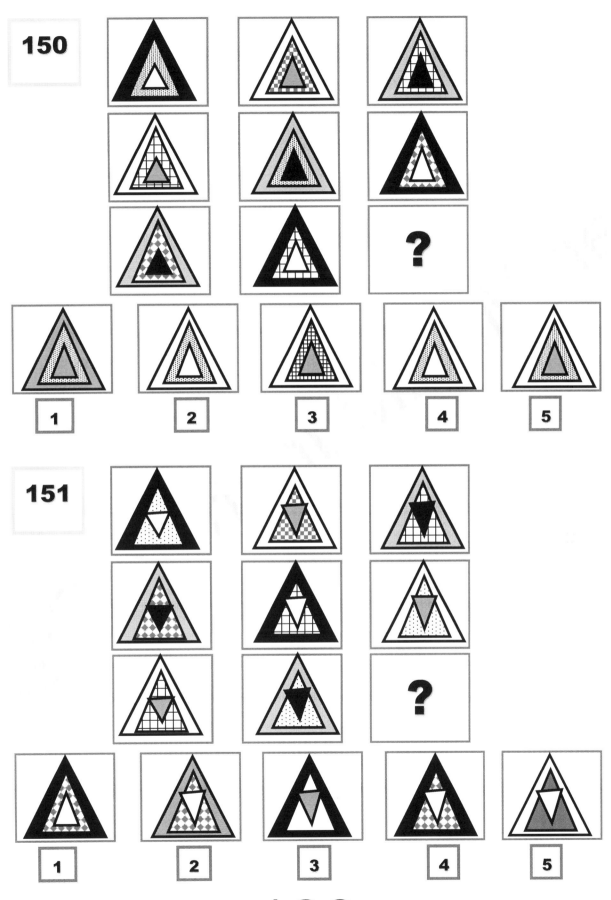

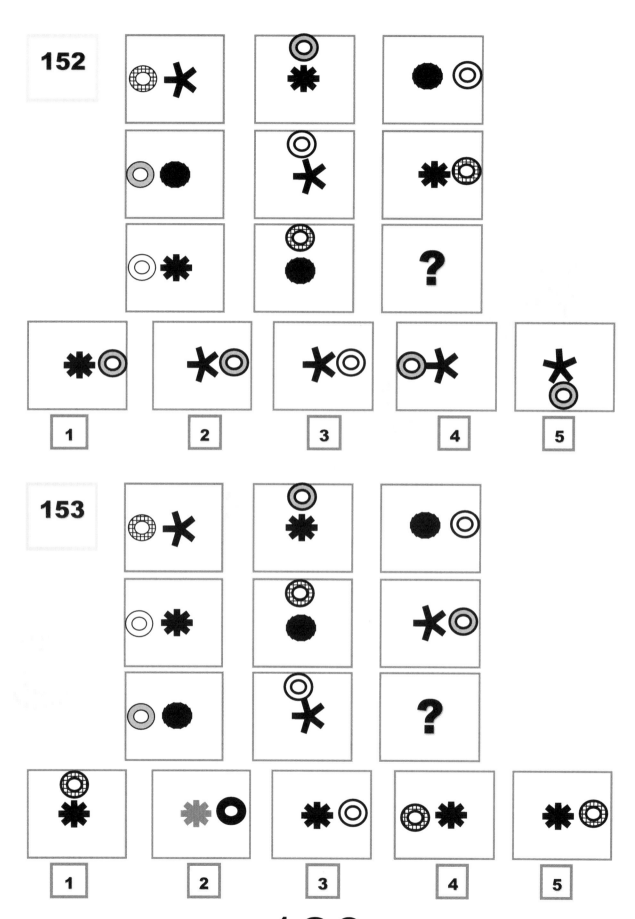

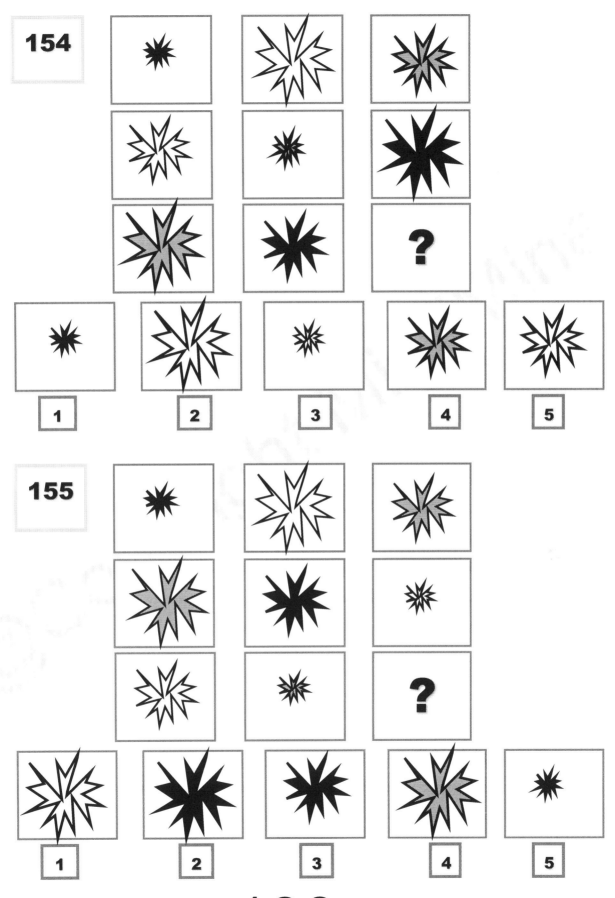

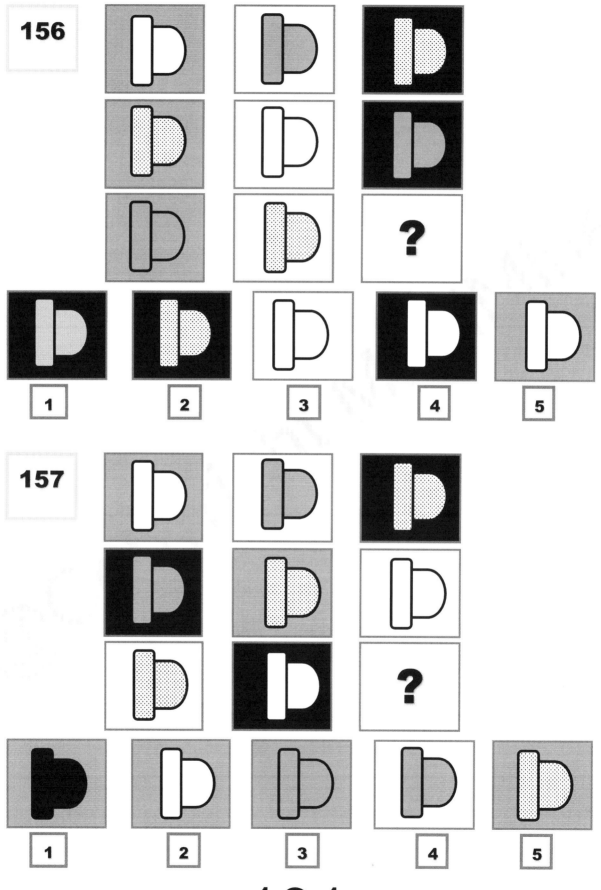

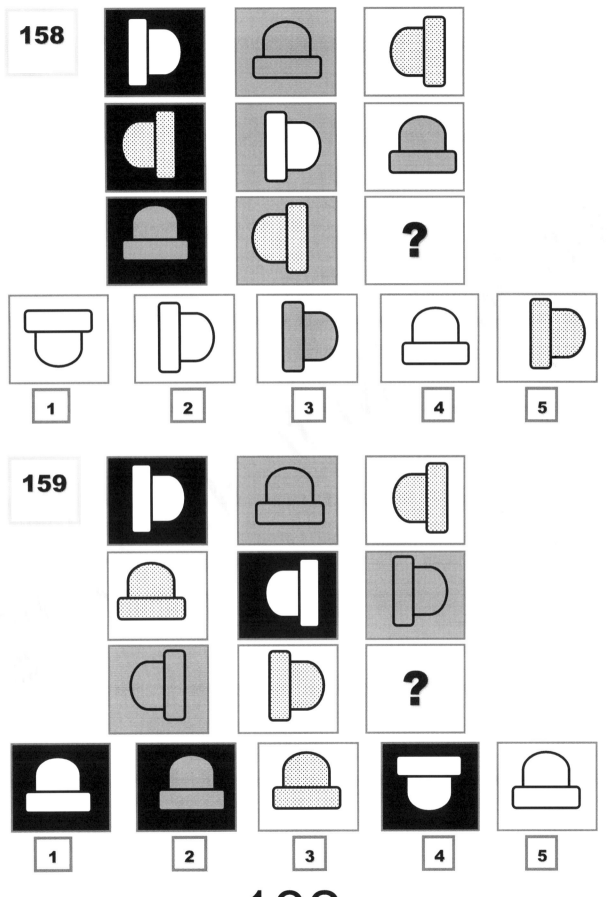

158

159

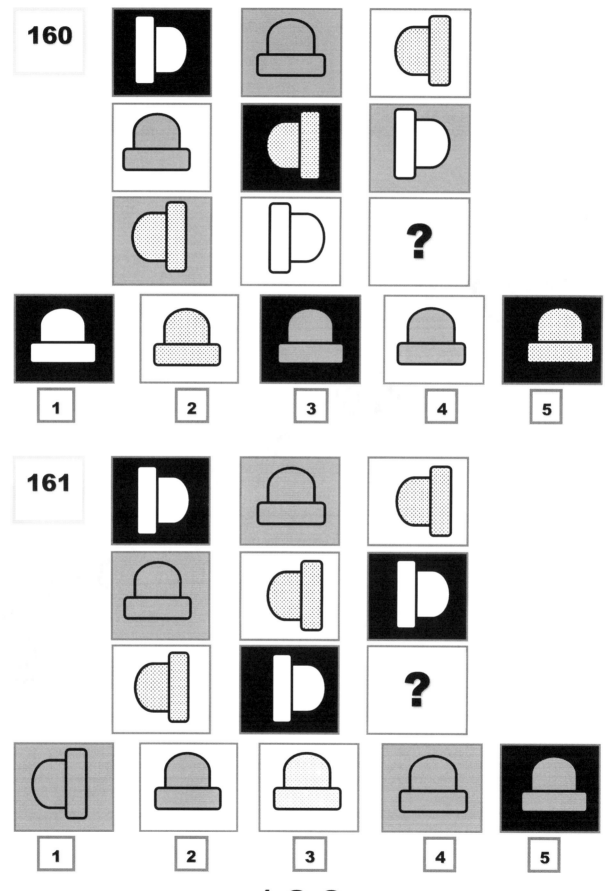

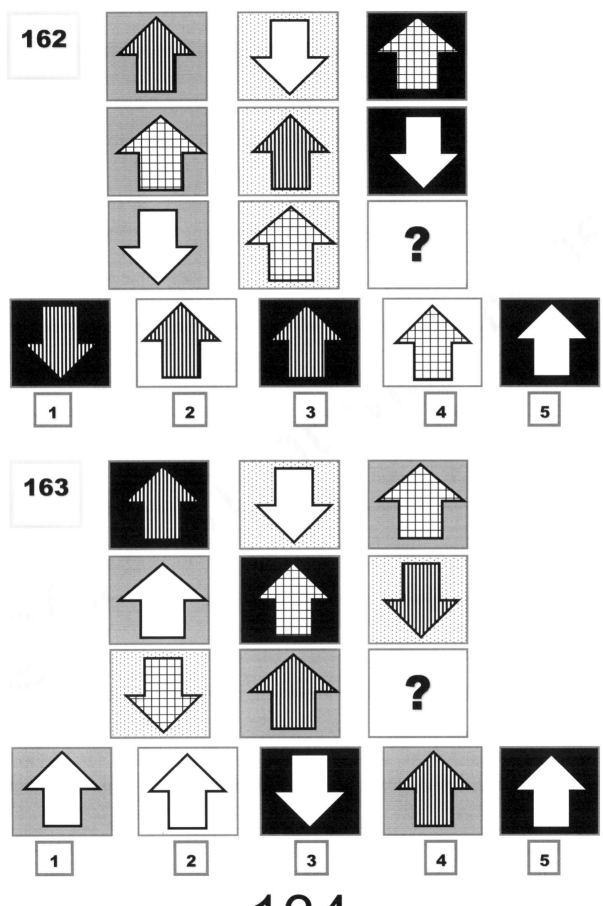

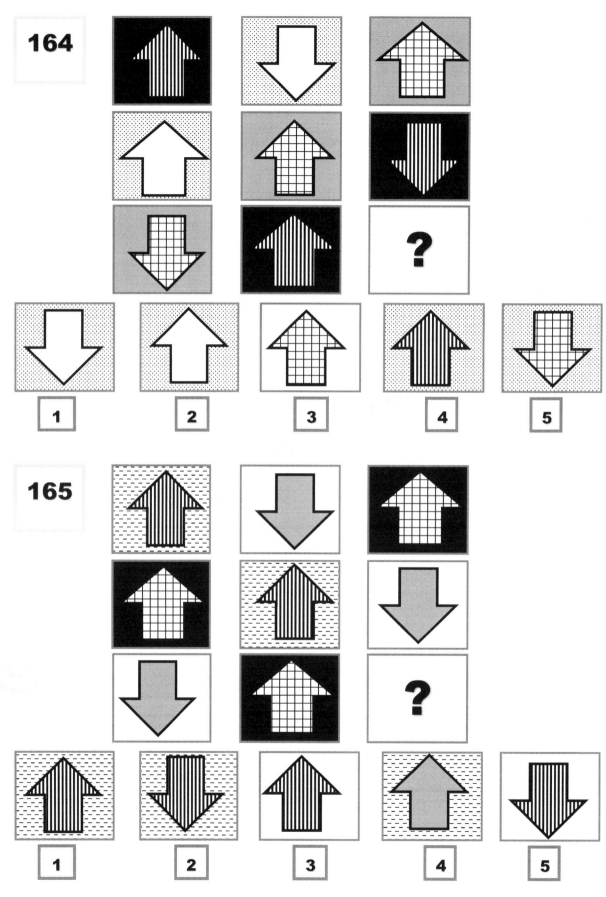

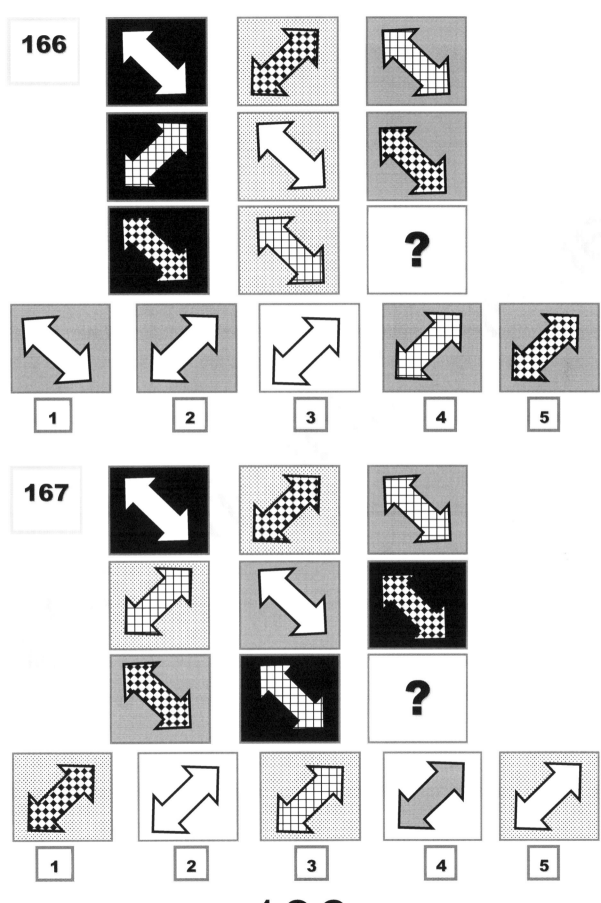

168

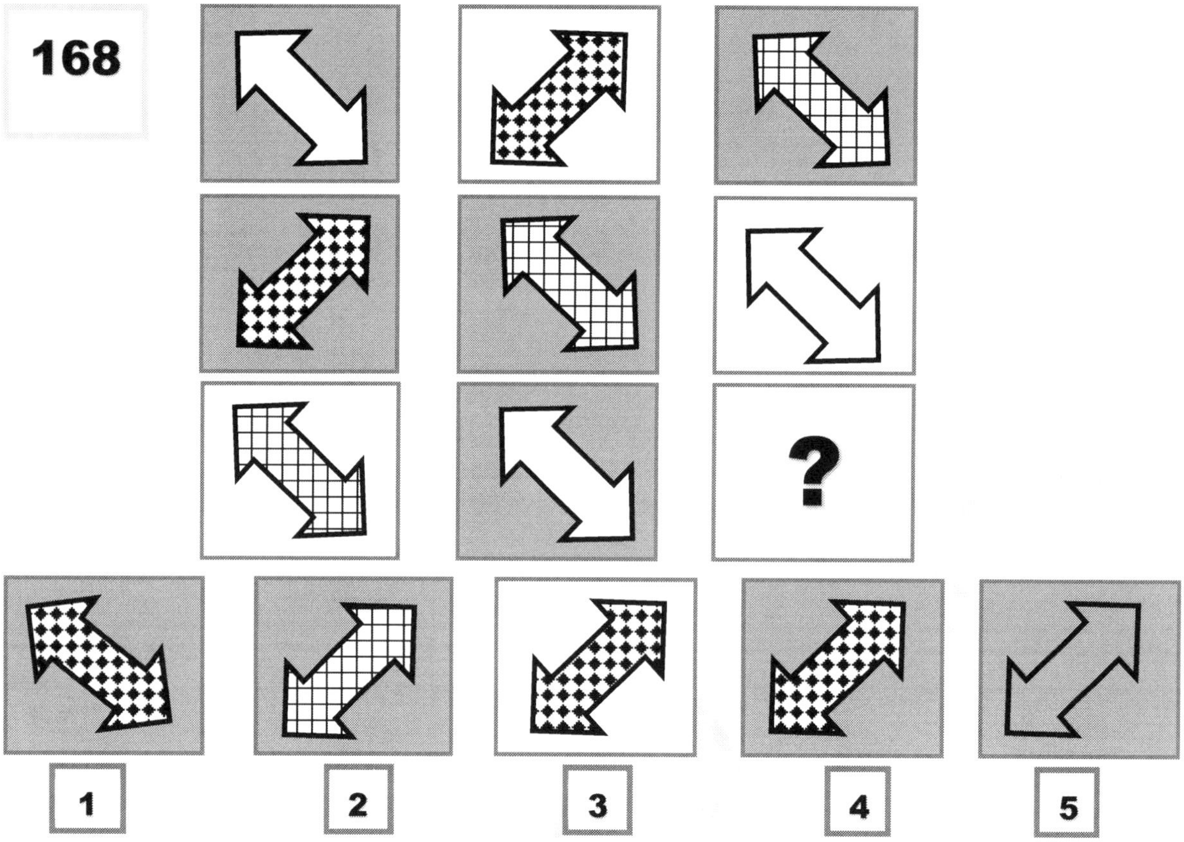

1 2 3 4 5

169

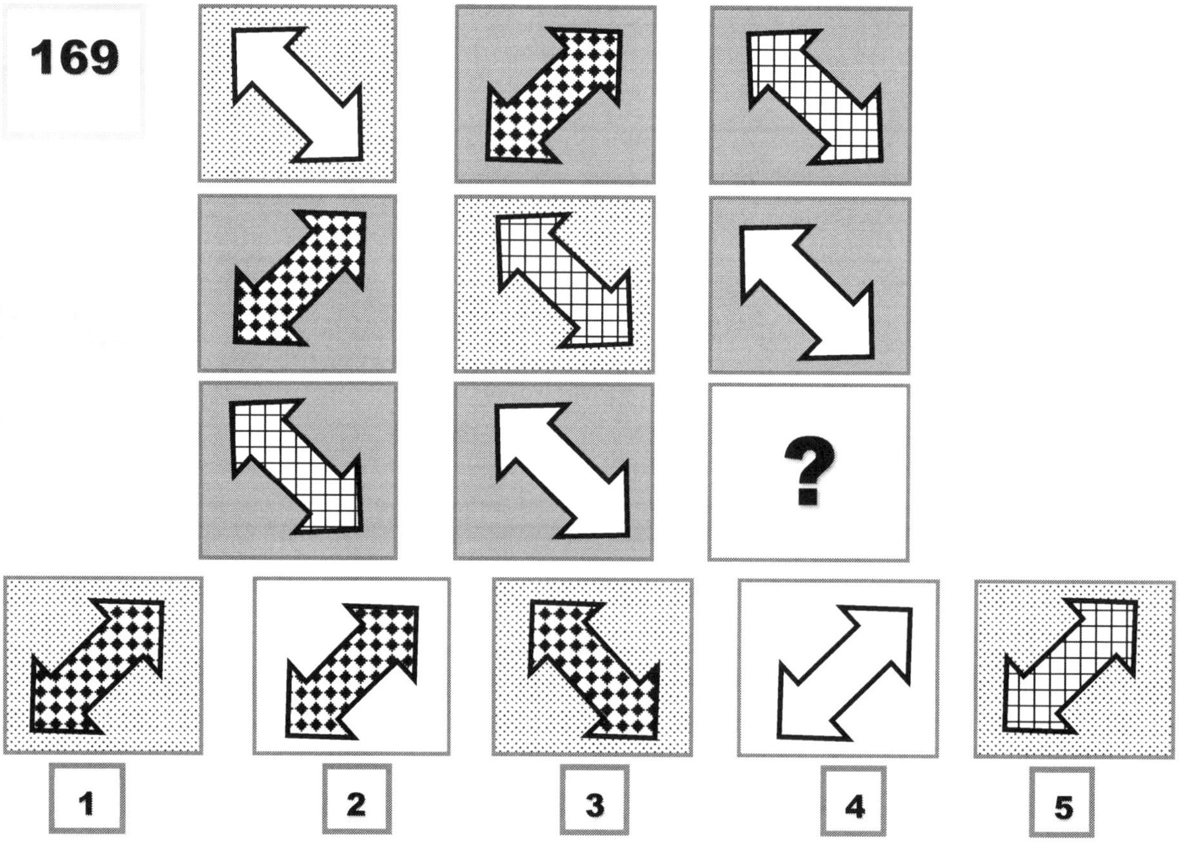

1 2 3 4 5

137

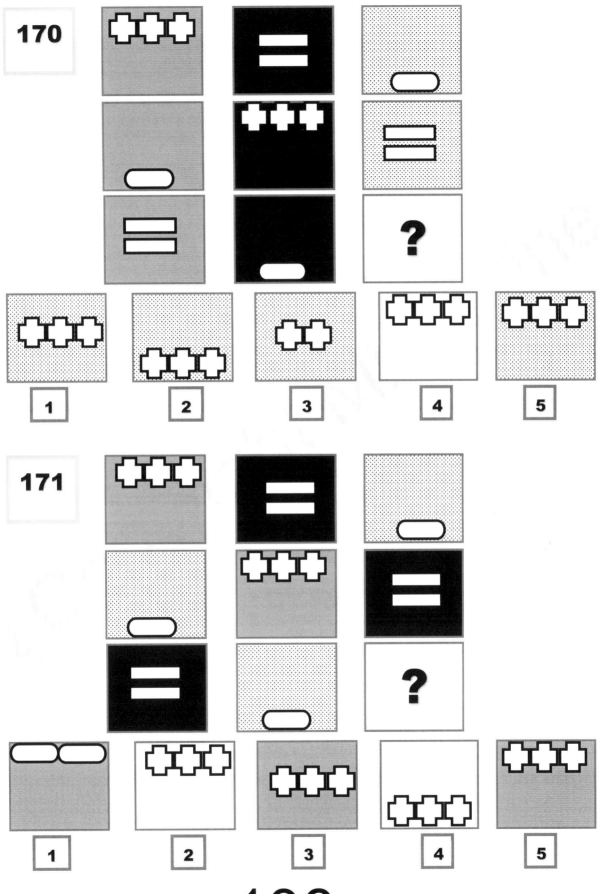

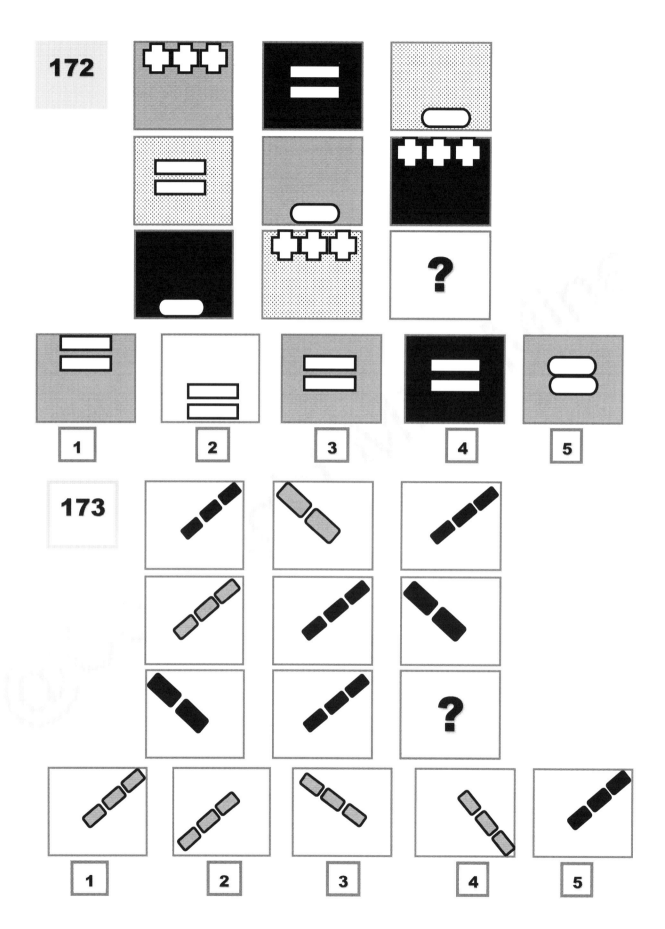

172

173

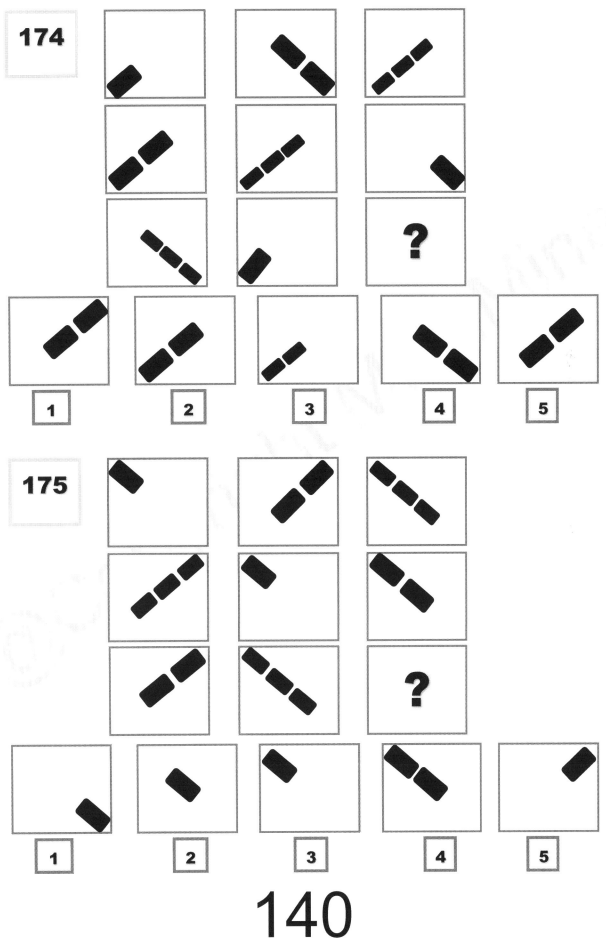

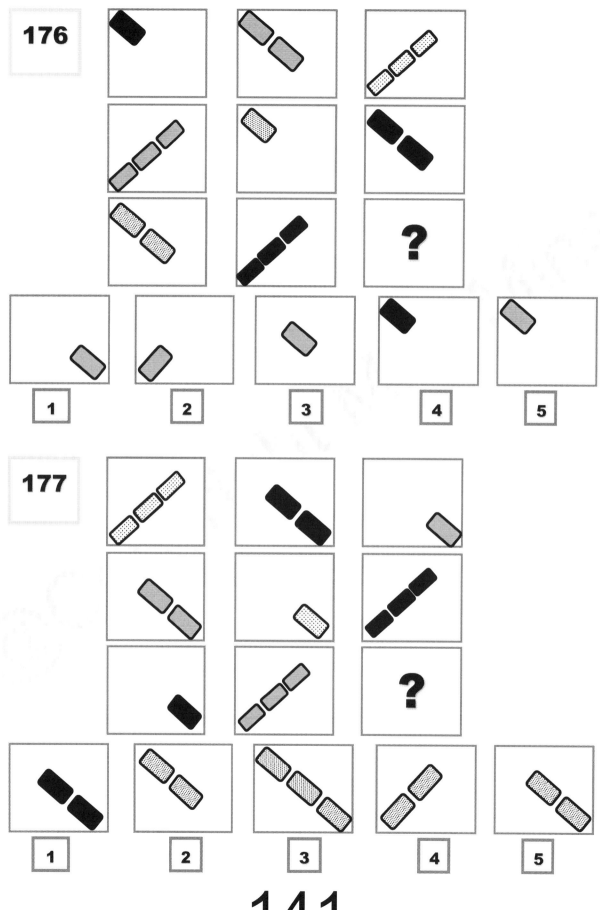

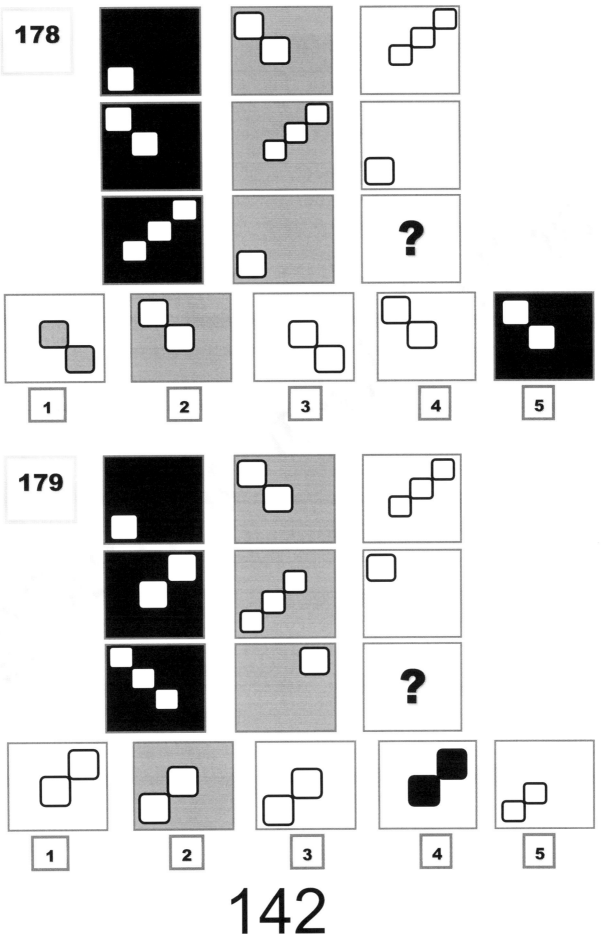

142

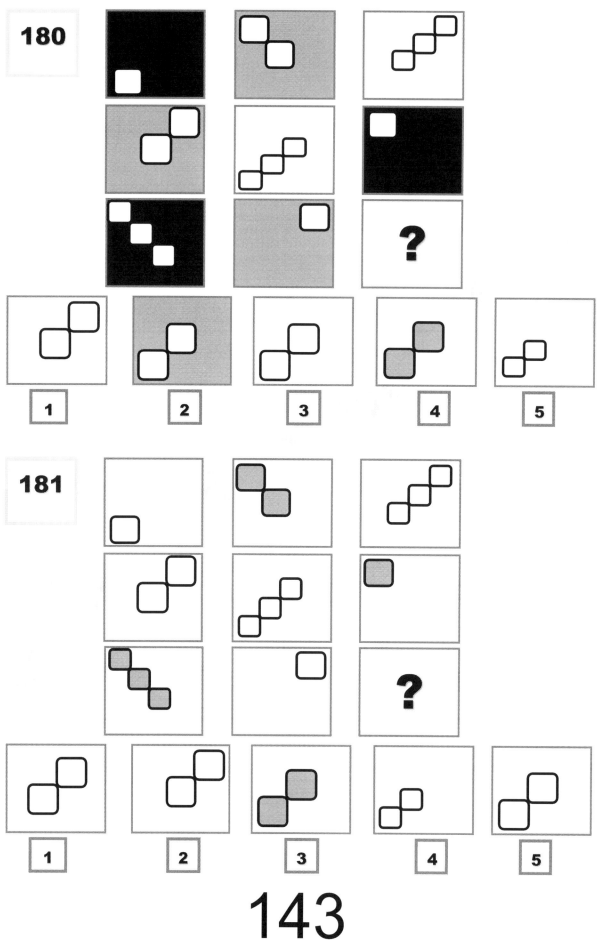

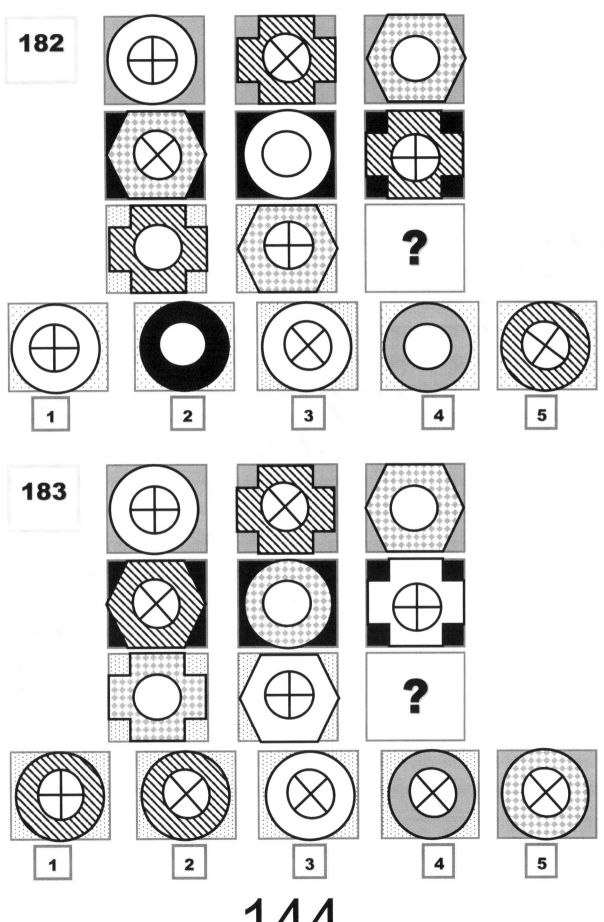

144

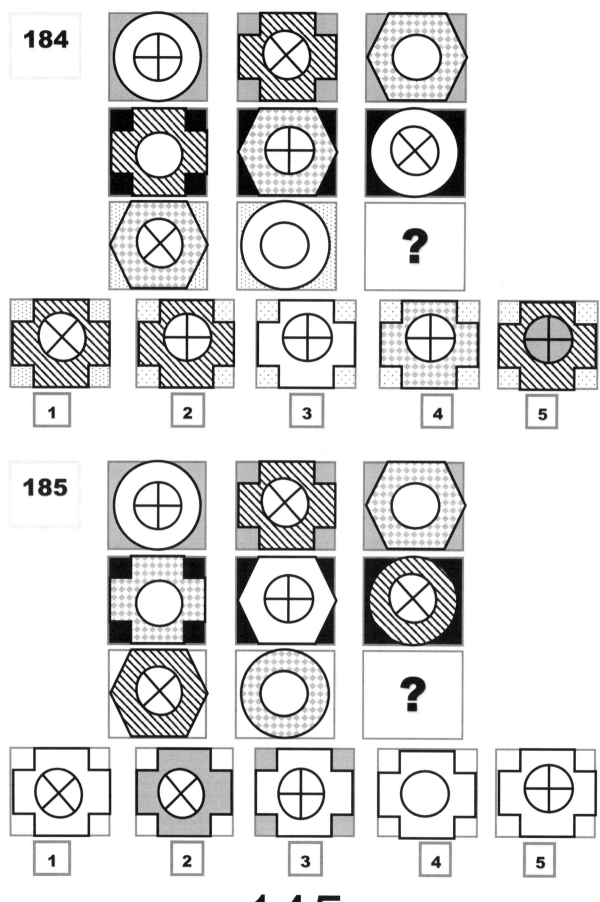

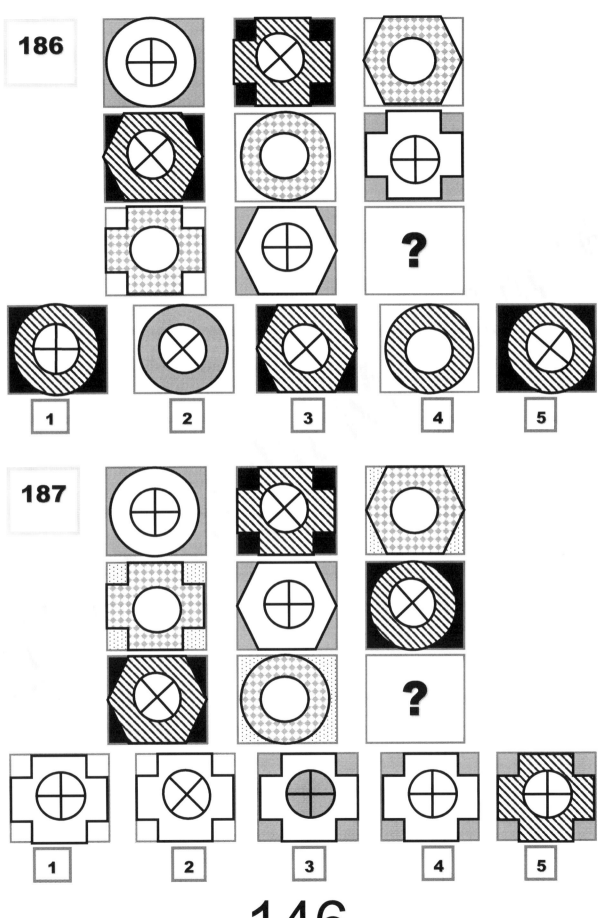

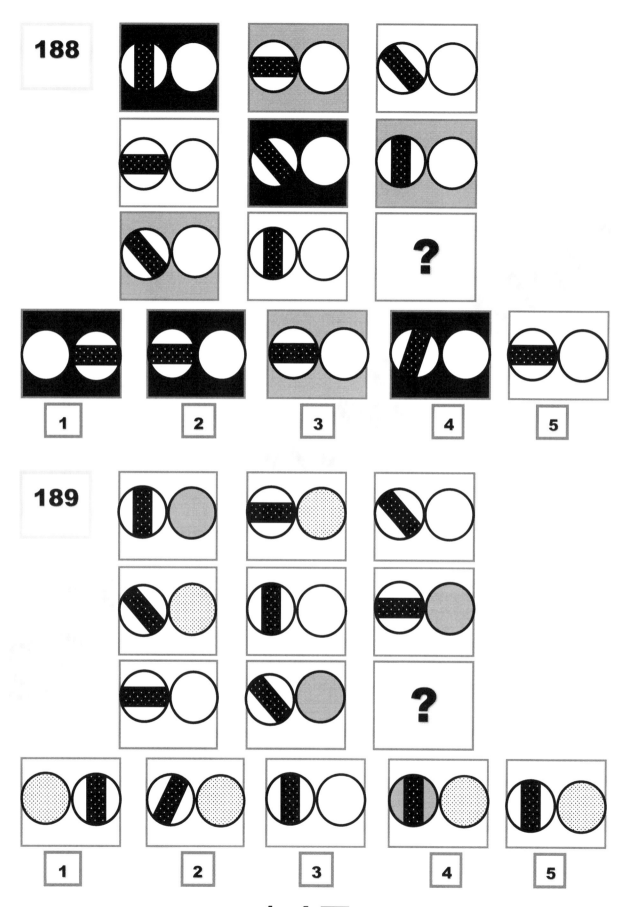

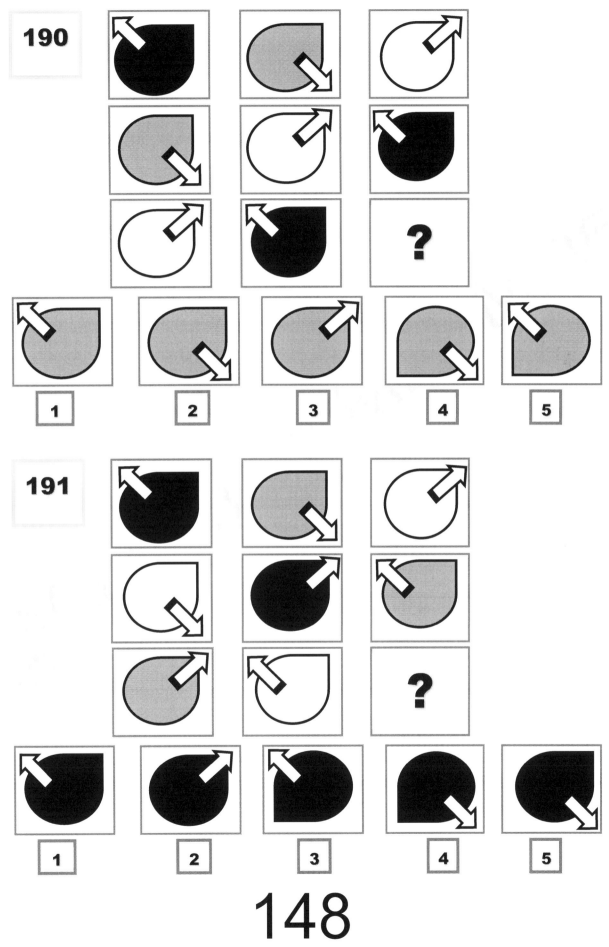

148

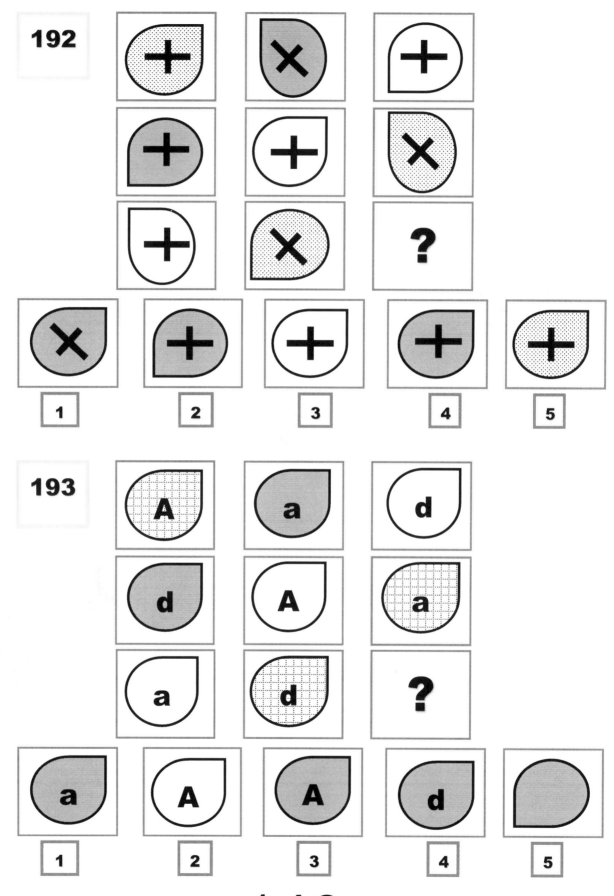

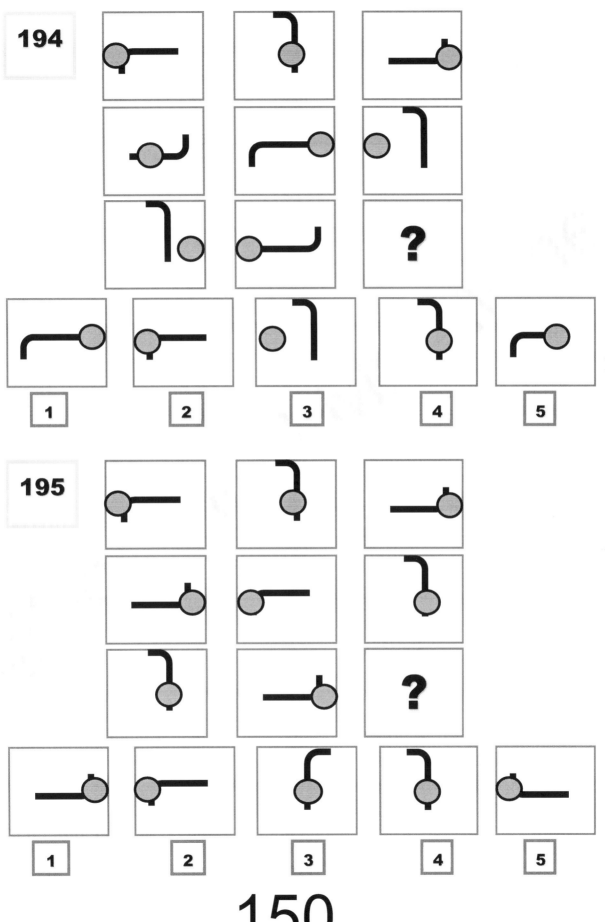

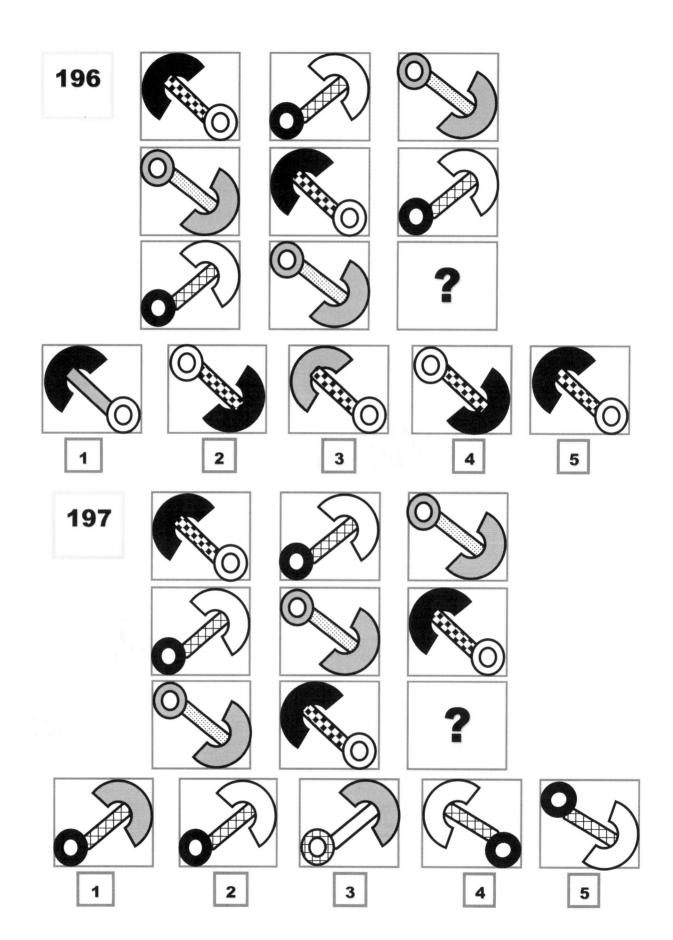

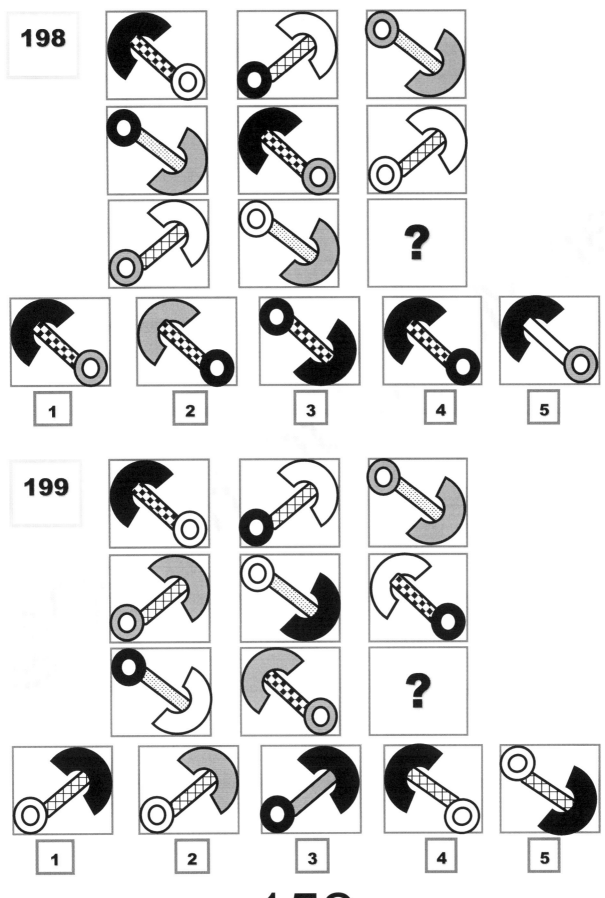

152

200

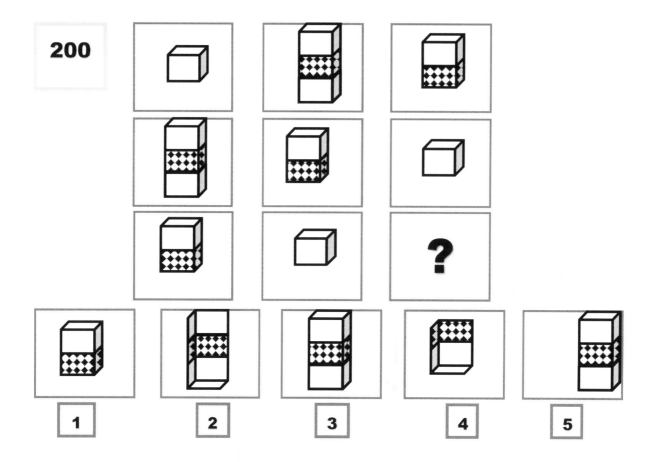

153

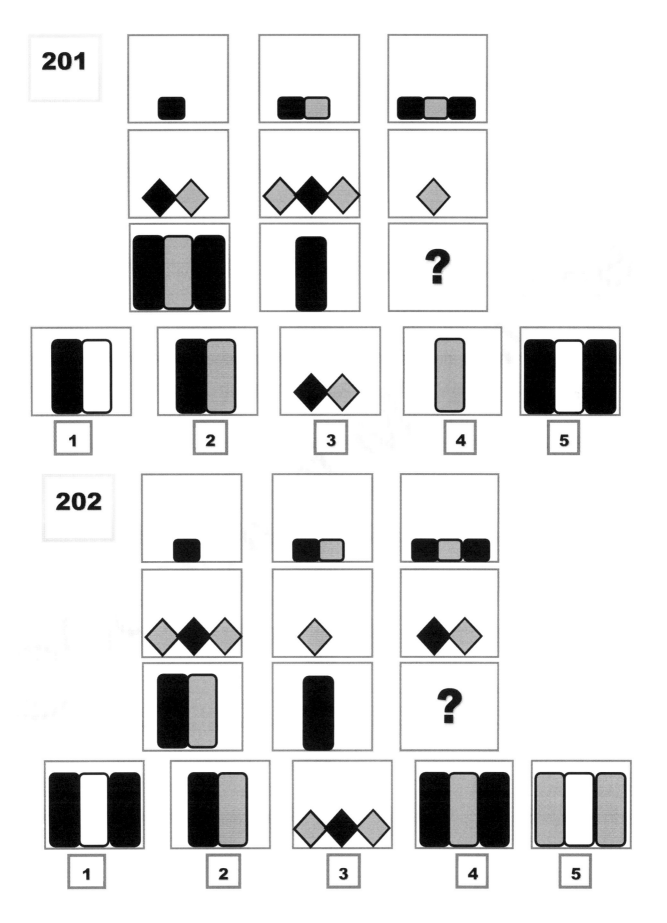

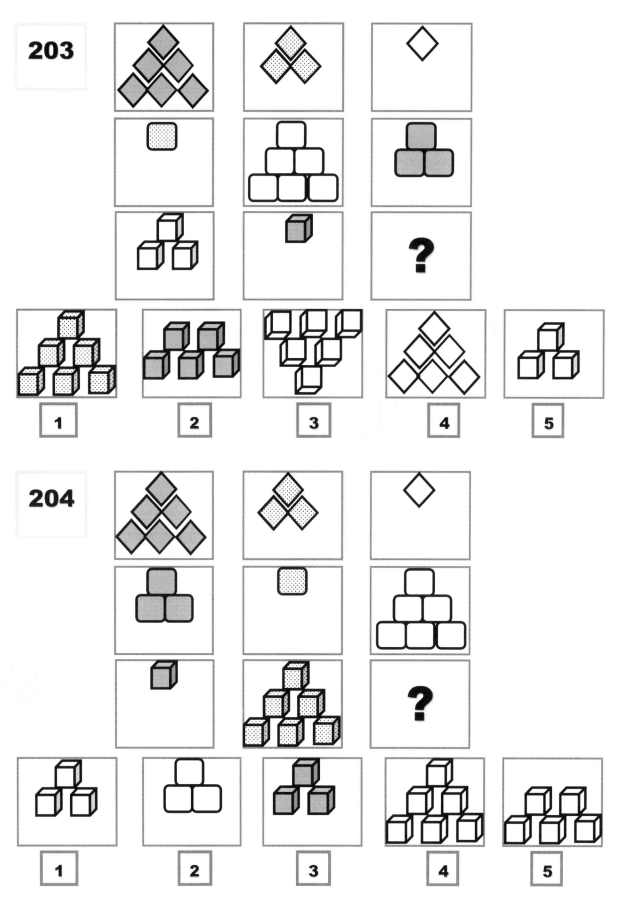

155

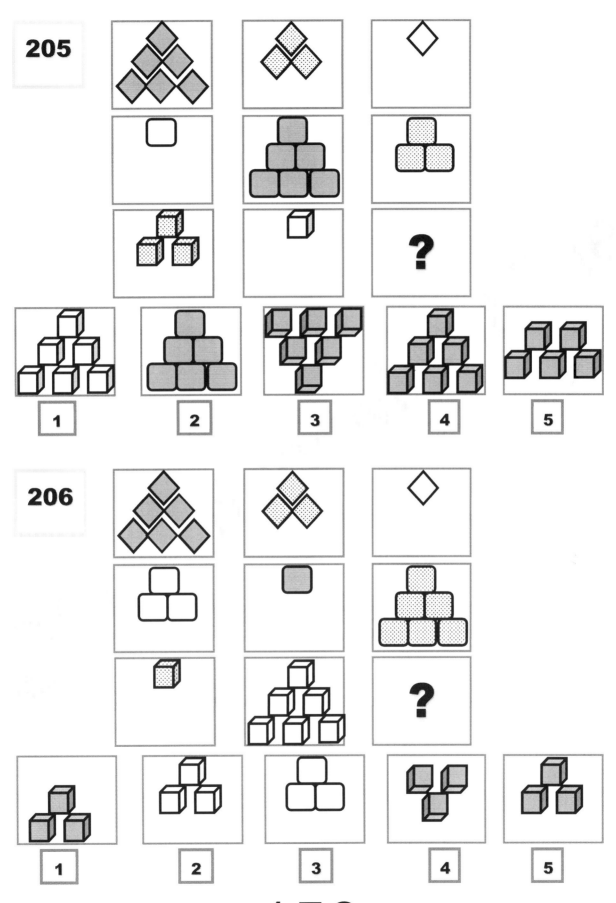

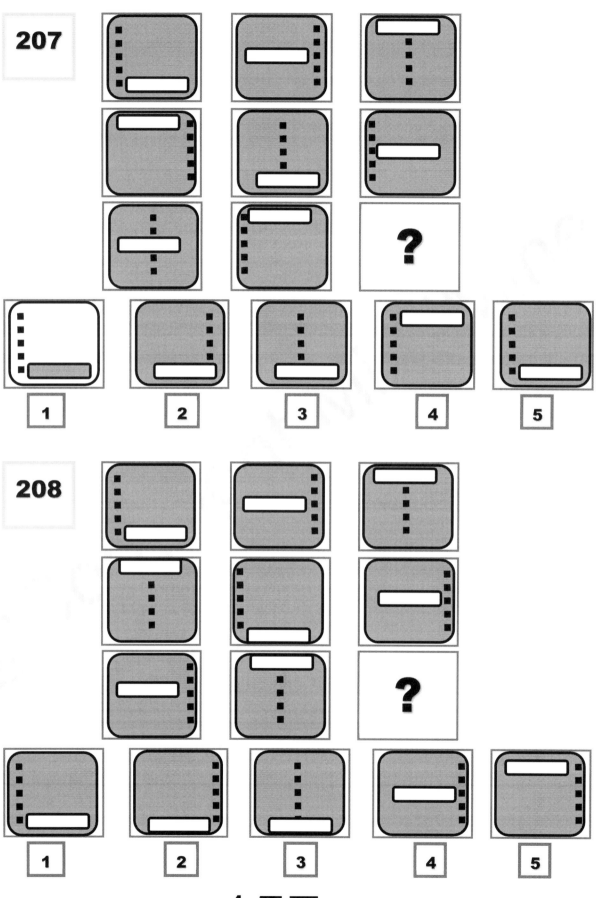

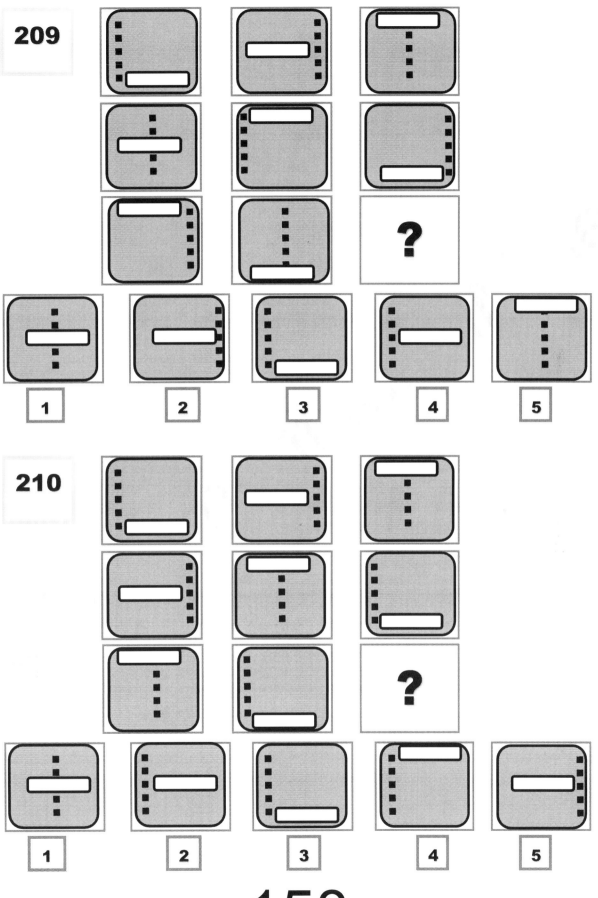

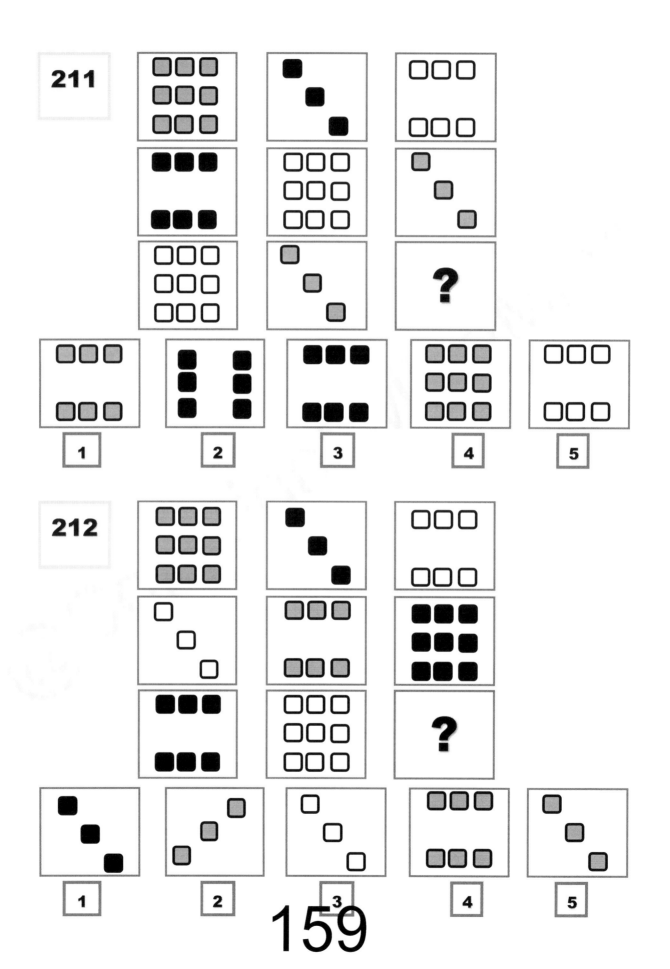

159

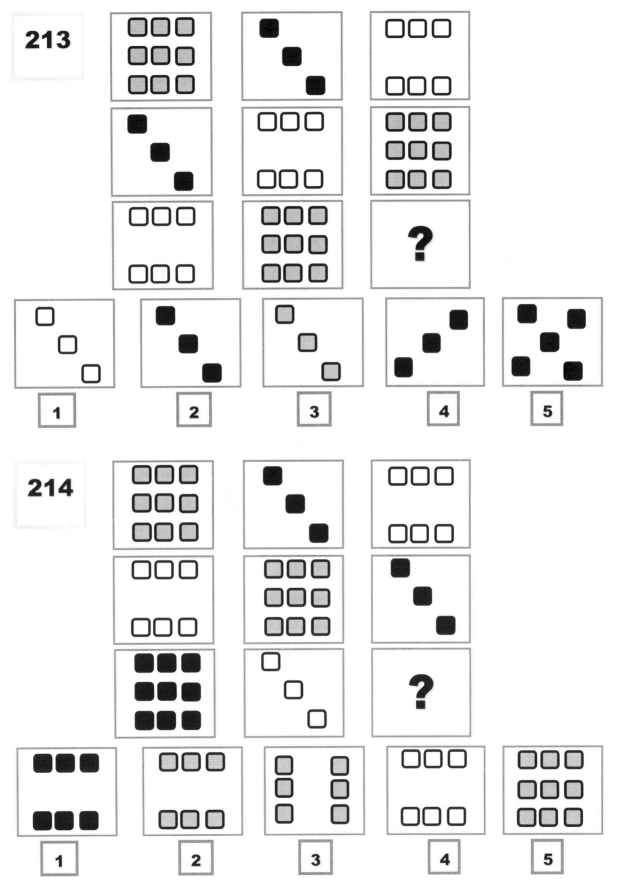

213

214

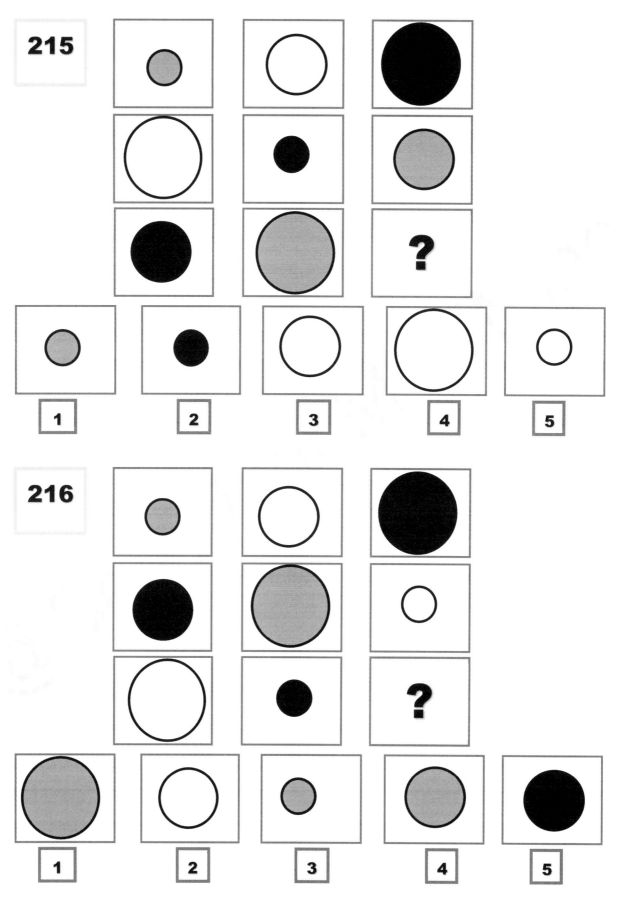

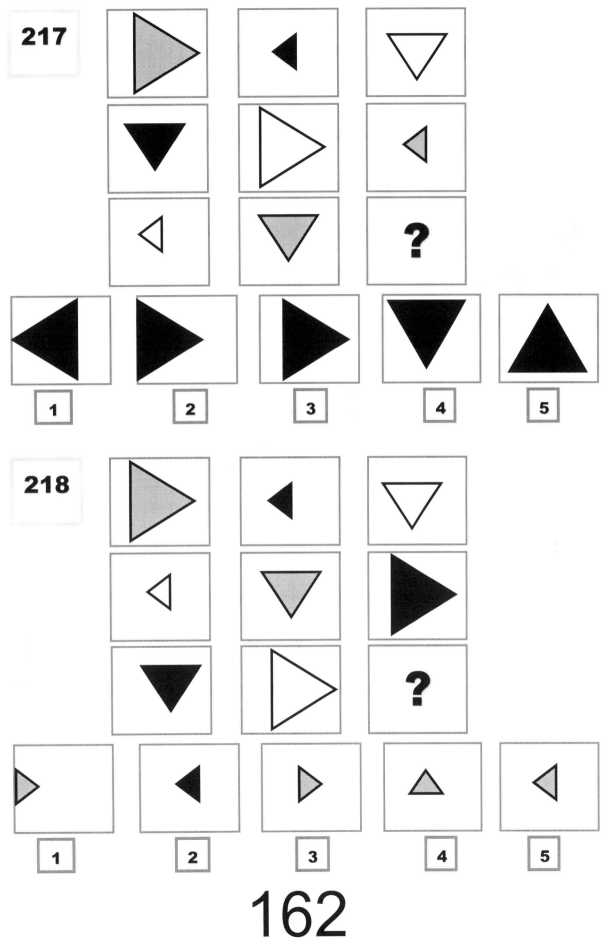

217

218

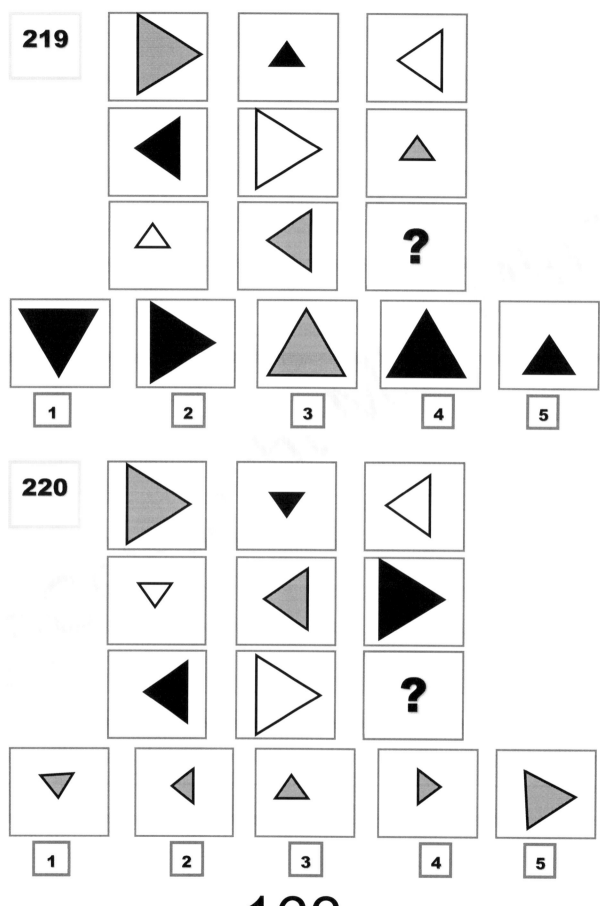

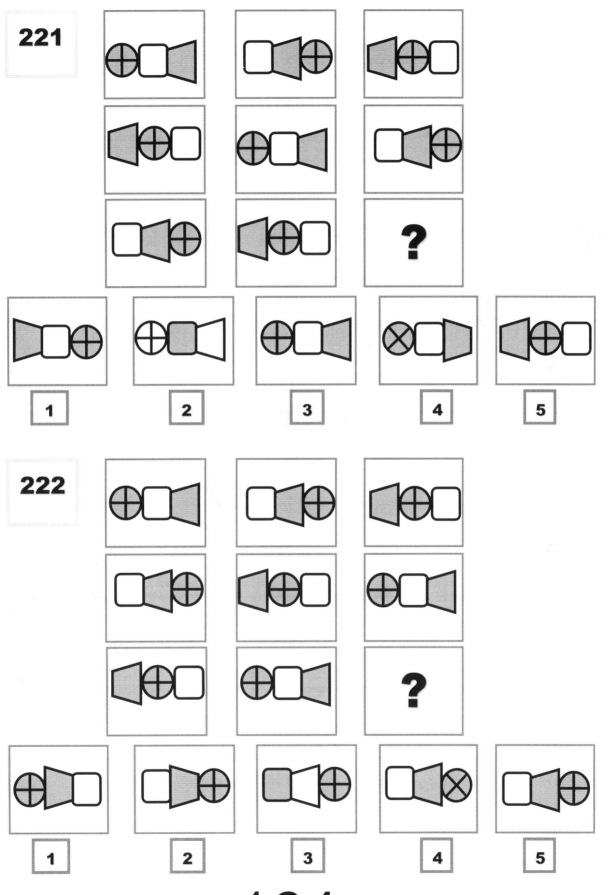

221

222

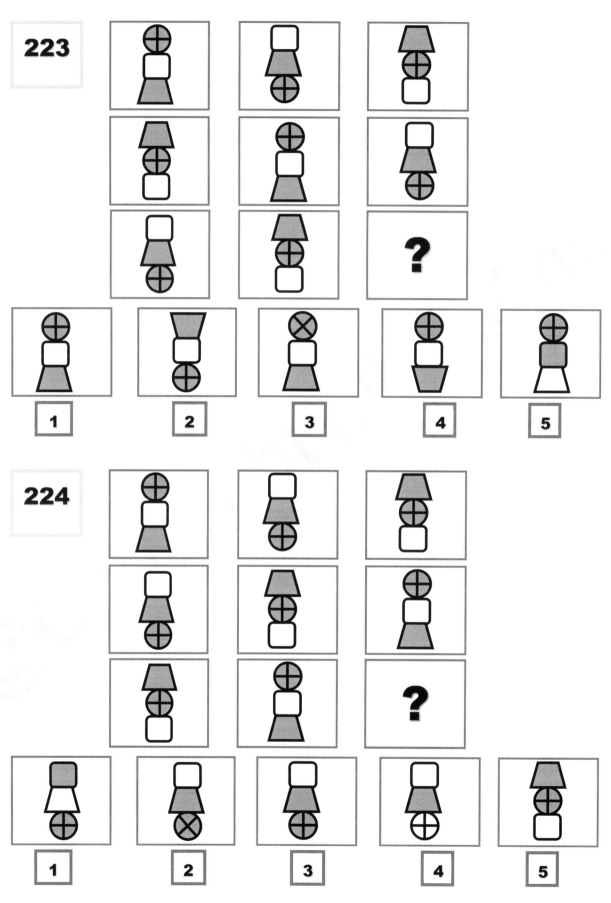

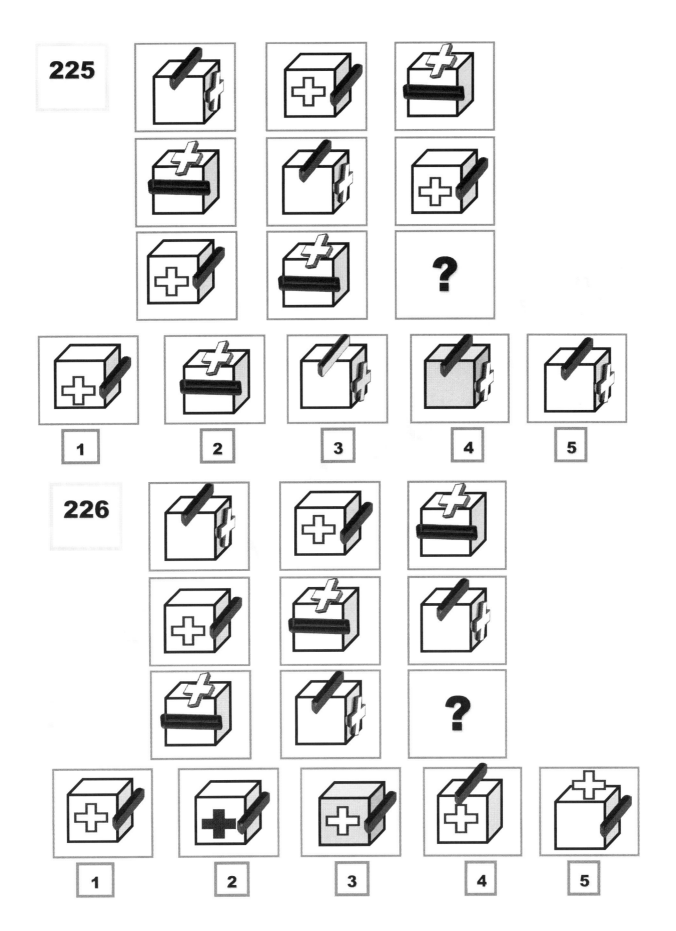

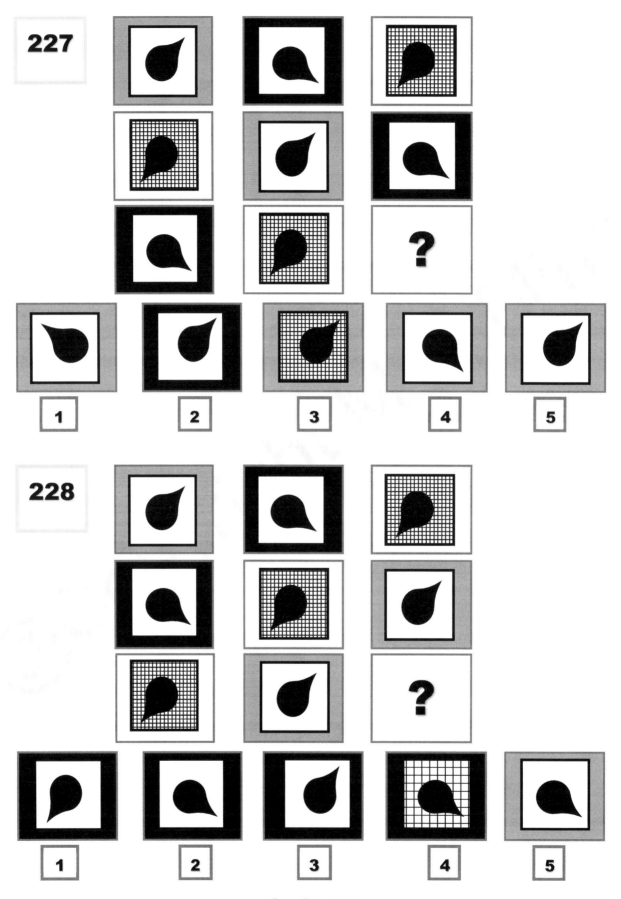

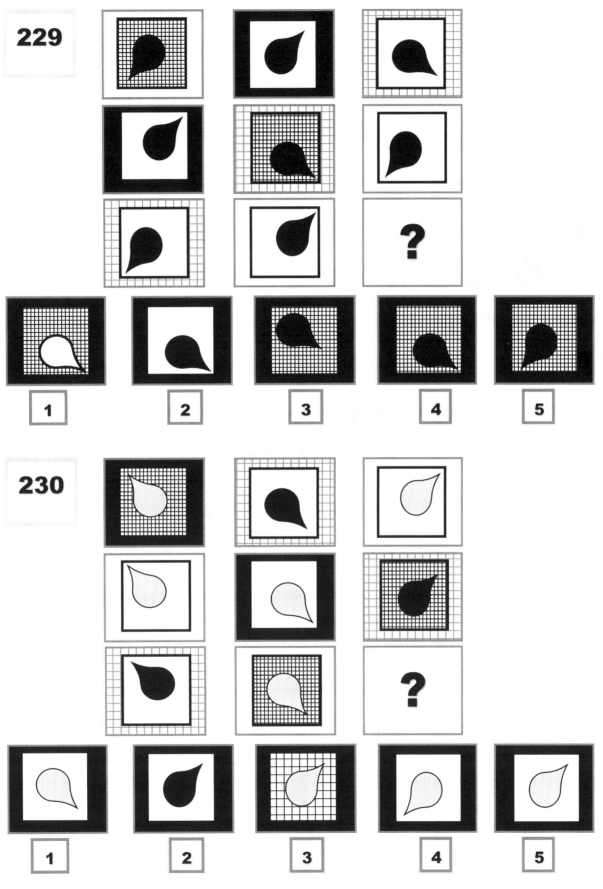

168

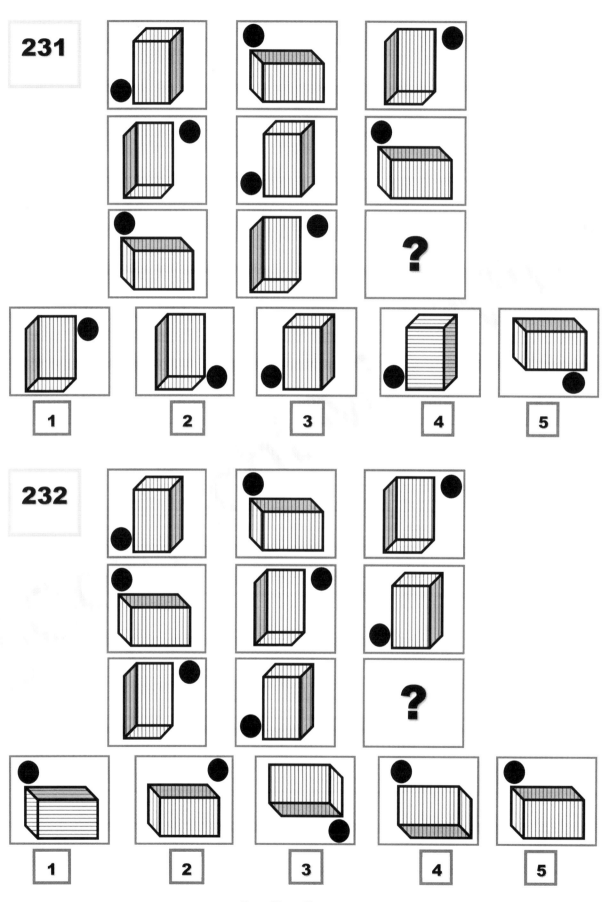

231

232

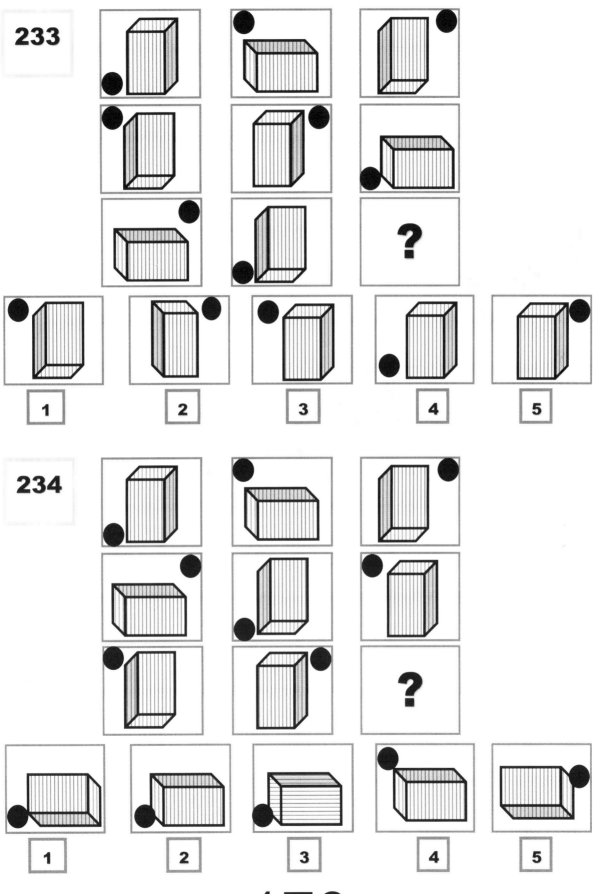

233

234

170

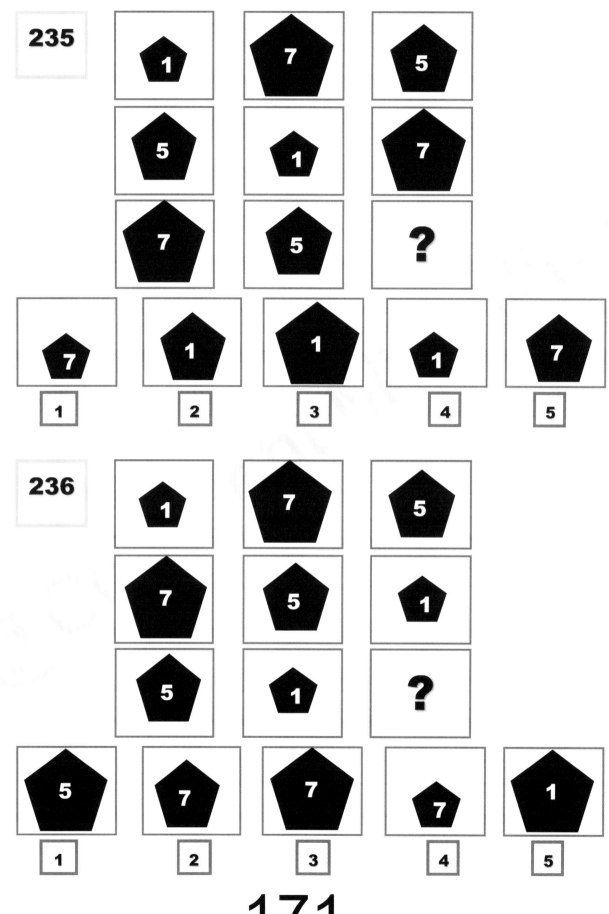

235

236

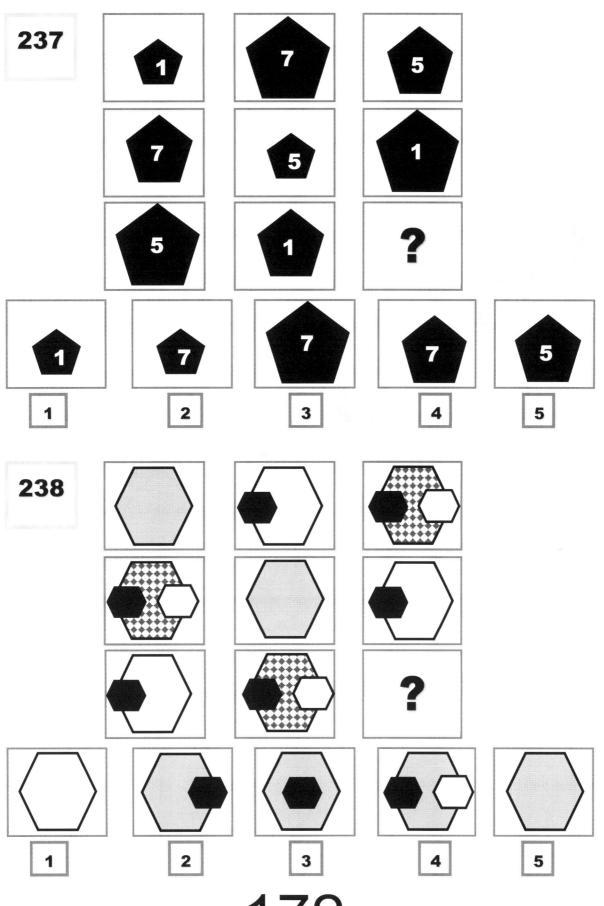

237

238

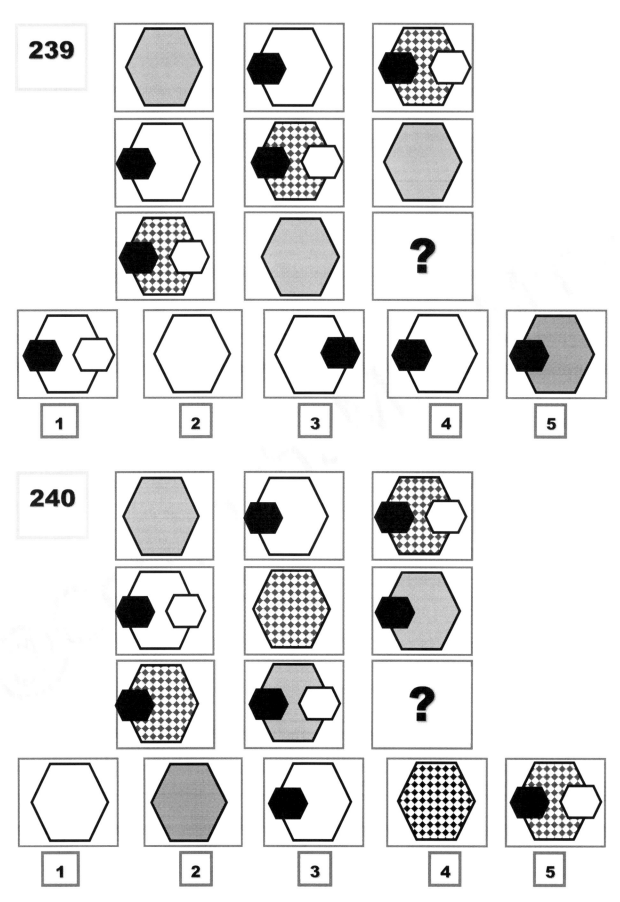

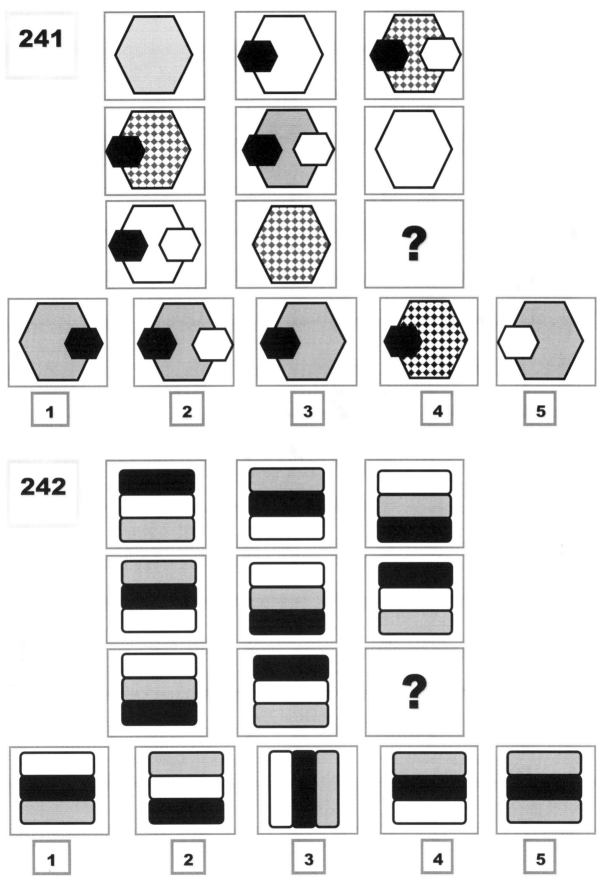

241

242

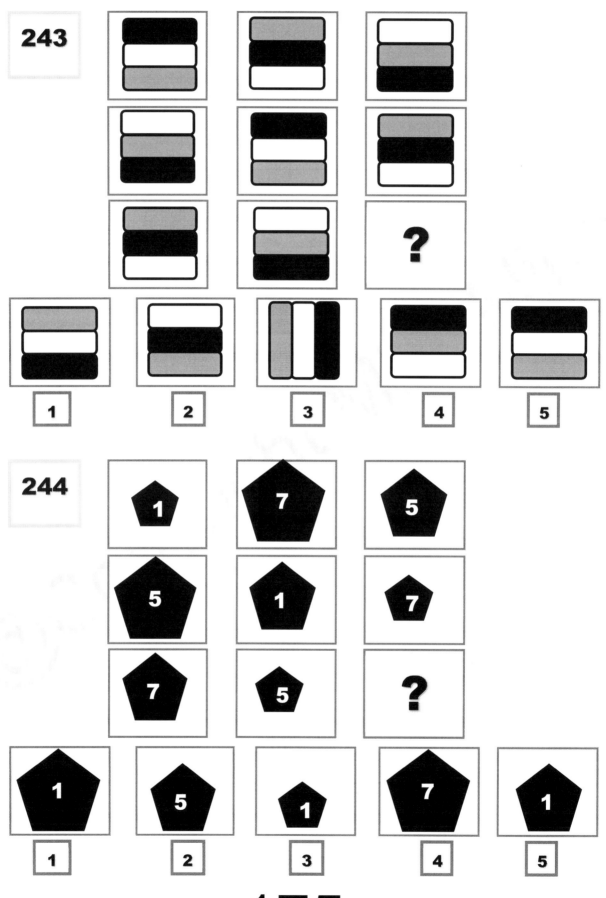

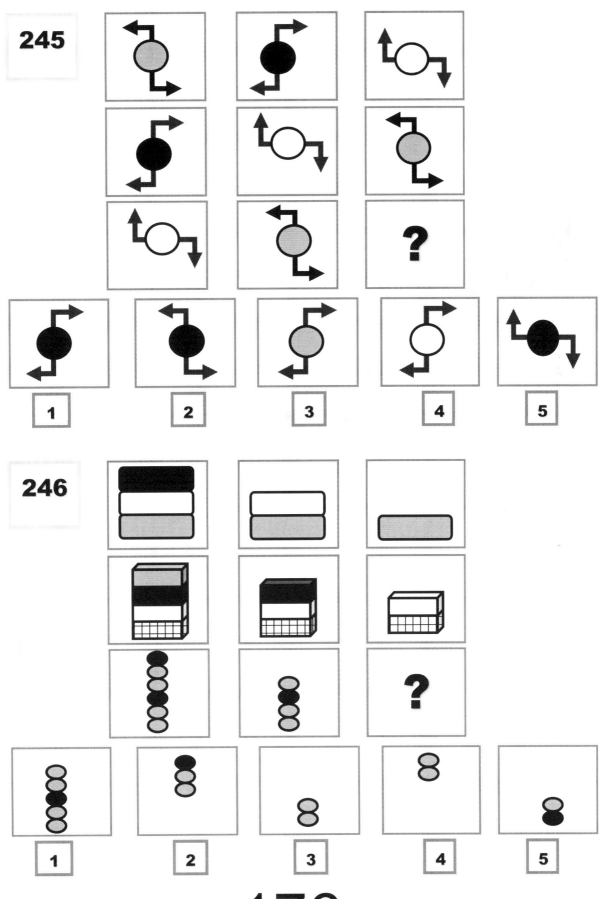

245

246

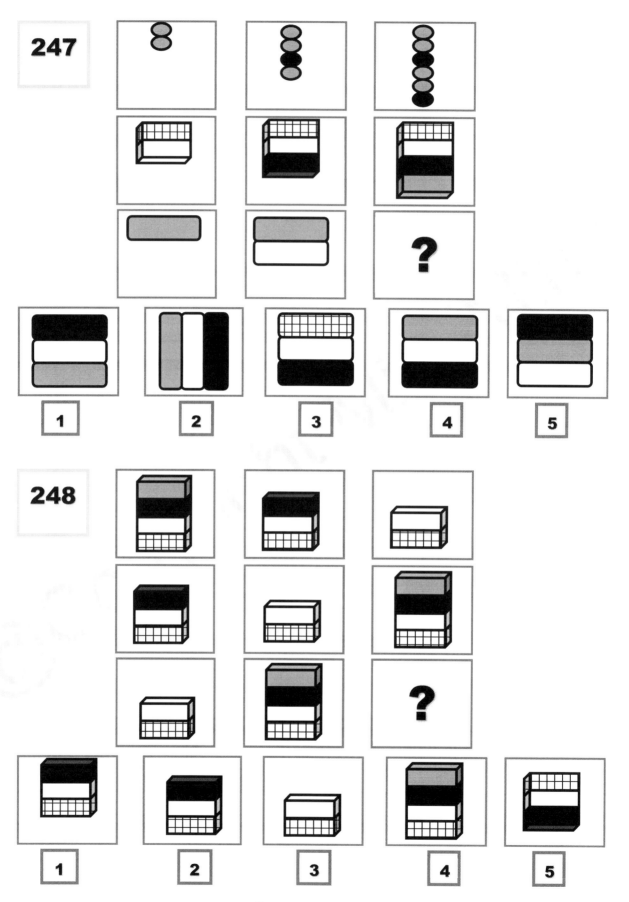

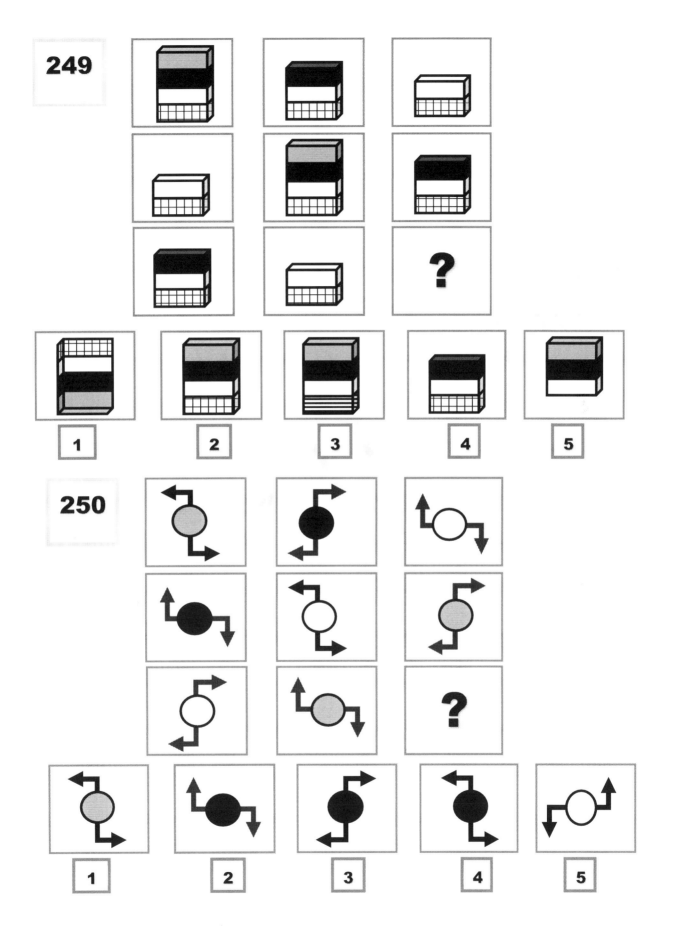

179

Practice

Test # 1

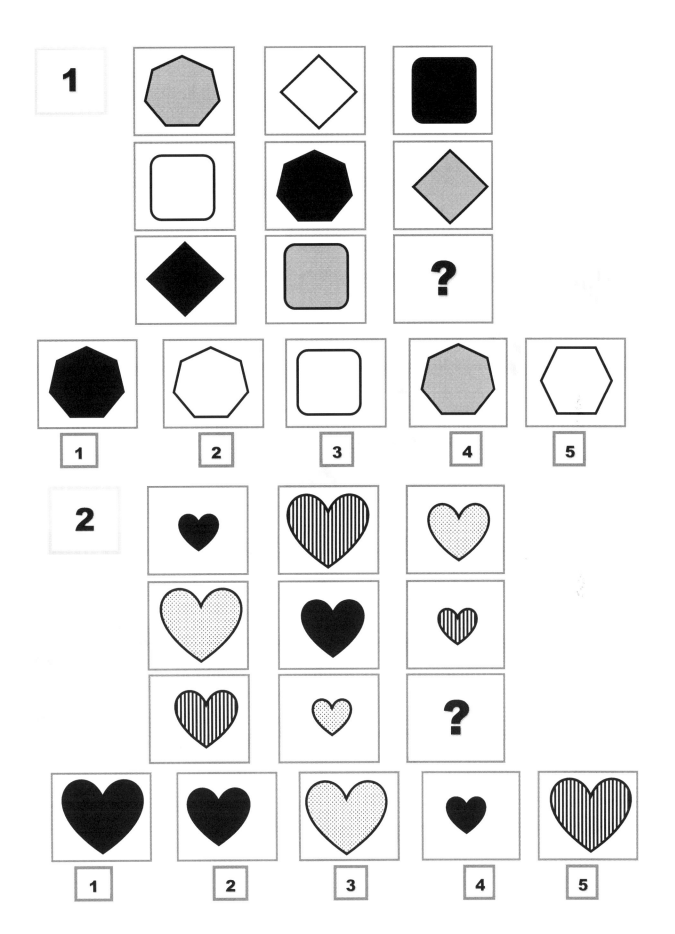

182

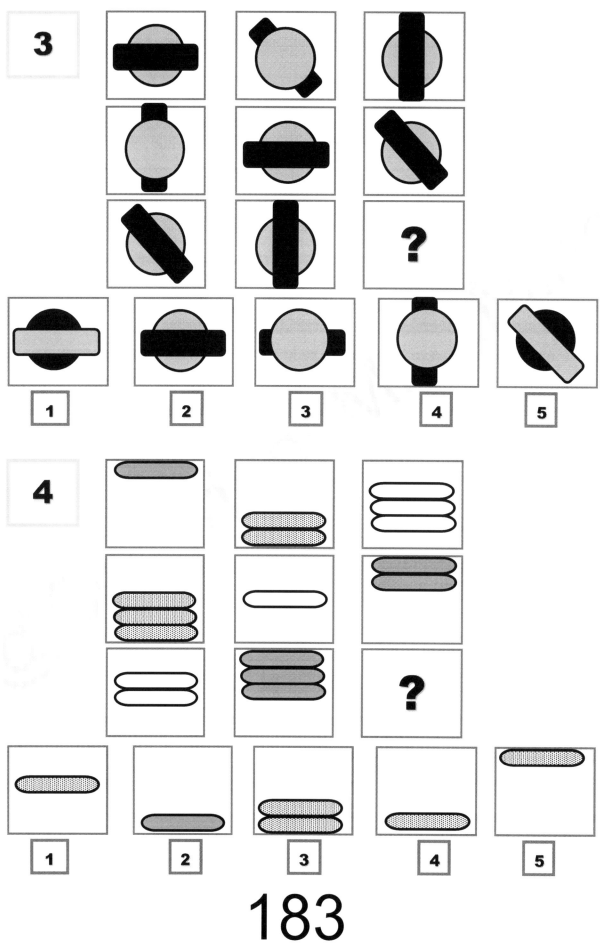

183

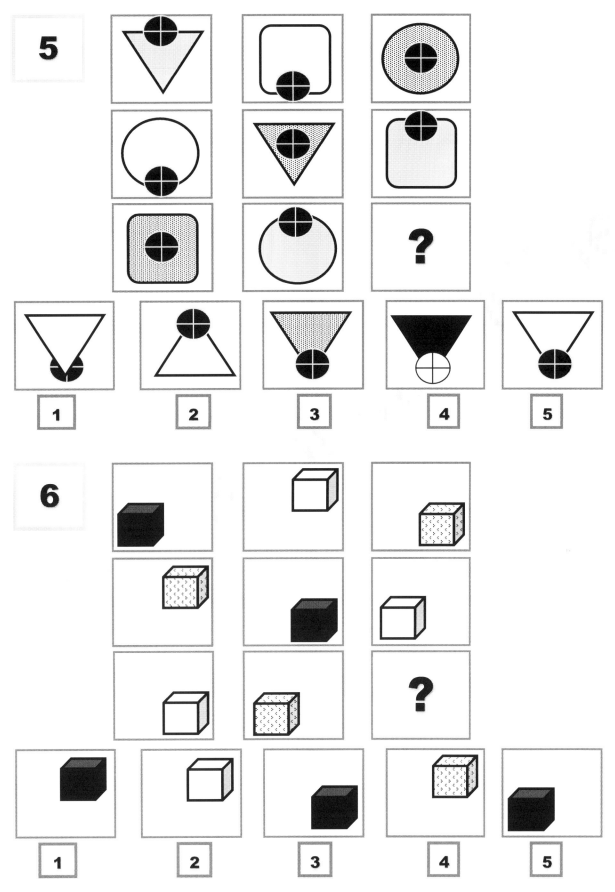

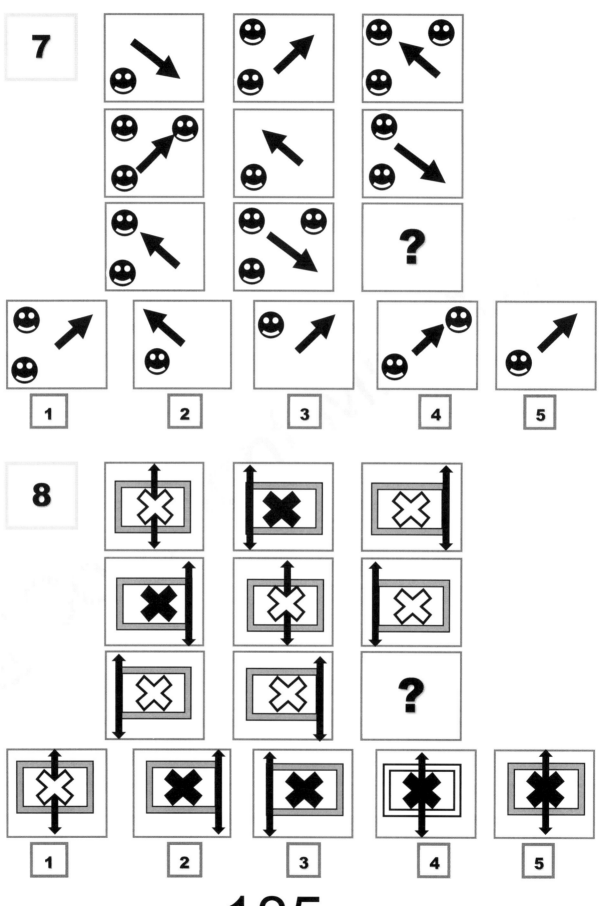

185

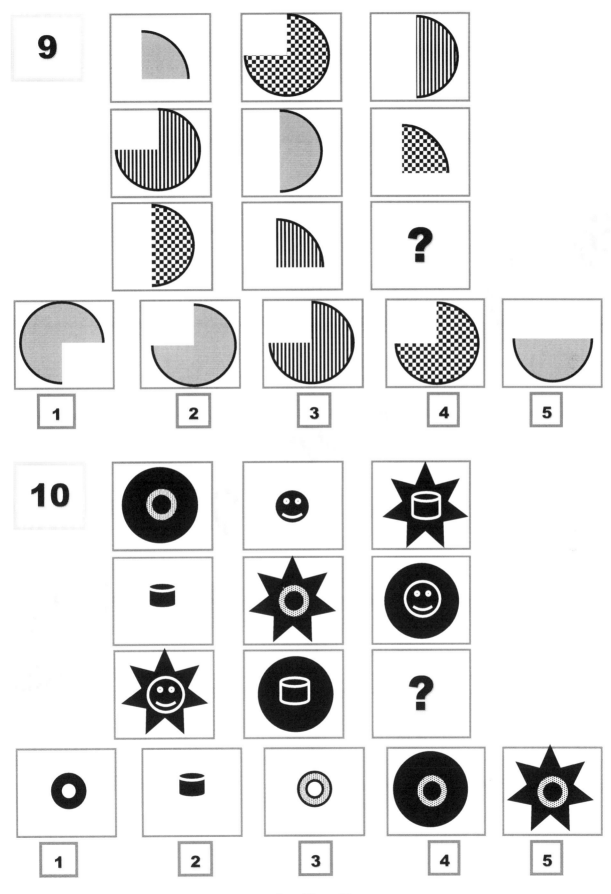

186

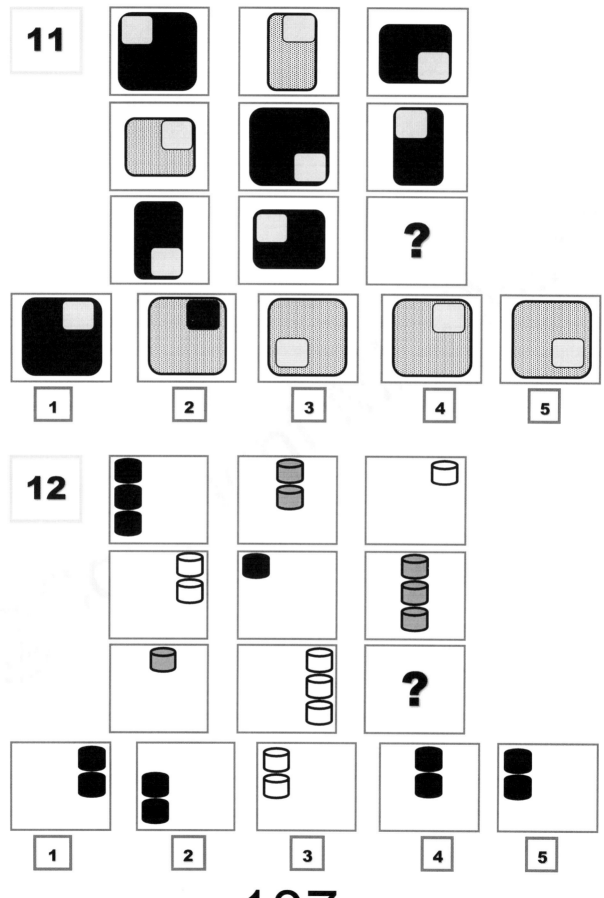

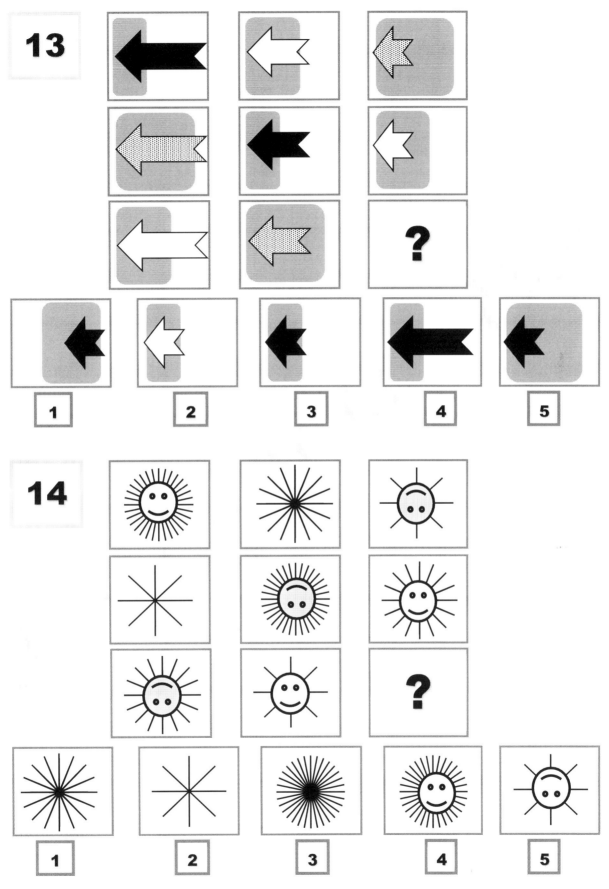

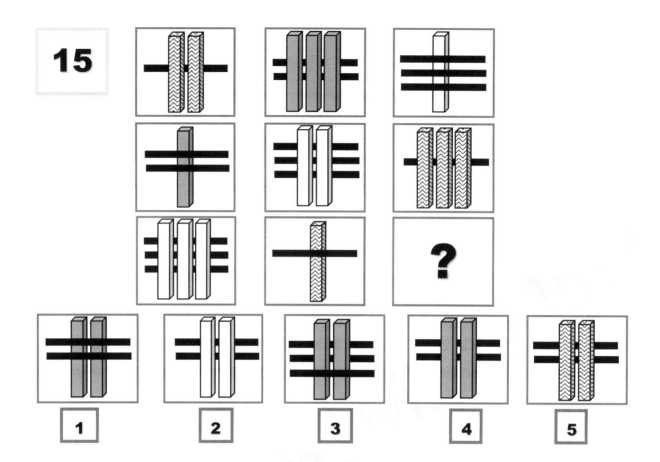

# Practice
# Test # 2

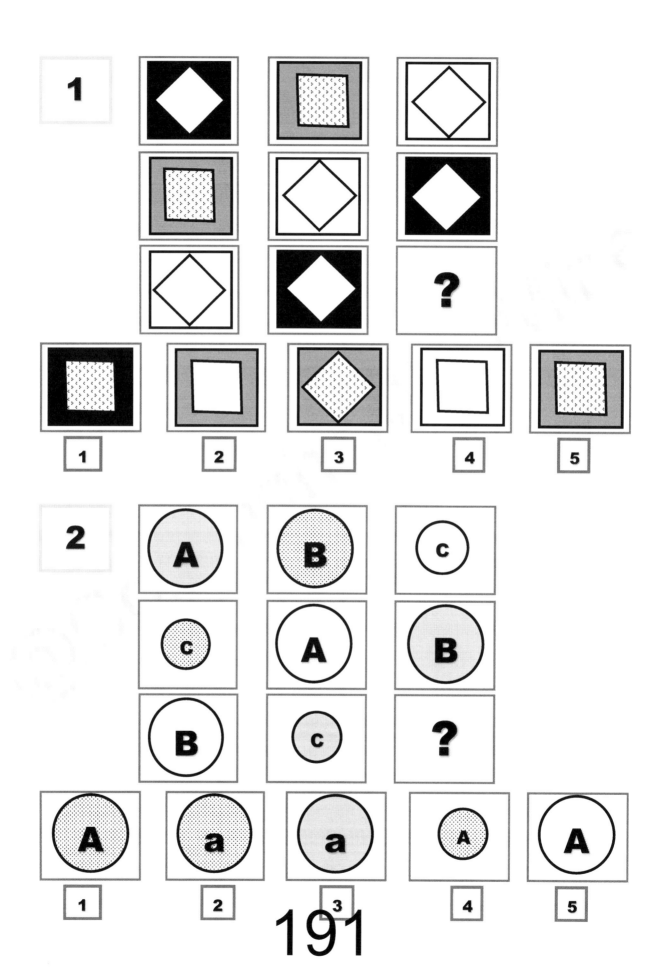

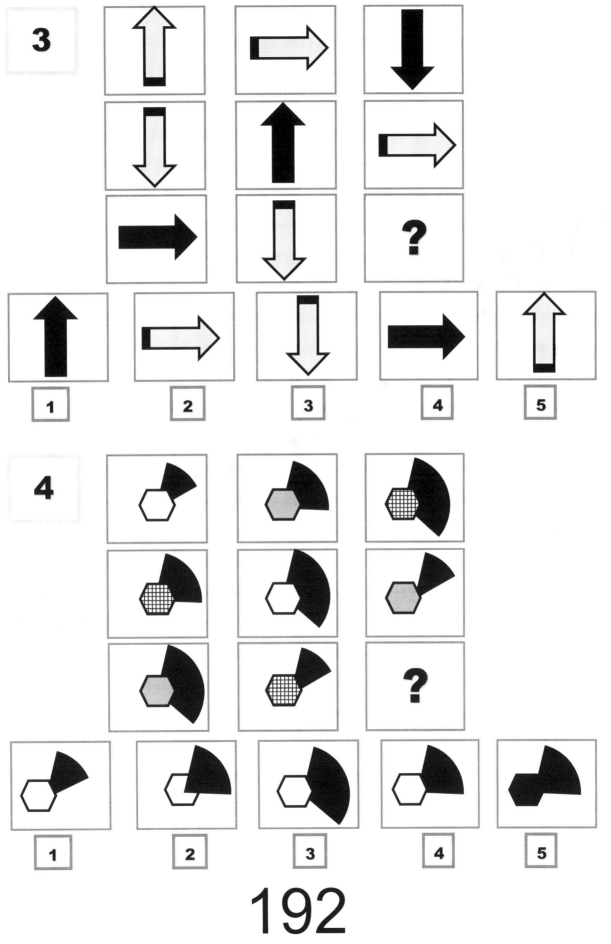

192

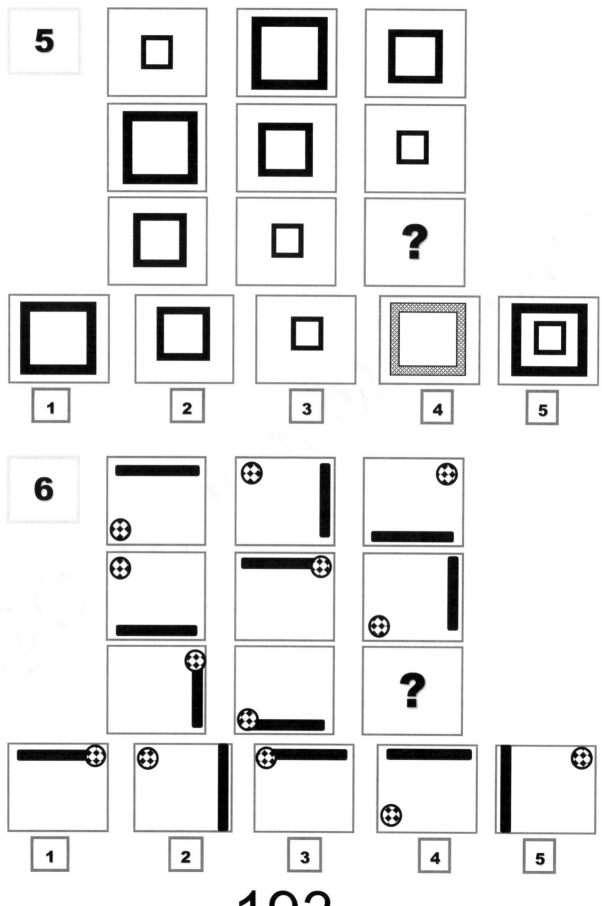

193

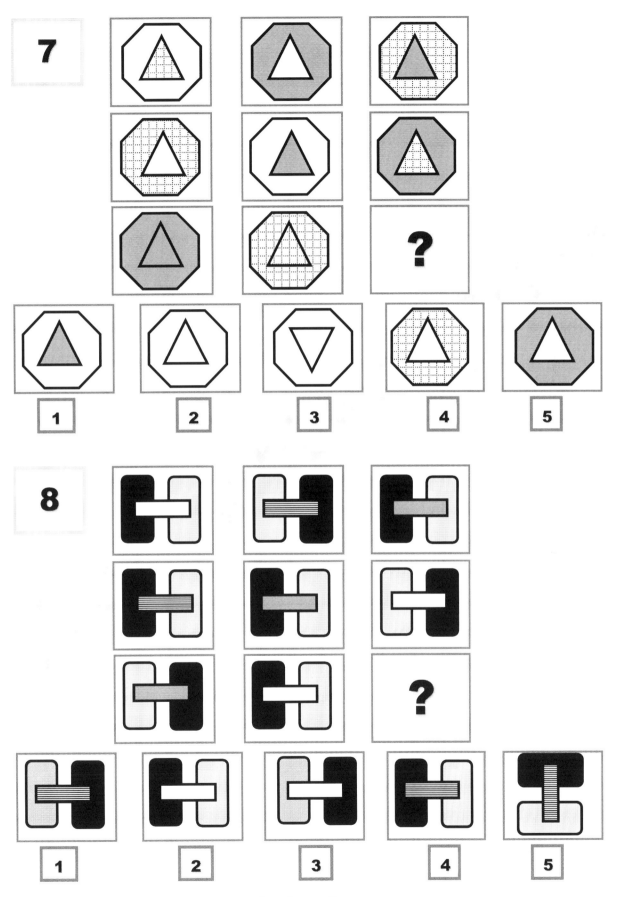

194

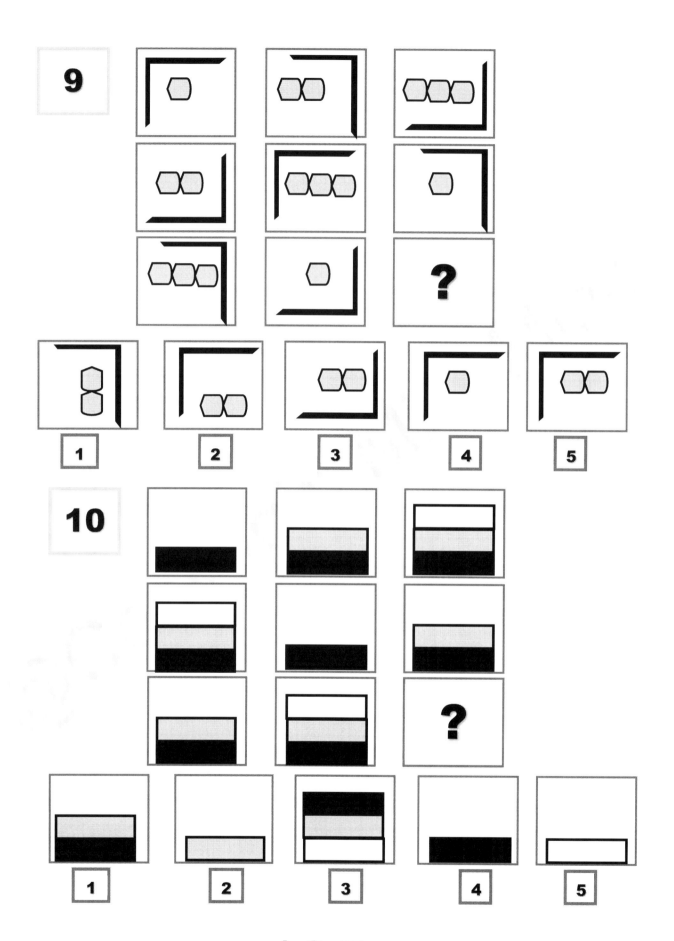

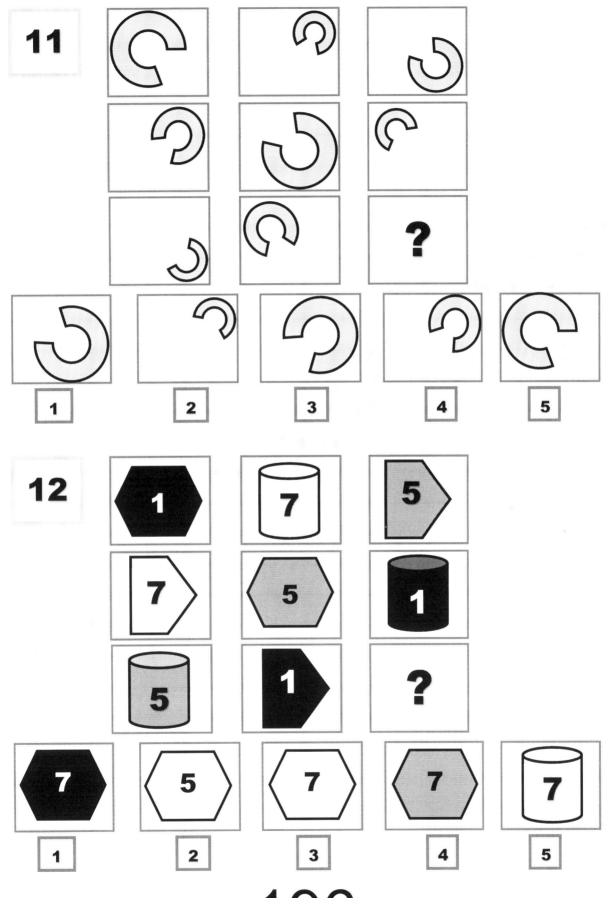

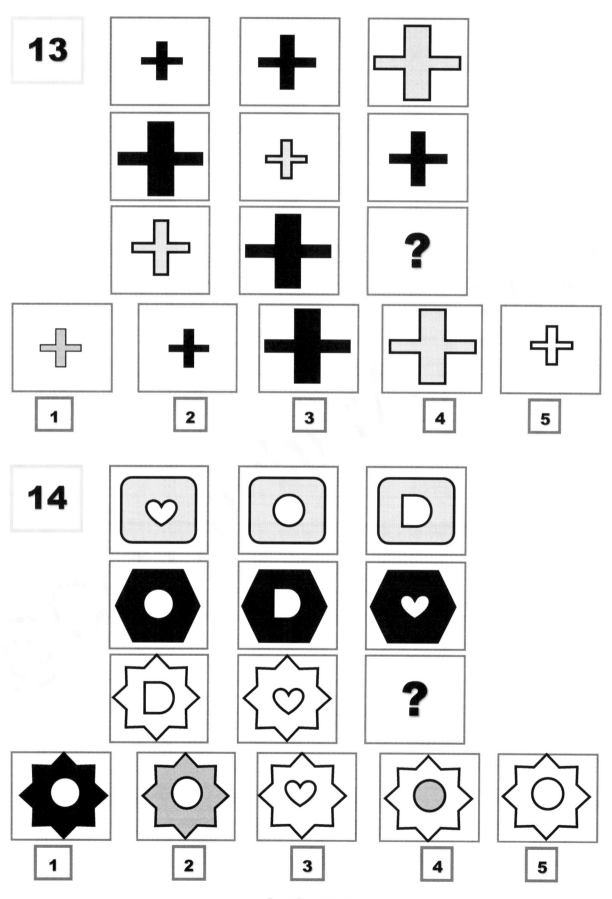

**15**

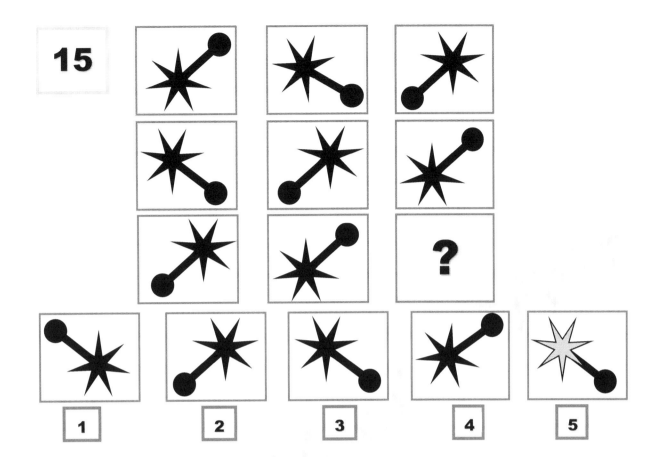

# ANSWERS

# ANSWERS TO SERIAL REASONING QUESTIONS

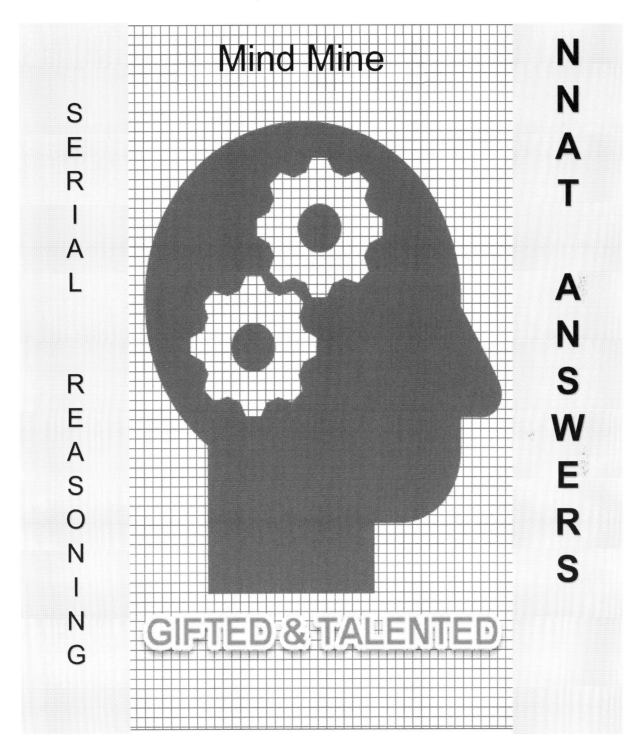

Mind Mine

S E R I A L   R E A S O N I N G

N N A T   A N S W E R S

GIFTED & TALENTED

200

| QUESTION | ANSWER | REASONING |
|---|---|---|
| **1** | **2** | Missing Shape is<br><br>• Color is "*Gray*" |
| **2** | **4** | Missing Shape is<br><br>• Size is "*Small*"<br><br>(Answer choice #2 is incorrect because of size) |
| **3** | **3** | Missing Shape is<br><br>• Pattern is "*Dots*" |
| **4** | **5** | Missing Shape is<br><br>• Pattern is "*Dots*" |

# 201

| QUESTION | ANSWER | REASONING |
|---|---|---|
| 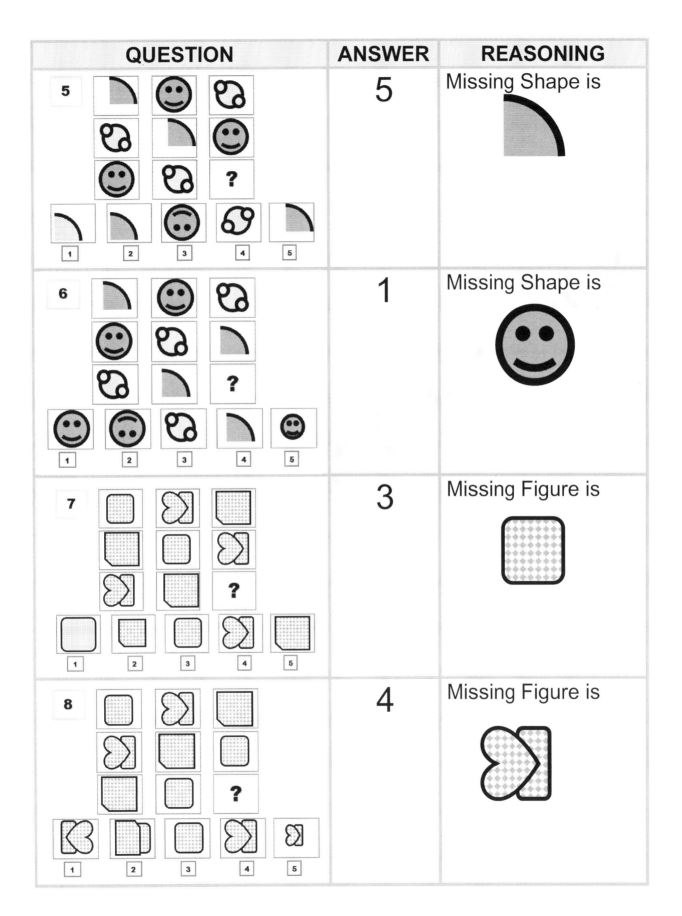 | 5 | Missing Shape is |
| | 1 | Missing Shape is |
| | 3 | Missing Figure is |
| | 4 | Missing Figure is |

202

| QUESTION | ANSWER | REASONING |
|---|---|---|
| 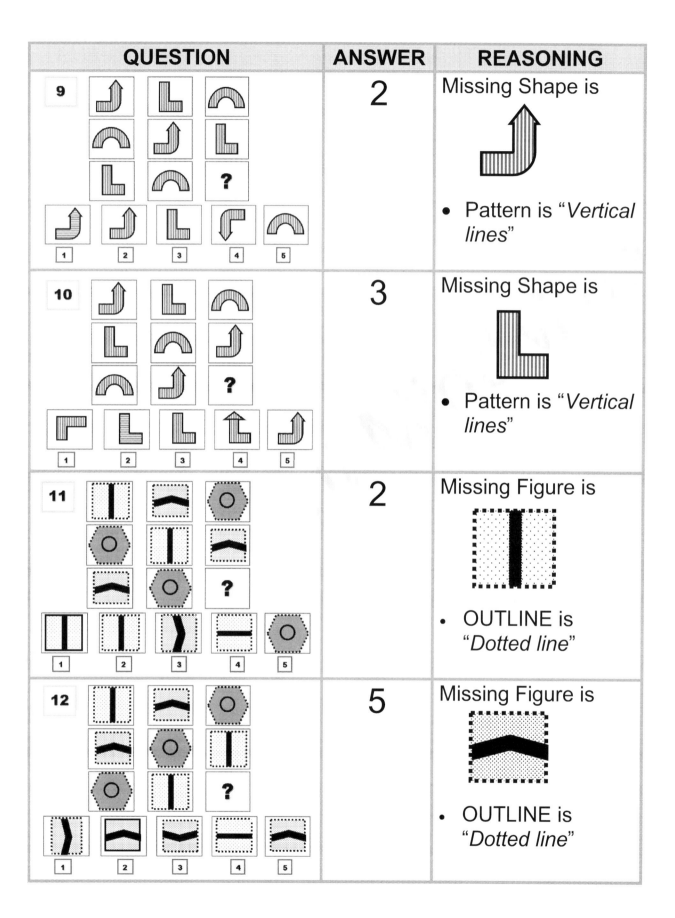 | | |

**9** — 2 — Missing Shape is

Pattern is "*Vertical lines*"

**10** — 3 — Missing Shape is

Pattern is "*Vertical lines*"

**11** — 2 — Missing Figure is

OUTLINE is "*Dotted line*"

**12** — 5 — Missing Figure is

OUTLINE is "*Dotted line*"

| QUESTION | ANSWER | REASONING |
|---|---|---|
| **13** | 1 | Missing Figure is<br><br>• Pattern is "*Dots*" |
| **14** | 3 | Missing Figure is<br><br>• Pattern is "*Dots*" |
| **15** | 1 | Missing Shape is<br><br>• Pattern is "*Gray diagonal lines pointing from Bottom-Left to Top-Right*" |

| QUESTION | ANSWER | REASONING |
|---|---|---|
| **16** | 2 | Missing Shape is <br><br>• Pattern is "*Gray diagonal lines pointing from Bottom-Left to Top-Right*" |
| **17** | 4 | Missing Shape is <br><br>• Outline is "*Broken line with dots*" |
| **18** | 3 | Missing Shape is <br><br>• Outline is "*Borken line with dots*" |

205

| QUESTION | ANSWER | REASONING |
|----------|--------|-----------|
| **19** | 5 | Missing Shape is |
| **20** | 1 | Missing Shape is |
| **21** | 3 | Missing Shape is <br><br> • Triangle is *"Pointing down"* <br> • Size is *"Medium"* <br> • Pattern is *"vertical lines"* |

206

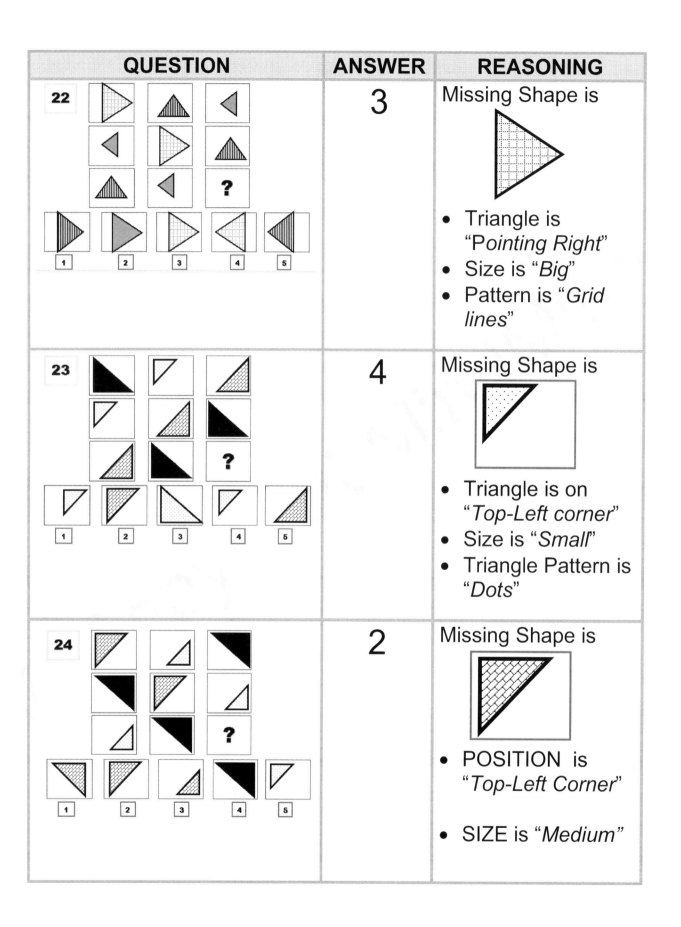

| QUESTION | ANSWER | REASONING |
|---|---|---|
| **22** | **3** | Missing Shape is<br><br>• Triangle is "Pointing Right"<br>• Size is "Big"<br>• Pattern is "Grid lines" |
| **23** | **4** | Missing Shape is<br><br>• Triangle is on "Top-Left corner"<br>• Size is "Small"<br>• Triangle Pattern is "Dots" |
| **24** | **2** | Missing Shape is<br><br>• POSITION is "Top-Left Corner"<br><br>• SIZE is "Medium" |

207

| QUESTION | ANSWER | REASONING |
|---|---|---|
| 25 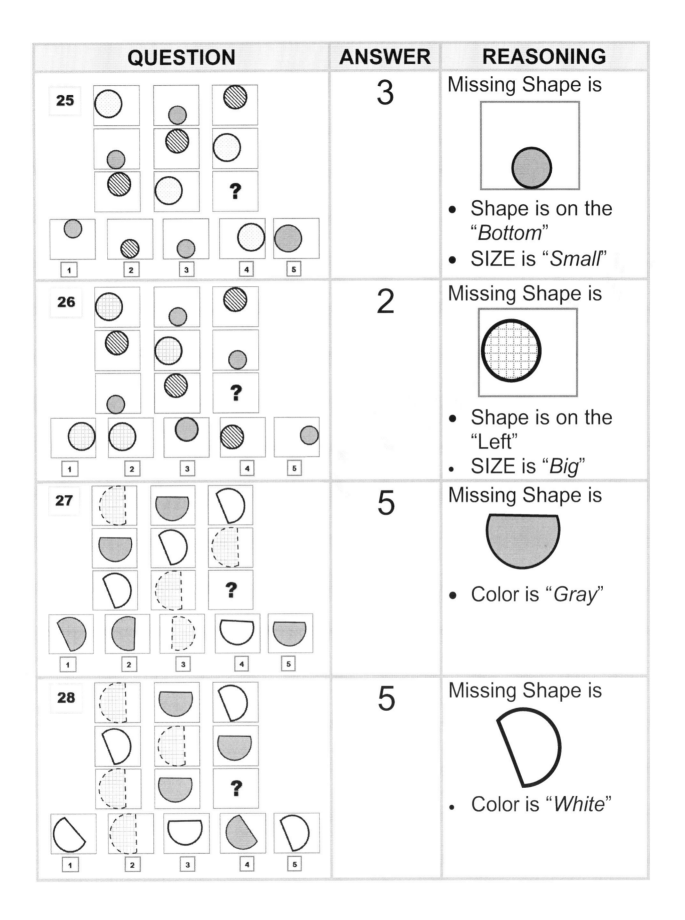 | 3 | Missing Shape is<br><br>• Shape is on the "Bottom"<br>• SIZE is "Small" |
| 26 | 2 | Missing Shape is<br><br>• Shape is on the "Left"<br>• SIZE is "Big" |
| 27 | 5 | Missing Shape is<br><br>• Color is "Gray" |
| 28 | 5 | Missing Shape is<br><br>• Color is "White" |

208

| QUESTION | ANSWER | REASONING |
|---|---|---|
| **29** | 3 | Missing Shape is • Pattern is "*Dots*" |
| **30** | 1 | Missing Shape is • Pattern is "*Dots*" |
| **31** | 2 | Missing Shape is • NUMBER OF SIDES is "*8*" • Color is "*Dark Gray*" |

209

| QUESTION | ANSWER | REASONING |
|---|---|---|
| **32** | 5 | Missing Shape is <ul><li>NUMBER OF SIDES is "*8*"</li><li>Color is "*Dark Gray*"</li></ul> |
| **33** | 1 | Missing Shape is <ul><li>NUMBER OF SIDES is "*8*"</li><li>Pattern is "*Dots*"</li></ul> |
| **34** | 3 | Missing Shape is <ul><li>NUMBER OF SIDES is "*8*"</li></ul> |

| QUESTION | ANSWER | REASONING |
|---|---|---|
| **35** | 4 | Missing Shape is<br><br>• Shape is "*Pointing Up*"<br>• Pattern is "*Horizontal lines*" |
| **36** | 5 | Missing Shape is<br><br>• Shape is "*Pointing Up*"<br>• Pattern is "*Vertical lines*" |
| **37** | 5 | Missing Shape is<br><br>• Shape is "*Pointing towards Right*" |

211

| QUESTION | ANSWER | REASONING |
|---|---|---|
| 38 | 3 | Missing Shape is <br><br> • Black part is "*Pointing towards RIGHT*" |
| 39 | 2 | Missing Shape is <br><br> • Black middle block is "P*ointing towards LEFT*" |
| 40 | 4 | Missing Shape is <br><br> • Shape is "*Pointing Upwards*" |
| 41 | 5 | Missing Shape is <br><br> • Number of sides is "*5*" <br> • Pattern is "*Dots*" |

212

| QUESTION | ANSWER | REASONING |
|----------|--------|-----------|
| **42** | **1** | Missing Shape is<br><br>• Shape has a pattern inside<br><br>Note that all Shapes in question have either Color or Pattern. Answer choice 2 is incorrect. |
| **43** | **3** | Missing Shape is<br><br>• Shape has "*No sides*"<br><br>Note that all Shapes in answer choices have some sides except #3. Answer choice 5 is not a solid shape. |
| **44** | **3** | Missing Shape is<br><br>• Shape has "*pattern*" |
| **45** | **5** | Missing Shape is<br><br>• Shape has "*Color/pattern*" |

213

| QUESTION | ANSWER | REASONING |
|---|---|---|
| 46 | 2 | Missing Shape is |
| 47 | 4 | Missing Shape is <br><br>• Shape has "*Color/pattern*" |
| 48 | 5 | Missing Shape is <br><br>• Color is "*White*"<br>• Triangle is on "*Top-Right Corner*" |

214

| QUESTION | ANSWER | REASONING |
|---|---|---|
| **49** | 2 | Missing Shape is <br><br>• Shape is "Pointing Upwards"<br>• SIZE is "Small"<br>• Pattern is "Dots" |
| **50** | 3 | Missing Shape is <br><br>• Shape is "Pointing Downwards"<br>• Color is "Gray"<br>• SIZE is "Big" |
| **51** | 5 | Missing Figure is <br><br>• Number of blocks is "4" |
| **52** | 3 | Missing Figure is <br><br>• Number of blocks is "6"<br>• Pattern is "Dots" |

| QUESTION | ANSWER | REASONING |
|---|---|---|
| 53 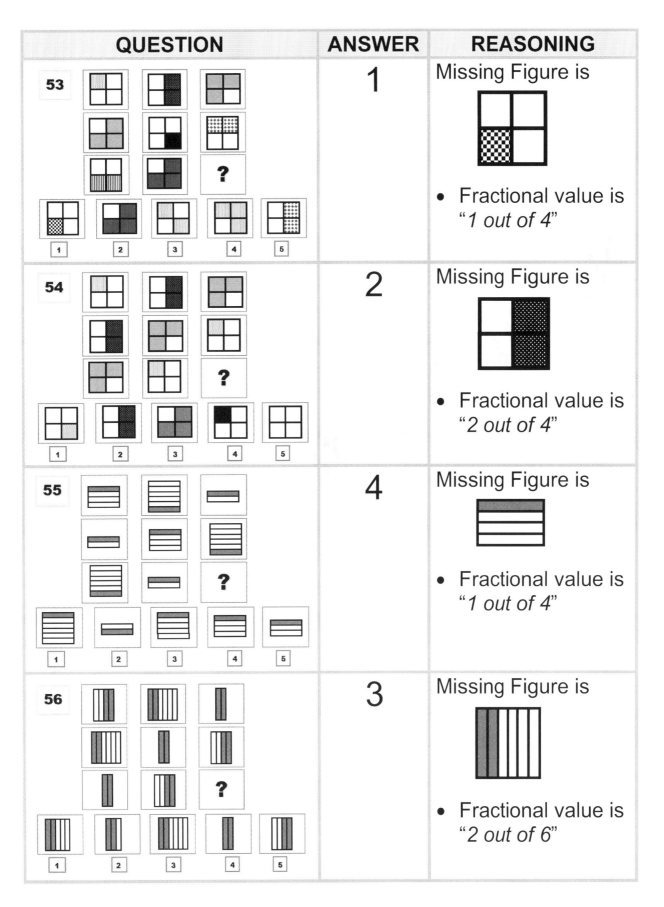 | 1 | Missing Figure is<br><br>• Fractional value is "1 out of 4" |
| 54 | 2 | Missing Figure is<br><br>• Fractional value is "2 out of 4" |
| 55 | 4 | Missing Figure is<br><br>• Fractional value is "1 out of 4" |
| 56 | 3 | Missing Figure is<br><br>• Fractional value is "2 out of 6" |

216

| QUESTION | ANSWER | REASONING |
|---|---|---|
| 57 | 5 | Missing Figure is<br><br>• Fractional value is "5 out of 9"<br>• Parts are shaded in "Black" |
| 58 | 3 | Missing Figure is<br><br>• Fractional value is "3 out of 9"<br>• Parts are shaded in "Black" |
| 59 | 3 | Missing Figure is<br><br>• Fractional value is "4 out of 8"<br>• Parts are shaded in "Gray" |

217

| QUESTION | ANSWER | REASONING |
|---|---|---|
| 60 | 4 | Missing Figure is <br><br>• Fractional value is "12 out of 16"<br>• 4 white donuts are diagonally placed from "Top-Left to Bottom-Right" |
| 61 | 4 | Missing Figure is <br><br>Note: Answer choices 2 and 4 are incorrect. Outside shape is not matching. |
| 62 | 4 | Missing Figure is <br><br>Note: Pattern/color inside shapes is a distraction |

| QUESTION | ANSWER | REASONING |
|----------|--------|-----------|
| **63** | 5 | Missing Figure is<br><br>• Shapes are *TURNING Clockwise* from row to row |
| **64** | 1 | Missing Figure is<br><br>• Shape has "*Black and White circles*" |
| **65** | 3 | Missing Figure is<br><br>Shape has "*Black squares and squares with dots*" |

219

| QUESTION | ANSWER | REASONING |
|---|---|---|
| **66** | 4 | Missing Figure is Shape has "*Black squares and squares with vertical lines pattern*" |
| **67** | 2 | Missing Figure is Note: Shape in answer choice 5 has incorrect size |
| **68** | 2 | Missing Figure is |

220

| QUESTION | ANSWER | REASONING |
|---|---|---|
| 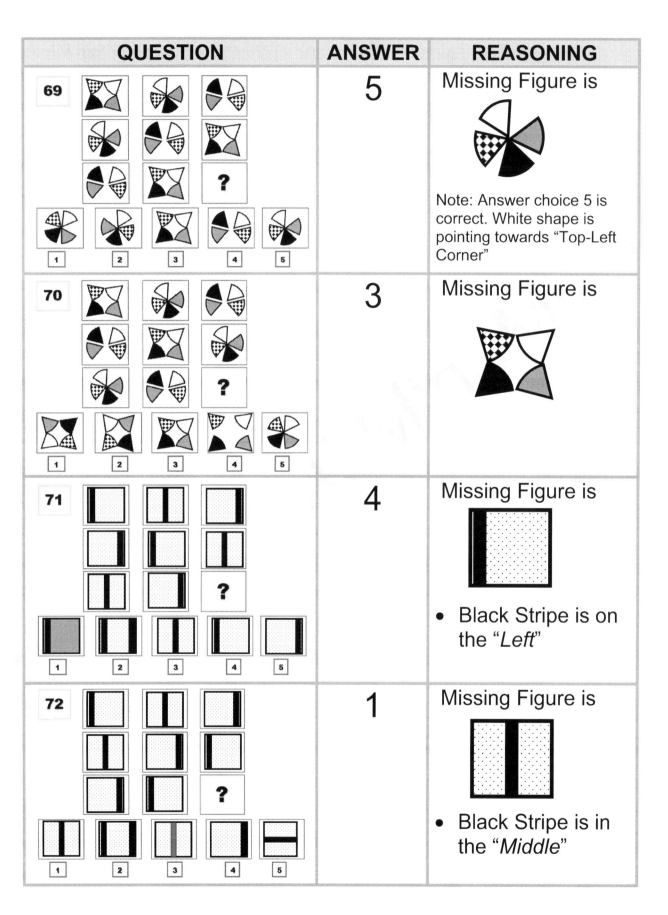 69 | 5 | Missing Figure is <br><br> Note: Answer choice 5 is correct. White shape is pointing towards "Top-Left Corner" |
| 70 | 3 | Missing Figure is |
| 71 | 4 | Missing Figure is <br><br> • Black Stripe is on the "*Left*" |
| 72 | 1 | Missing Figure is <br><br> • Black Stripe is in the "*Middle*" |

| QUESTION | ANSWER | REASONING |
|---|---|---|
| 73 | 3 | Missing Figure is<br>• Gray stripe is on the "*Top*" |
| 74 | 5 | Missing Figure is<br>• Gray stripe is in the "*Middle*" |
| 75 | 5 | Missing Figure is<br>• Inside shape is on "*Top-Left corner*" |
| 76 | 5 | Missing Figure is<br>• Inside shape is in the "*Middle*" |

222

| QUESTION | ANSWER | REASONING |
|---|---|---|
| 77 | 2 | Missing Shape is <br> • Triangle is "Gray" <br> • Triangle is on the "*Top-Left* corner" |
| 78 | 5 | Missing Shape is <br> • Triangle's pattern is "*Gray Squares*" <br> • Triangle is on the "*Bottom-Right corner*" |
| 79 | 3 | Missing Figure is <br> • Shape is on the "*Bottom-Right corner*" |

| QUESTION | ANSWER | REASONING |
|---|---|---|
| **80** 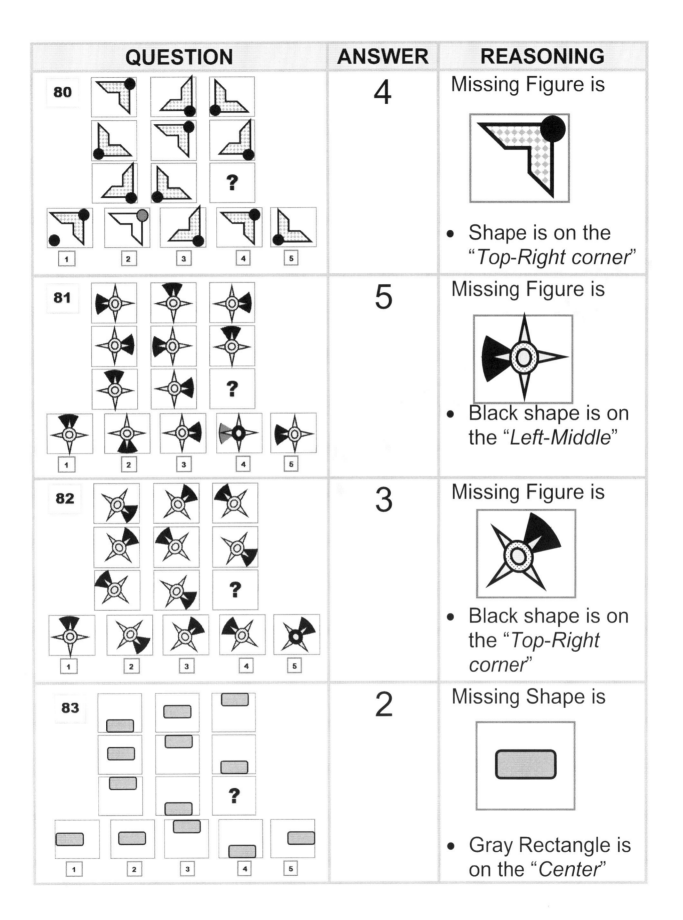 | 4 | Missing Figure is<br><br>• Shape is on the "*Top-Right corner*" |
| **81** | 5 | Missing Figure is<br><br>• Black shape is on the "*Left-Middle*" |
| **82** | 3 | Missing Figure is<br><br>• Black shape is on the "*Top-Right corner*" |
| **83** | 2 | Missing Shape is<br><br>• Gray Rectangle is on the "*Center*" |

224

| QUESTION | ANSWER | REASONING |
|---|---|---|
| 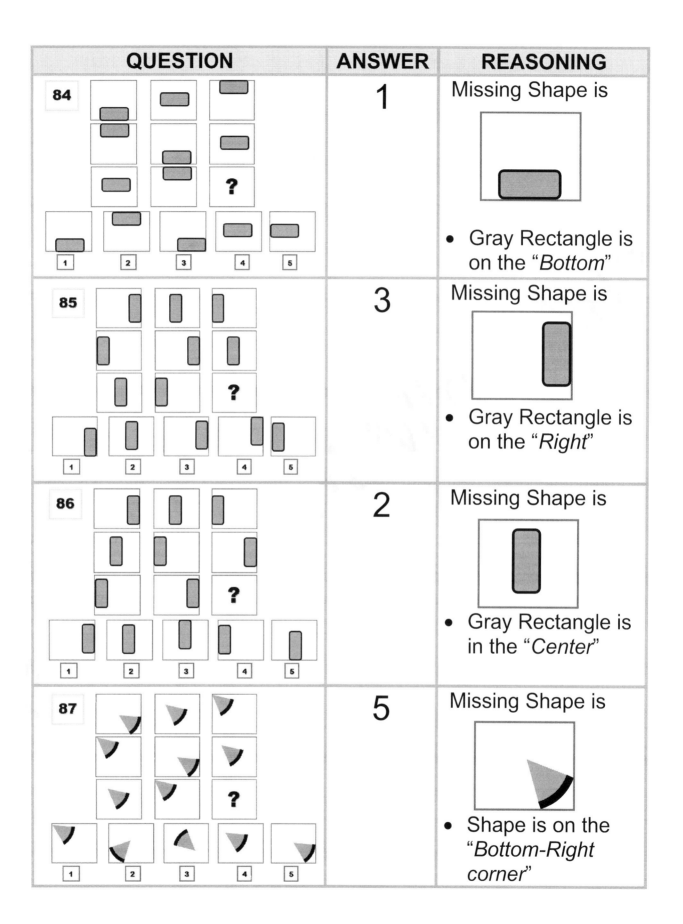 **84** | 1 | Missing Shape is<br><br>• Gray Rectangle is on the "*Bottom*" |
| **85** | 3 | Missing Shape is<br><br>• Gray Rectangle is on the "*Right*" |
| **86** | 2 | Missing Shape is<br><br>• Gray Rectangle is in the "*Center*" |
| **87** | 5 | Missing Shape is<br><br>• Shape is on the "*Bottom-Right corner*" |

| QUESTION | ANSWER | REASONING |
|---|---|---|
| 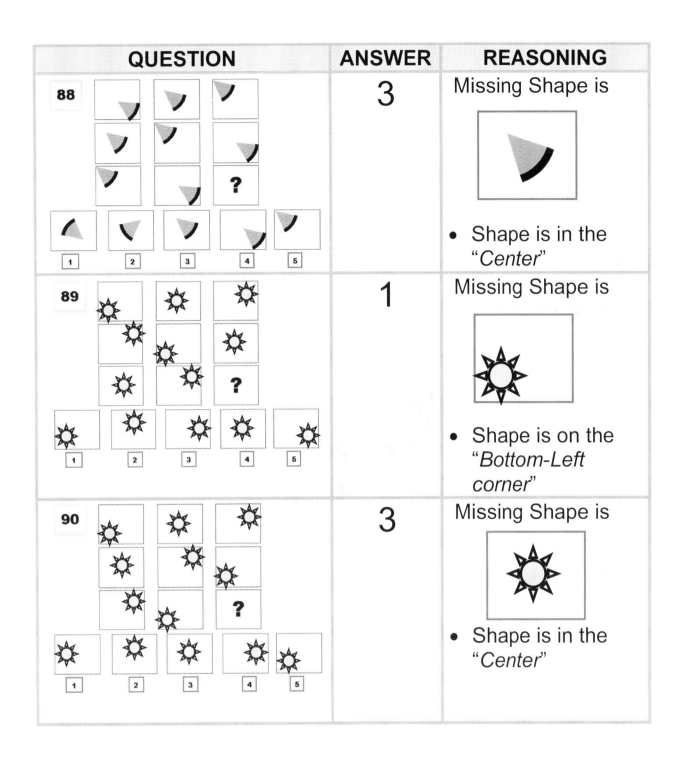 **88** | 3 | Missing Shape is<br><br>• Shape is in the "*Center*" |
| **89** | 1 | Missing Shape is<br><br>• Shape is on the "*Bottom-Left corner*" |
| **90** | 3 | Missing Shape is<br><br>• Shape is in the "*Center*" |

226

| QUESTION | ANSWER | REASONING |
|---|---|---|
| **91** L T I / I L T / T I **?** / 1: l  2: L  3: I  4: T  5: t | 2 | Missing LETTER is **L** |
| **92** P Z D / Z D P / D P **?** / 1: z  2: P  3: d  4: p  5: Z | 5 | Missing LETTER is **Z** |
| **93** p d q / q p d / d q **?** / 1: p  2: q  3: d  4: P  5: r | 1 | Missing LETTER is **p** |
| **94** p d q / d q p / q p **?** / 1: q  2: d  3: D  4: p  5: r | 2 | Missing LETTER is **d** |

227

| QUESTION | ANSWER | REASONING |
|---|---|---|
| 95 | 4 | Missing Figure is <br><br>• Black stripe is "*Horizontal*"<br>• Black stripe is in the "*Front and middle*" |
| 96 | 2 | Missing Figure is <br><br>• Black stripe is "*Vertical*"<br>• Black vertical stripe is in the "*Front and middle*" |
| 97 | 1 | Missing Figure is <br><br>• Black stripe is diagonally positioned from "*Top-Left to Bottom-Right*"<br>• Black stripe is in the "*Front*" |

228

| QUESTION | ANSWER | REASONING |
|---|---|---|
| **98** | 1 | Missing Figure is <br><br>• Black stripe is *"Horizontal"*<br>• Black stripe is *"Small"*<br>• Small black stripe is in the *"Front and middle"* |
| **99** | 5 | Missing Figure is <br><br>• Numbe of cubes is *"1"*<br>• Cube is *"Gray"*<br>• Cube is in the *"Center"* |
| **100** | 5 | Missing Figure is <br><br>• Square is *"White"*<br>• Inside shape is *"Circle"*<br>• Circle is *"Gray"* |

| QUESTION | ANSWER | REASONING |
|---|---|---|
| **101** | 2 | Missing Figure is <br> • Square is "*Gray*" <br> • Triangle is "*Gray*" <br> • Triangle is "*Pointing Up*" |
| **102** | 1 | Missing Figure is <br> • Square is "*White*" <br> • Triangle is "*Gray*" <br> • Triangle is "*Pointing Up*" |
| **103** | 1 | Missing Figure is <br> • Square is "*Gray*" <br> • Circle is "*Gray*" |

230

| QUESTION | ANSWER | REASONING |
|---|---|---|
| 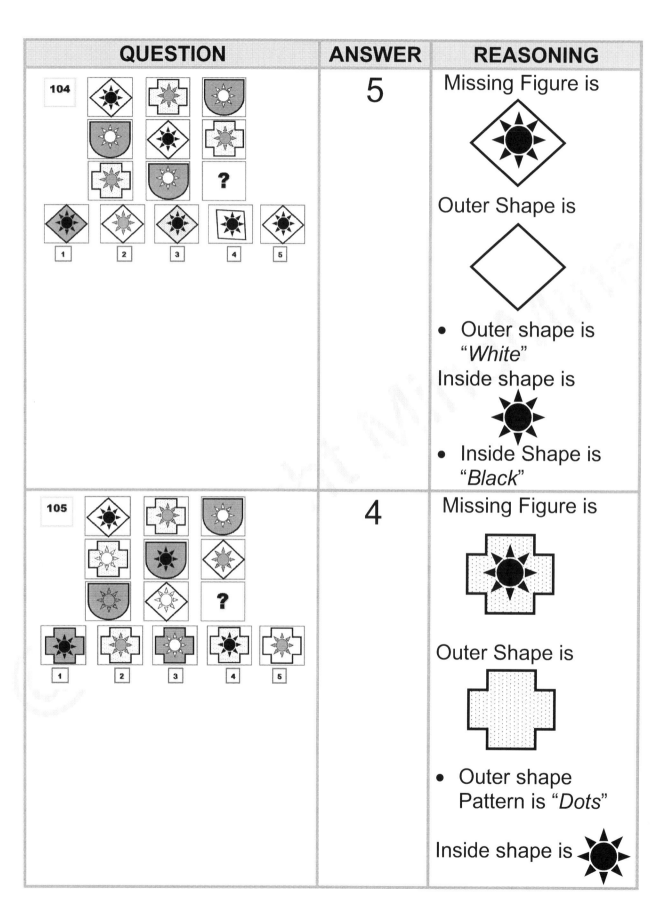 | 5 | Missing Figure is<br><br>Outer Shape is<br><br>• Outer shape is "*White*"<br>Inside shape is<br><br>• Inside Shape is "*Black*" |
| | 4 | Missing Figure is<br><br>Outer Shape is<br><br>• Outer shape Pattern is "*Dots*"<br><br>Inside shape is |

| QUESTION | ANSWER | REASONING |
|---|---|---|
| | | • Inside Shape is *"Black"* |
| **106** | 3 | Missing Figure is Outer Shape is • Outer shape is *"White"* Inside shape is • Inside Shape is *"Gray"* |
| **107** | 5 | Missing Figure is Outer Shape is • Outer shape Pattern is *"Dots"* |

| QUESTION | ANSWER | REASONING |
|---|---|---|
| | | Inside shape is • Inside Shape is "*Gray*" |
| **108** | 2 | Missing Figure is Outer shape is • Outer shape pattern is "*Dots*" • Number of sticks inside is "*1*" • Stick is on the "*Left*" |
| **109** | 1 | Missing Figure is Outer shape is |

233

| QUESTION | ANSWER | REASONING |
|----------|--------|-----------|
| | | • Outer shape is "*Gray*" <br> • Number of sticks inside is "*2*" <br> • Sticks are on the "*Left*" |
| 110 | 4 | Missing Figure is <br><br> Outer shape is <br><br> • Outer shape Pattern is "*Dots*" <br> • Number of sticks inside is "*1*" <br> • Stick is on the "*Left*" |
| 111 | 3 | Missing Figure is <br><br> • Outer shape is |

| QUESTION | ANSWER | REASONING |
|---|---|---|
| | | • Outer shape is "*Gray*"<br>• Number of sticks inside is "*2*"<br>• Sticks are in the "*Middle*" |
| **112** | 3 | Missing Figure is<br><br>• Outer shape is<br><br>• Outer shape Pattern is "*Dots*"<br>• Number of sticks inside is "*1*"<br>• Stick is in the "*Middle*" |
| **113** | 2 | Missing Figure is<br><br>• Outer shape is<br> |

235

| QUESTION | ANSWER | REASONING |
|---|---|---|
| | | • Outer shape is "*Gray*" <br> • Number of sticks inside is "*2*" <br> • Sticks are on the "*Left*" |
| 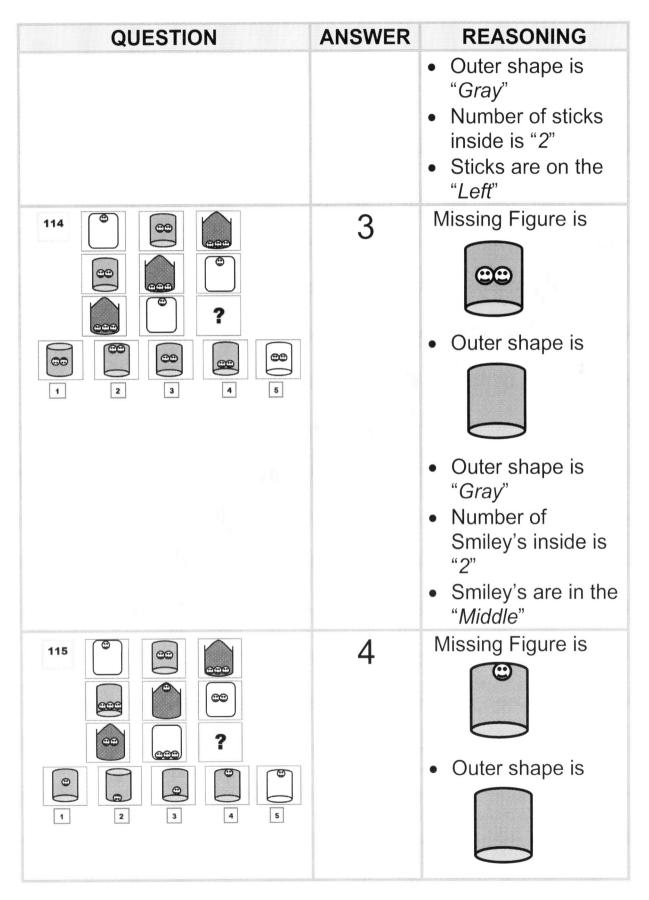 114 | 3 | Missing Figure is <br><br> • Outer shape is <br><br> • Outer shape is "*Gray*" <br> • Number of Smiley's inside is "*2*" <br> • Smiley's are in the "*Middle*" |
| 115 | 4 | Missing Figure is <br><br> • Outer shape is |

236

| QUESTION | ANSWER | REASONING |
|---|---|---|
| | | • Outer shape is "*Gray*"<br>• Number of Smiley's inside is "*1*"<br>• Smiley is on the "*Top*" |
| **116** | 4 | Missing Figure is<br><br>• Outer shape is<br><br>• Outer shape is "*Gray*"<br>• Number of Smiley's inside is "*1*"<br>• Smiley is in the "*Middle*" |
| **117** | 3 | Missing Figure is<br><br>• Outer shape is<br> |

237

| QUESTION | ANSWER | REASONING |
|---|---|---|
| | | • Outer shape is "*Gray*" |
| | | • Number of Smiley's inside is "*2*" |
| | | • Smiley's are on the "*Top*" |
| 118 | 2 | Missing Figure is |
| | | • Outer shape is |
| | | • Outer shape is "*White*" |
| | | • Number of Smiley's inside is "*2*" |
| | | • Smiley's are in the "*Middle*" |
| 119 | 1 | Missing Figure is |
| | | • Outer shape is |

238

| QUESTION | ANSWER | REASONING |
|---|---|---|
| | | - Outer shape is "*White*"<br>- Number of Smiley's inside is "*1*"<br>- Smiley is on the "*Top*" |
| 120 | 3 | Missing Figure is<br><br>- Outer shape is<br><br>- Outer shape is "*White*"<br>- Number of Smiley's inside is "*1*"<br>- Smiley is in the "*Middle*" |
| 121 | 1 | Missing Figure is<br><br>- Outer shape is<br> |

239

| QUESTION | ANSWER | REASONING |
|---|---|---|
| | | • Outer shape is "*White*"<br>• Number of Smiley's inside is "*2*"<br>• Smiley's are on the "*Top*" |
| 122 | 1 | Missing Figure is<br><br>• Outer most shape is<br><br>• Outer most shape is "*Dark Gray*"<br><br>Inner shape is<br><br>• Inner shape pattern is "*Vertical Lines*"<br>• Number of sticks inside is "*3*" |

240

| QUESTION | ANSWER | REASONING |
|---|---|---|
| 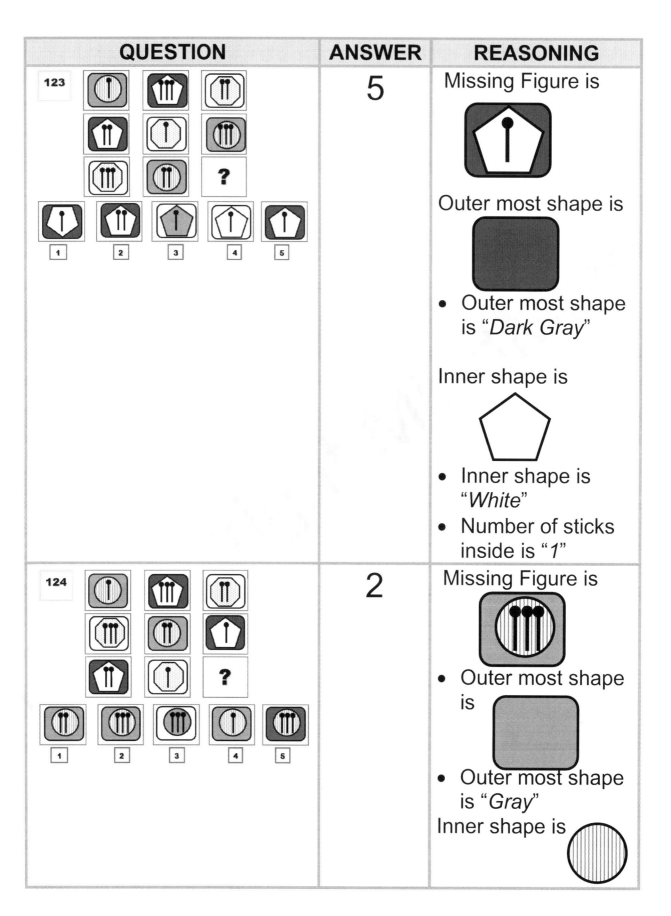 | 5 | Missing Figure is<br><br>Outer most shape is<br><br>• Outer most shape is "*Dark Gray*"<br><br>Inner shape is<br><br>• Inner shape is "*White*"<br>• Number of sticks inside is "*1*" |
| | 2 | Missing Figure is<br><br>• Outer most shape is<br><br>• Outer most shape is "*Gray*"<br>Inner shape is |

241

| QUESTION | ANSWER | REASONING |
|---|---|---|
| | | • Inner shape pattern is "*Vertical Lines*" <br> • Number of sticks inside is "*3*" |
| | 1 | Missing Figure is <br><br> • Outer most shape is <br><br> • Outer most shape is "*Gray*" <br><br> Inner shape is <br><br> • Inner shape is "*White*" <br> • Number of sticks inside is "*1*" |

242

| QUESTION | ANSWER | REASONING |
|---|---|---|
| 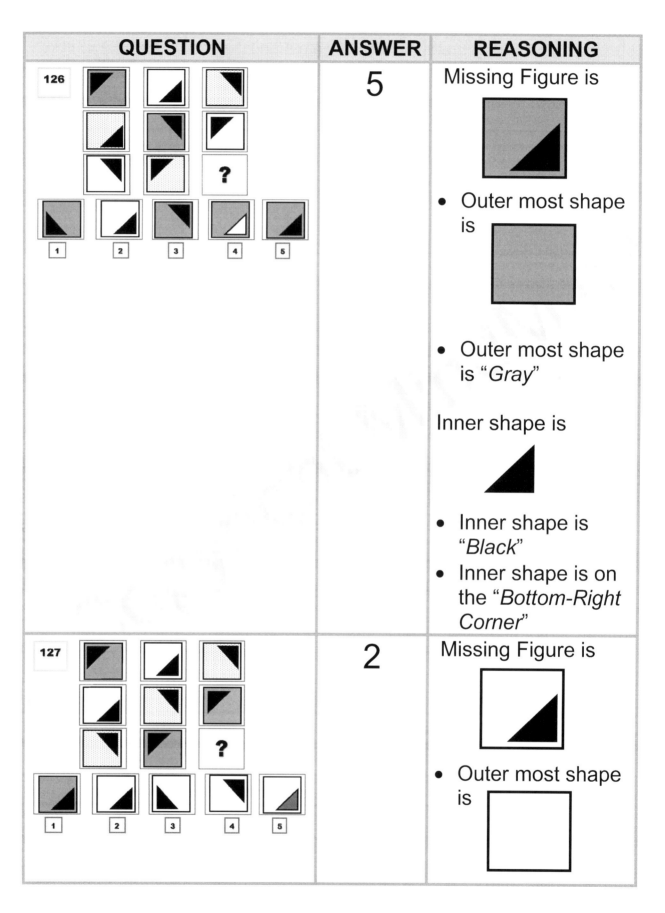 126 | 5 | Missing Figure is<br><br>• Outer most shape is<br><br>• Outer most shape is "*Gray*"<br><br>Inner shape is<br><br>• Inner shape is "*Black*"<br>• Inner shape is on the "*Bottom-Right Corner*" |
| 127 | 2 | Missing Figure is<br><br>• Outer most shape is |

| QUESTION | ANSWER | REASONING |
|---|---|---|
| | | • Outer most shape is "*White*" |
| | | Inner shape is |
| | | |
| | | • Inner shape is "*Black*" |
| | | • Inner shape is on the "*Bottom-Right Corner*" |
| 128 | 2 | Missing Figure is |
| | | Outer most shape is |
| | | • Outer most shape Pattern is "*Dots*" |
| | | • Black Triangle on outer most shape is positioned on the "*Top-Right corner*" |
| | | • Inner shape is |

244

| QUESTION | ANSWER | REASONING |
|---|---|---|
| | | • Inner shape is "*White*" |
| **129** | 4 | Missing Figure is  • Outer most shape is  • Outer most shape is "*White*"  • Black Triangle on outer most shape is positioned on the "*Top-Right corner*"  • Inner shape is  • Inner shape is "*White*" |
| **130** | 3 | Missing Figure is |

245

| QUESTION | ANSWER | REASONING |
|---|---|---|
| | | • Outer most shape is <br><br>• Outer most shape Pattern is "*Dots*"<br>• Black Triangle on outer most shape is positioned on the "*Bottom-Right corner*"<br>• Inner shape is <br>• Inner shape is "*White*" |
| 131 | 5 | Missing Figure is <br><br>Outer most shape is <br><br>• Outer most shape is "*White*"<br>• Black Triangle on outer most shape is positioned on |

| QUESTION | ANSWER | REASONING |
|---|---|---|
| | | the "*Top-Left corner*"<br>• Inner shape is<br><br>◯<br><br>• Inner shape is "*White*" |
| 132 | 5 | Missing Figure is<br><br><br><br>• Number of vertical stripes is "*3*"<br>• Vertical stripes are "*Black*"<br>• Number of Horizontal stripes is "*1*"<br>• Horizontal stripe is "*Gray*"<br>• Horizontal stripe is "*in the Front*" |
| 133 | 4 | Missing Figure is<br><br><br><br>• Number of vertical stripes is "*4*"<br>• Vertical stripes are "*Black*" |

| QUESTION | ANSWER | REASONING |
|---|---|---|
| | | • Number of Horizontal stripes is "*1*" |
| | | • Horizontal stripe is "*Gray*" |
| | | • Horizontal stripe is "*in the Back*" |
| 134 | 4 | Missing Figure is • Number of vertical stripes is "*2*" • Vertical stripes pattern is "*Dots*" • Number of Horizontal stripes is "*1*" • Horizontal stripe is "*Gray*" • Horizontal stripe is "*in the Front*" |
| 135 | 3 | Missing Figure is • Number of vertical stripes is "*4*" • Vertical stripes are "*Black*" |

248

| QUESTION | ANSWER | REASONING |
|---|---|---|
| | | • Number of Horizontal stripes is "*1*" <br> • Horizontal stripe is "*Gray*" <br> • Horizontal stripe is "*in the Back*" |
| **136** | 3 | Missing Figure is <br><br> • Number of vertical stripes is "*2*" <br> • Vertical stripes pattern is "*Dots*" <br> • Number of Horizontal stripes is "*1*" <br> • Horizontal stripe is "*Black*" <br> • Horizontal stripe is "*in the Front*" |
| **137** | 2 | Missing Figure is <br><br> • Number of vertical stripes is "*4*" <br> • Vertical stripes are "*Black*" |

| QUESTION | ANSWER | REASONING |
|---|---|---|
| | | • Number of Horizontal stripes is "1"<br>• Horizontal stripe is "White"<br>• Horizontal stripe is "in the Back" |
| 138 | 5 | Missing Figure is<br><br>• Shape is on the "Bottom-Right corner" |
| 139 | 3 | Missing Figure is<br><br>• Smiley is on the "Top-Left corner"<br>• Size of ⬚ is "Small" |

| QUESTION | ANSWER | REASONING |
|----------|--------|-----------|
| 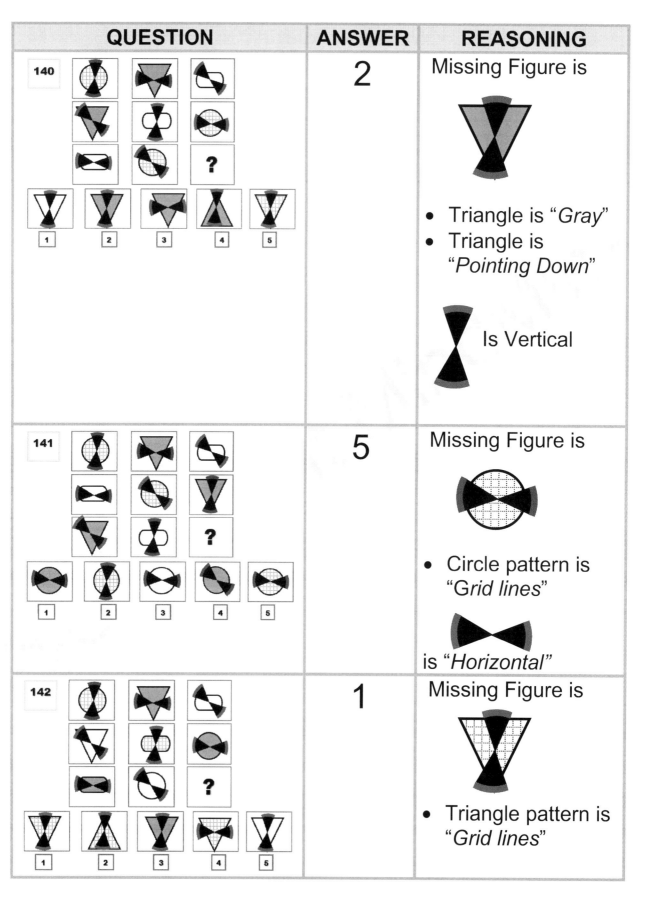 140 | 2 | Missing Figure is<br><br>• Triangle is "*Gray*"<br>• Triangle is "*Pointing Down*"<br><br>Is Vertical |
| 141 | 5 | Missing Figure is<br><br>• Circle pattern is "*Grid lines*"<br><br>is "*Horizontal*" |
| 142 | 1 | Missing Figure is<br><br>• Triangle pattern is "*Grid lines*" |

| QUESTION | ANSWER | REASONING |
|---|---|---|
| | | - Triangle is "*Pointing Down*"<br><br>is "*Vertical*" |
| 143 | 4 | Missing Figure is<br><br><br><br>- Circle is "*Gray*"<br><br>is "*Horizontal*" |
| 144 | 3 | Missing Figure is<br><br><br><br>- Triangle is "*Black*"<br>- Triangle is "*Pointing Up*"<br>- Inside shape is "*Gray Diamond*" |

| QUESTION | ANSWER | REASONING |
|---|---|---|
| **145** | 1 | Missing Figure is <br> • Triangle is *"Black"* <br> • Triangle is *"Pointing towards Right"* <br> • Inside shape is *"Gray Hexagon"* |
| **146** | 2 | Missing Figure is <br> • Triangle is *"Black"* <br> • Triangle is *"Pointing towards Right"* <br> • Inside shape is *"Gray Hexagon"* |
| **147** | 3 | Missing Figure is <br> • Triangle is *"White"* <br> • Triangle is *"Pointing towards Right"* <br> • Inside shape is *"White Hexagon"* |

| QUESTION | ANSWER | REASONING |
|---|---|---|
| 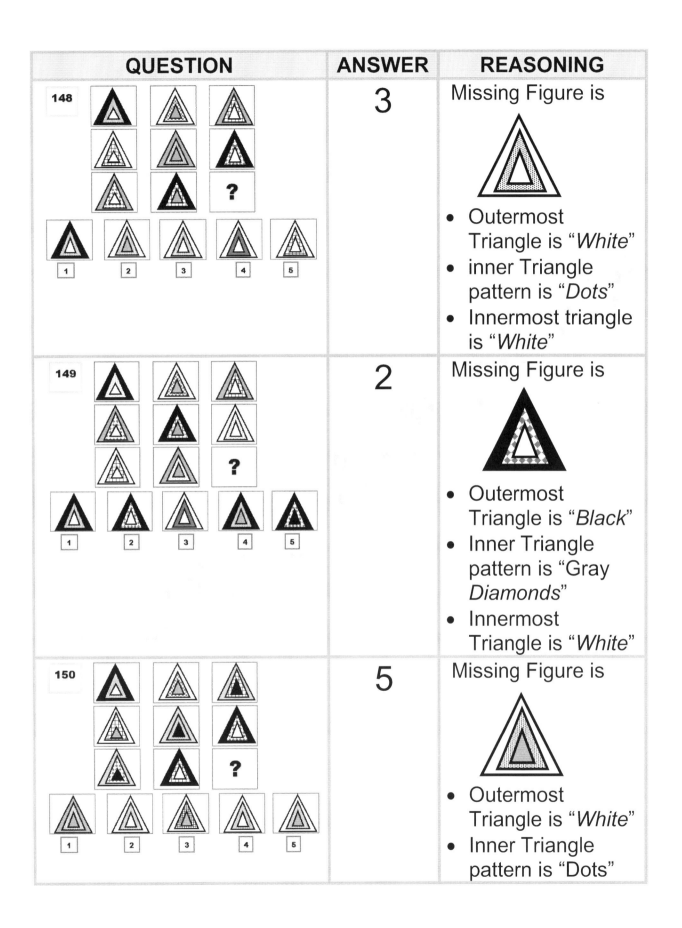 | | |

148 — 3 — Missing Figure is
- Outermost Triangle is "*White*"
- inner Triangle pattern is "*Dots*"
- Innermost triangle is "*White*"

149 — 2 — Missing Figure is
- Outermost Triangle is "*Black*"
- Inner Triangle pattern is "Gray *Diamonds*"
- Innermost Triangle is "*White*"

150 — 5 — Missing Figure is
- Outermost Triangle is "*White*"
- Inner Triangle pattern is "Dots"

| QUESTION | ANSWER | REASONING |
|---|---|---|
| | | • Innermost triangle is "*Gray*" |
| **151** | 4 | Missing Figure is <br>• Outermost Triangle is "*Black*" <br>• Inner Triangle pattern is "*Gray Diamonds*" <br>• Innermost triangle is "*White*" <br>• Innermost triangle is "*Pointing Downwards*" |
| **152** | 2 | Missing Figure is <br>• 1st Shape is <br>• 2nd Shape is <br>• 2nd Shape is "*Gray*" <br>• 2nd shape is on the "*Right*" |

255

| QUESTION | ANSWER | REASONING |
|---|---|---|
| **153** | 5 | Missing Figure is<br><br>❋ ◎<br><br>• 1st Shape is ❋<br><br>• 2nd Shape is ◎<br>• 2nd Shape pattern is "*Grid lines*"<br><br>• 2nd shape is on the "*Right*" |
| **154** | 3 | Missing Figure is<br><br>❋<br><br>• Color is "*White*"<br>• Size is "*Small*" |
| **155** | 2 | Missing Figure is<br><br>✦<br><br>• Color is "*Black*"<br>• Size is "*Big*" |

| QUESTION | ANSWER | REASONING |
|---|---|---|
| 156 | 4 | Missing Figure is <br><br> • Outer box is "*Black*" <br> • Inside shape is "*White*" |
| 157 | 3 | Missing Figure is <br><br> • Outer box is "*Gray*" <br> • Inside shape is "*Gray*" |
| 158 | 2 | Missing Figure is <br><br> • Outer box is "*White*" <br> • Inside shape is "*White*" <br> • Shape is "*Pointing towards Right*" |

257

| QUESTION | ANSWER | REASONING |
|---|---|---|
| 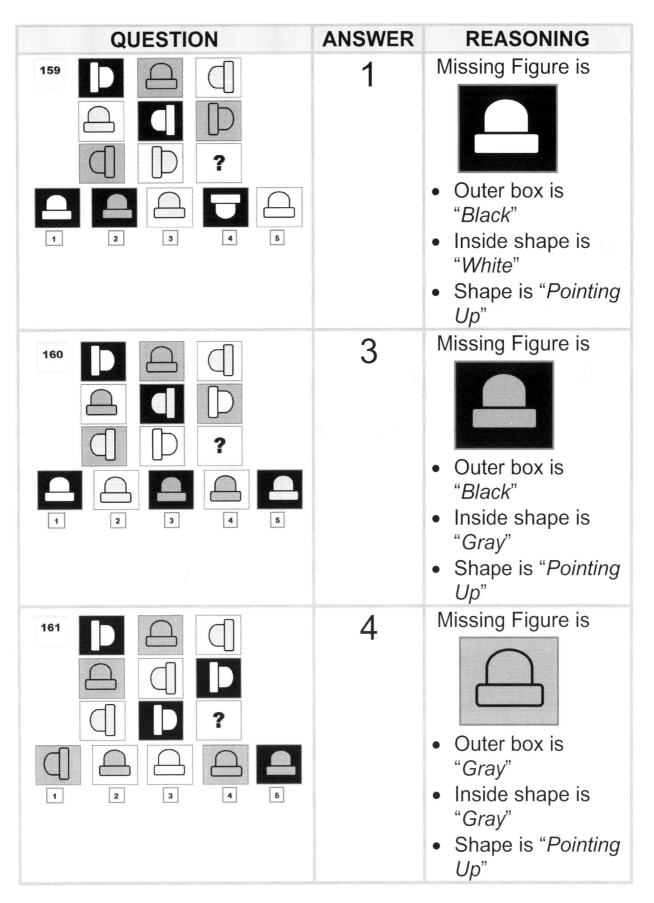 | 1 | Missing Figure is<br><br>• Outer box is "*Black*"<br>• Inside shape is "*White*"<br>• Shape is "*Pointing Up*" |
| | 3 | Missing Figure is<br><br>• Outer box is "*Black*"<br>• Inside shape is "*Gray*"<br>• Shape is "*Pointing Up*" |
| | 4 | Missing Figure is<br><br>• Outer box is "*Gray*"<br>• Inside shape is "*Gray*"<br>• Shape is "*Pointing Up*" |

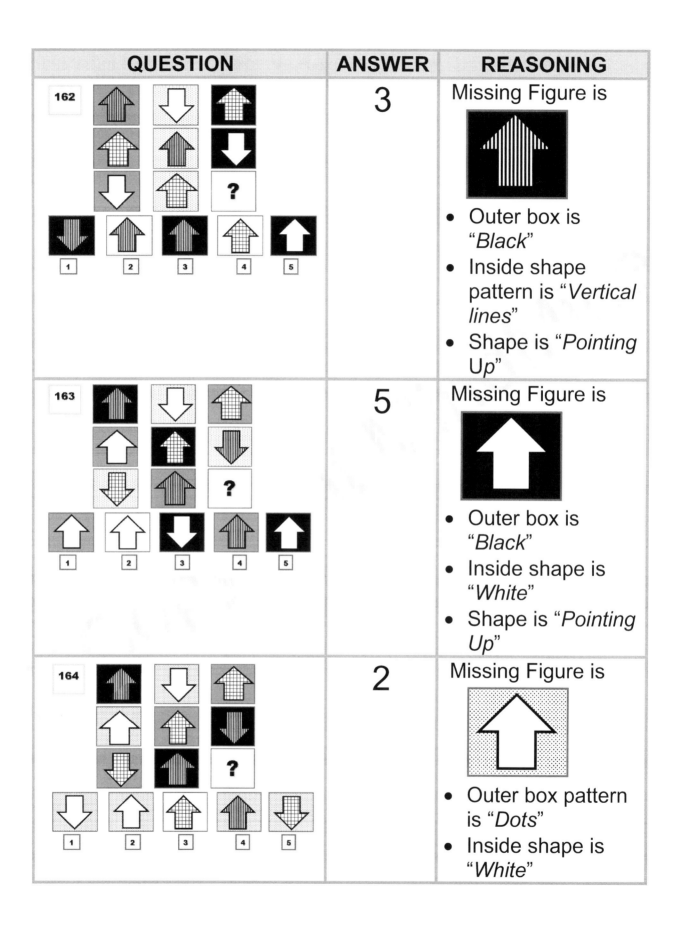

| QUESTION | ANSWER | REASONING |
|---|---|---|
| 162 | 3 | Missing Figure is<br><br>• Outer box is "*Black*"<br>• Inside shape pattern is "*Vertical lines*"<br>• Shape is "*Pointing Up*" |
| 163 | 5 | Missing Figure is<br><br>• Outer box is "*Black*"<br>• Inside shape is "*White*"<br>• Shape is "*Pointing Up*" |
| 164 | 2 | Missing Figure is<br><br>• Outer box pattern is "*Dots*"<br>• Inside shape is "*White*" |

| QUESTION | ANSWER | REASONING |
|---|---|---|
| | | • Shape is "*Pointing Up*" |
| 165 | 1 | Missing Figure is • Outer box pattern is "*Horizontal broken lines*" • Inside shape pattern is "*Vertical lines*" • Shape is "*Pointing Up*" |
| 166 | 2 | Missing Figure is • Outer box is "*Gray*" • Inside shape is "*White*" • Arrow is "*Diagonally positioned from Bottom-Left to Top-Right*" |

| QUESTION | ANSWER | REASONING |
|---|---|---|
| 167 | 5 | Missing Figure is <br><br>• Outer box pattern is "*Dots*"<br>• Inside shape is "*White*"<br>• Shape is "*Pointed diagonally from Bottom-Left to Top-Right*" |
| 168 | 4 | Missing Figure is <br><br>• Outer box is "*Gray*"<br>• Inside shape pattern is "*black diamonds*"<br>• Arrow is "*Diagonally positioned from Bottom-Left to Top-Right*" |

261

| QUESTION | ANSWER | REASONING |
|---|---|---|
| 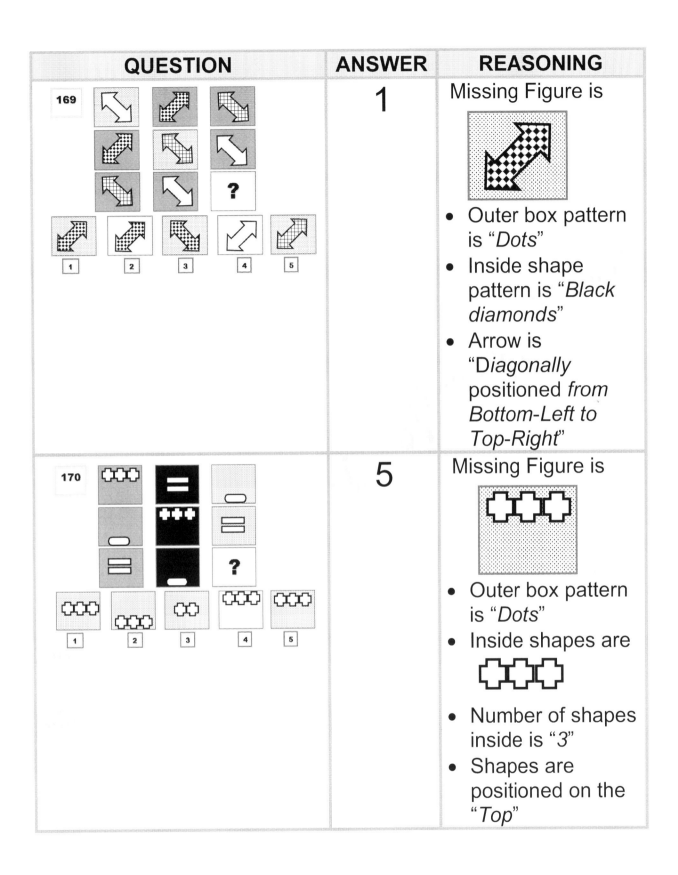 | 1 | Missing Figure is<br><br>- Outer box pattern is "*Dots*"<br>- Inside shape pattern is "*Black diamonds*"<br>- Arrow is "D*iagonally positioned from Bottom-Left to Top-Right*" |
| | 5 | Missing Figure is<br><br>- Outer box pattern is "*Dots*"<br>- Inside shapes are<br><br>- Number of shapes inside is "*3*"<br>- Shapes are positioned on the "*Top*" |

262

| QUESTION | ANSWER | REASONING |
|----------|--------|-----------|
| 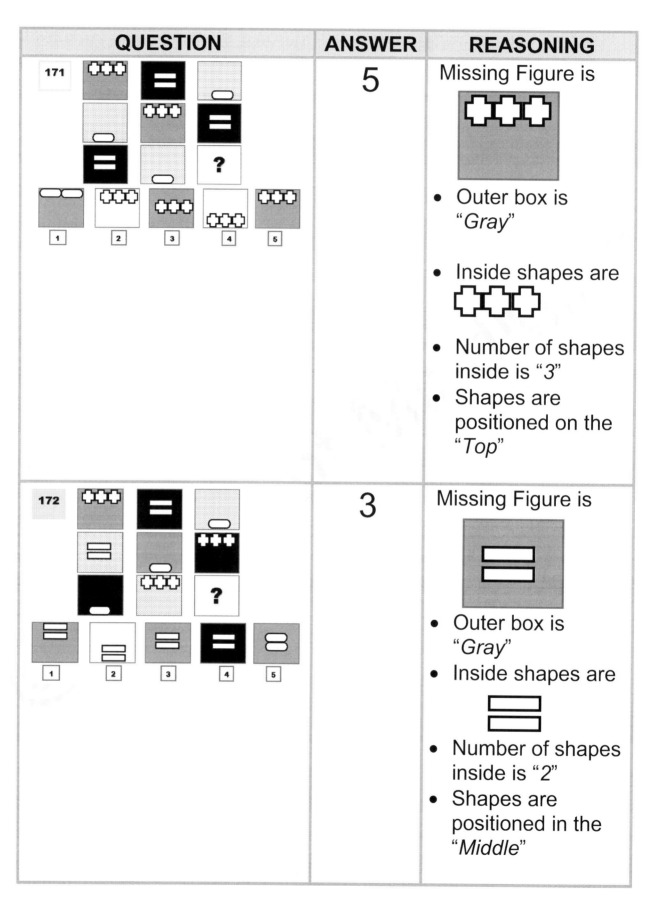 **171** | 5 | Missing Figure is<br><br>• Outer box is "*Gray*"<br><br>• Inside shapes are<br><br>• Number of shapes inside is "*3*"<br>• Shapes are positioned on the "*Top*" |
| **172** | 3 | Missing Figure is<br><br>• Outer box is "*Gray*"<br>• Inside shapes are<br><br>• Number of shapes inside is "*2*"<br>• Shapes are positioned in the "*Middle*" |

263

| QUESTION | ANSWER | REASONING |
|---|---|---|
| 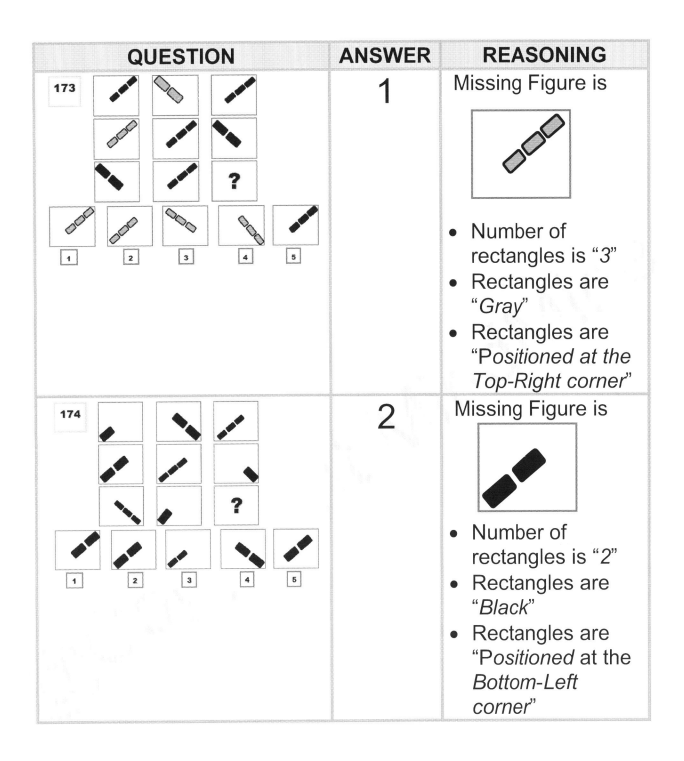 173 | 1 | Missing Figure is<br><br>• Number of rectangles is "*3*"<br>• Rectangles are "*Gray*"<br>• Rectangles are "*Positioned at the Top-Right corner*" |
| 174 | 2 | Missing Figure is<br><br>• Number of rectangles is "*2*"<br>• Rectangles are "*Black*"<br>• Rectangles are "*Positioned at the Bottom-Left corner*" |

| QUESTION | ANSWER | REASONING |
|---|---|---|
| **175** 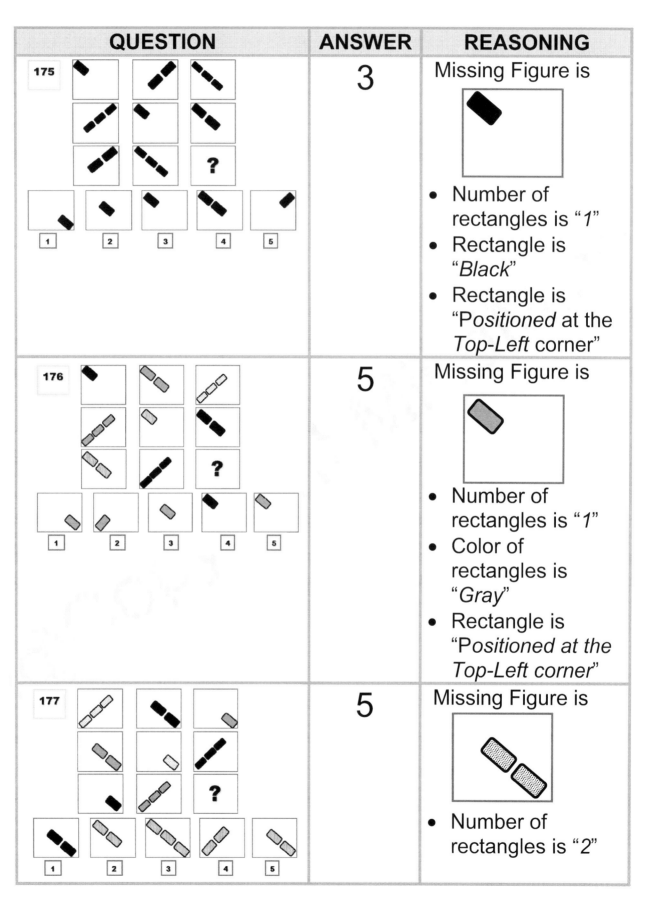 | 3 | Missing Figure is<br><br>• Number of rectangles is "*1*"<br>• Rectangle is "*Black*"<br>• Rectangle is "*Positioned* at the *Top-Left* corner" |
| **176** | 5 | Missing Figure is<br><br>• Number of rectangles is "*1*"<br>• Color of rectangles is "*Gray*"<br>• Rectangle is "*Positioned at the Top-Left corner*" |
| **177** | 5 | Missing Figure is<br><br>• Number of rectangles is "*2*" |

| QUESTION | ANSWER | REASONING |
|---|---|---|
| | | • Rectangles pattern is "*Dots*" <br> • Rectangles are "*Positioned at the Bottom-Right corner*" |
| 178 | 4 | Missing Figure is <br> • Outer box is "*White*" <br> • Number of squares inside is "*2*" <br> • Rectangles are "*White*" <br> • Rectangles are "*Positioned at the Top-Left corner*" |
| 179 | 3 | Missing Figure is <br> • Outer box is "*White*" <br> • Number of squares inside is "*2*" <br> • Rectangles are "*White*" |

| QUESTION | ANSWER | REASONING |
|---|---|---|
| | | • Rectangles are "Positioned at the Bottom-Left corner" |
| 180 | 3 | Missing Figure is <br>• Outer box is "White" <br>• Number of squares is "2" <br>• Rectangles are "White" <br>• Rectangles are "Positioned at the Bottom-Left corner" |
| 181 | 5 | Missing Figure is <br>• Outer box is "White" <br>• Number of squares inside is "2" <br>• Rectangles are "White" <br>• Rectangles are "Positioned at the |

| QUESTION | ANSWER | REASONING |
|---|---|---|
| | | *Bottom-Left corner"* |
| 182 | 3 | Missing Figure is Outermost box pattern is *"Dots"* Inner shape is Inner shape is *"White"* Innermost Shape is |
| 183 | 2 | Missing Figure is • Outermost box pattern is *"Dots"* Inner shape is |

268

| QUESTION | ANSWER | REASONING |
|---|---|---|
| | | • Inner shape Pattern is "*Diagonal lines*"<br>• Innermost Shape is<br> |
| 184 | 2 | Missing Figure is<br><br>• Outermost box pattern is "*Dots*"<br><br>Inner shape is<br><br>• Inner shape Pattern is "*Diagonal lines*"<br><br>Innermost Shape is<br> |

269

| QUESTION | ANSWER | REASONING |
|---|---|---|
| **185** 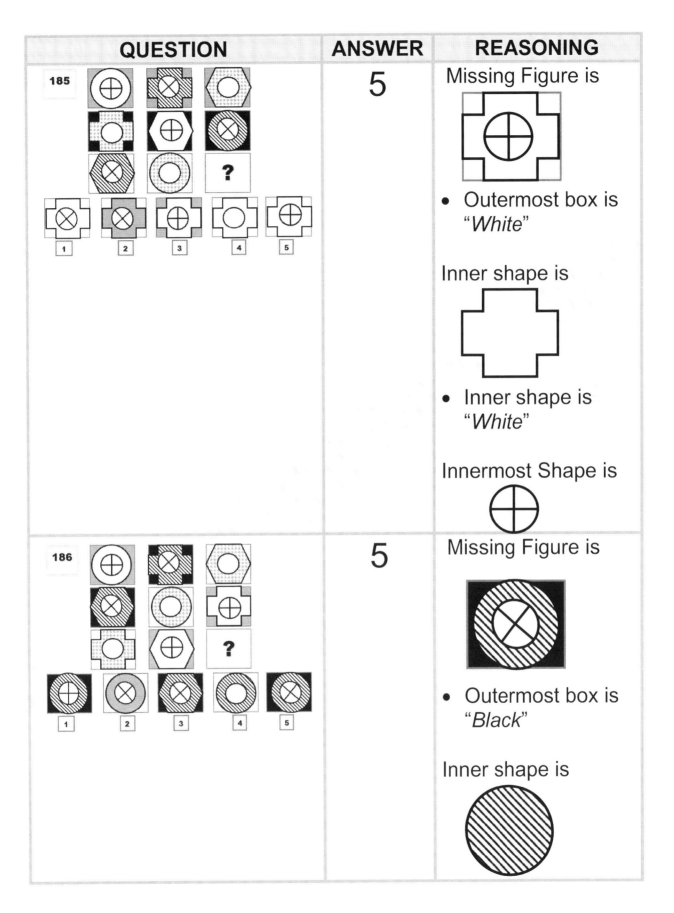 | 5 | Missing Figure is<br><br>• Outermost box is "*White*"<br><br>Inner shape is<br><br>• Inner shape is "*White*"<br><br>Innermost Shape is |
| **186** | 5 | Missing Figure is<br><br>• Outermost box is "*Black*"<br><br>Inner shape is |

270

| QUESTION | ANSWER | REASONING |
|---|---|---|
| | | • Inner shape Pattern is *"Diagonal lines"*<br><br>Innermost Shape is<br> |
| 187<br> | 4 | Missing Figure is<br><br><br>• Outermost box is *"Gray"*<br><br><br>Inner shape is<br><br><br>• Inner shape is *"White"*<br><br>Innermost Shape is<br> |

| QUESTION | ANSWER | REASONING |
|---|---|---|
| 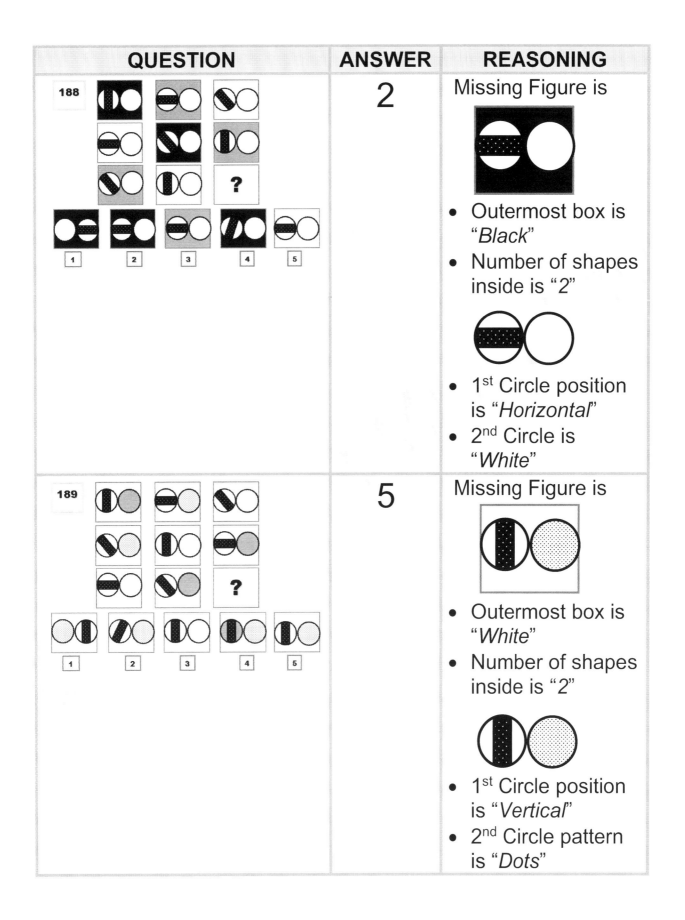 | 2 | Missing Figure is<br><br>• Outermost box is "*Black*"<br>• Number of shapes inside is "*2*"<br><br>• 1st Circle position is "*Horizontal*"<br>• 2nd Circle is "*White*" |
| | 5 | Missing Figure is<br><br>• Outermost box is "*White*"<br>• Number of shapes inside is "*2*"<br><br>• 1st Circle position is "*Vertical*"<br>• 2nd Circle pattern is "*Dots*" |

272

| QUESTION | ANSWER | REASONING |
|---|---|---|
| 190 | 2 | Missing Figure is <br><br>• Droplet shape is "*Gray*"<br>• Droplet shape is pointing towards "*Top-Right corner*"<br>• Arrow is pointing towards "*Bottom-Right corner*" |
| 191 | 5 | Missing Figure is <br><br>• Droplet shape is "*Black*"<br>• Droplet shape is "*Pointing* towards *Top-Right corner*"<br>• Arrow is "*Pointing towards Bottom-Right corner*" |

273

| QUESTION | ANSWER | REASONING |
|---|---|---|

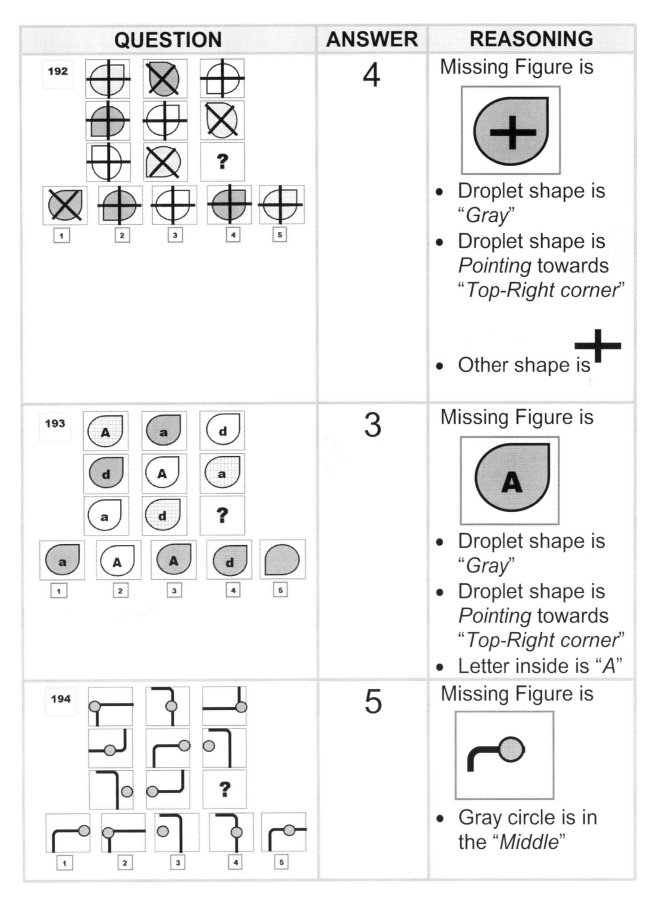

**192** — Answer: **4**

Missing Figure is

- Droplet shape is "*Gray*"
- Droplet shape is *Pointing* towards "*Top-Right corner*"
- Other shape is

**193** — Answer: **3**

Missing Figure is

- Droplet shape is "*Gray*"
- Droplet shape is *Pointing* towards "*Top-Right corner*"
- Letter inside is "*A*"

**194** — Answer: **5**

Missing Figure is

- Gray circle is in the "*Middle*"

| QUESTION | ANSWER | REASONING |
|---|---|---|
| | | • Is the other shape |
| 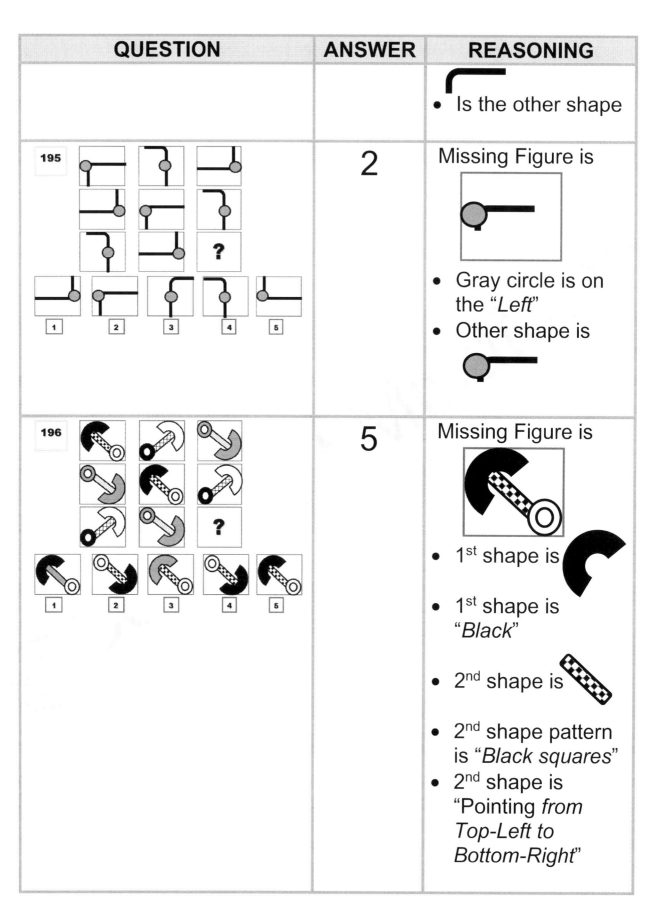 | 2 | Missing Figure is<br><br>• Gray circle is on the "*Left*"<br>• Other shape is |
| | 5 | Missing Figure is<br><br>• 1st shape is<br><br>• 1st shape is "*Black*"<br><br>• 2nd shape is<br><br>• 2nd shape pattern is "*Black squares*"<br>• 2nd shape is "Pointing *from Top-Left to Bottom-Right*" |

275

| QUESTION | ANSWER | REASONING |
|---|---|---|
| | | • 3rd shape is ◎<br>• 3rd shape is "*White*" |
| 197 | 2 | • Missing Figure is<br><br>• 1st shape is<br>• 1st shape is "White"<br>• 2nd shape is<br>• 2nd shape pattern is "*Grid lines*"<br>• 2nd shape is "*Pointing from Bottom-Left to Top-Right*"<br>• 3rd shape is ●<br>• 3rd shape is "*Black*" |

| QUESTION | ANSWER | REASONING |
|---|---|---|
| 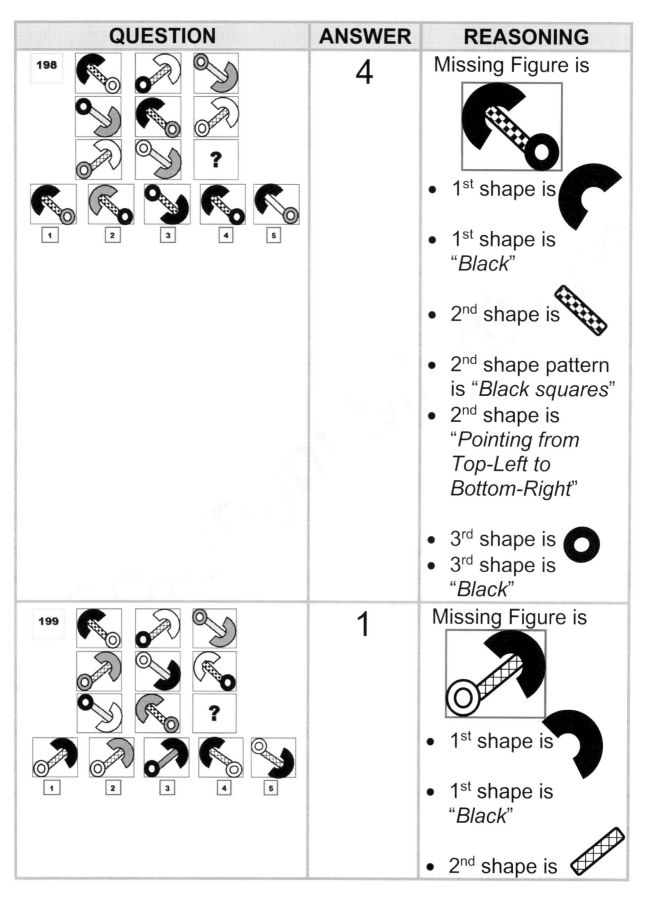 | 4 | Missing Figure is<br><br>• 1st shape is<br><br>• 1st shape is "*Black*"<br><br>• 2nd shape is<br><br>• 2nd shape pattern is "*Black squares*"<br>• 2nd shape is "*Pointing from Top-Left to Bottom-Right*"<br><br>• 3rd shape is<br>• 3rd shape is "*Black*" |
| | 1 | Missing Figure is<br><br>• 1st shape is<br><br>• 1st shape is "*Black*"<br><br>• 2nd shape is |

277

| QUESTION | ANSWER | REASONING |
|---|---|---|
| | | - 2nd shape pattern is "*Grid lines*" <br> - 2nd shape is "*Pointing from Bottom-Left to Top-Right*" <br><br> - 3rd shape is ◎ <br> - 3rd shape is "*White*" |
| **200** | 3 | Missing Figure is <br><br> - Number of cubes is "*3*" <br> - Cubes are stacked in the "*Middle*" |
| **201** | 2 | Missing Figure is <br><br> - Number of Rectangle boxes is "*2*" <br> - Rectangle boxes are "*Black and Gray*" |

| QUESTION | ANSWER | REASONING |
|---|---|---|
| **202** | 4 | Missing Figure is <br> • Number of Rectangle boxes is "*3*" <br> • Rectangle boxes are "*Black and Gray*" |
| **203** | 1 | Missing Figure is <br> • Number of rows is "*3*" <br> • Number of cubes are "*6*" <br> • Cubes pattern is "*Dotted*" |
| **204** | 1 | Missing Figure is <br> • Number of rows is "*2*" <br> • Number of cubes is "*3*" <br> • Cubes are "*White*" |

279

| QUESTION | ANSWER | REASONING |
|----------|--------|-----------|
| **205** | 4 | Missing Figure is <br>• Number of rows is "*3*"<br>• Number of cubes is "*6*"<br>• Cubes are "*Gray*" |
| **206** | 5 | Missing Figure is <br>• Number of rows is "*2*"<br>• Number of cubes is "*3*"<br>• Cubes are "*Gray*" |
| **207** | 2 | Missing Figure is <br>• Square box is "*Gray*"<br>• Dotted line is on the "*Left*"<br>• White Rectangle is on the "*Bottom*" |

| QUESTION | ANSWER | REASONING |
|---|---|---|
| **208** | 1 | Missing Figure is <br><br>• Square box is "*Gray*"<br>• Dotted line is on the "*Left*"<br>• White Rectangle is on the "*Bottom*" |
| **209** | 4 | Missing Figure is <br><br>• Square box is "*Gray*"<br>• Dotted line is on the "*Left*"<br>• White Rectangle is in the "*Middle*" |
| **210** | 5 | Missing Figure is <br><br>• Square box is "*Gray*"<br>• Dotted line is on the "*Right*"<br>• White Rectangle is in the "*Middle*" |

281

| QUESTION | ANSWER | REASONING |
|---|---|---|
| 211 | 3 | Missing Figure is<br><br>Number of squares is "6"<br>Squares are "Black" |
| 212 | 5 | Missing Figure is<br><br>Number of squares is "3"<br>Squares are "Gray"<br>Squares are "Positioned from Top-Left to Bottom-Right corner" |
| 213 | 2 | Missing Figure is<br><br>Number of squares is "3"<br>Squares are "Black" |

| QUESTION | ANSWER | REASONING |
|---|---|---|
| | | • Squares are "Positioned *from Top-Left to Bottom-Right corner*" |
| **214** | 2 | Missing Figure is <br> • Number of shapes is "*6*" <br> • Shapes are "*Gray*" |
| **215** | 5 | Missing Shape is <br> • Color is "*White*" <br> • Size is "*Small*" |
| **216** | 4 | Missing Shape is <br> • Color is "*Gray*" <br> • Size is "*Medium*" |

283

| QUESTION | ANSWER | REASONING |
|---|---|---|
| **217** | 3 | Missing Shape is <br> • Color is "*Black*" <br> • Size is "*Big*" <br> • Triangle is "*Pointing towards Right*" |
| **218** | 5 | Missing Shape is <br> • Color is "*Gray*" <br> • Size is "*Small*" <br> • Triangle is "*Pointing towards Left*" |
| **219** | 2 | Missing Shape is <br> • Color is "*Black*" <br> • Size is "*Big*" <br> • Triangle is "*Pointing Right*" |

284

| QUESTION | ANSWER | REASONING |
|----------|--------|-----------|
| **220** | 1 | Missing Shape is <br>• Color is "*Gray*" <br>• Size is "*Small*" <br>• Triangle is "*Pointing Down*" |
| **221** | 3 | Missing Figure is <br>• Order of shapes Left to Right is: "*Gray Circle, White rectangle, Gray Trapezoid*" |
| **222** | 5 | Missing Figure is <br>• Order of shapes Left to Right is: "*White Rectangle, Gray Trapezoid, Gray Circle*" |
| **223** | 1 | Missing Figure is <br>• Order of shapes from Top to Bottom is: |

285

| QUESTION | ANSWER | REASONING |
|---|---|---|
| | | *"Gray Circle, White Rectangle, Gray Trapezoid"* |
| **224** | 3 | Missing Figure is  • Order of shapes from Top to Bottom is: *"White Rectangle, Gray Trapezoid, Gray Circle"* |
| **225** | 5 | Missing Figure is  Cube is white  Is on the "*Right*"  Is on the "*Top*" |

| QUESTION | ANSWER | REASONING |
|---|---|---|
| 226 | 1 | Missing Figure is Is on the "*right*" Is on the "*front*" |
| 227 | 5 | Missing Figure is Outside box is "*Gray*" Inside box is "*White*" Droplet is "*Pointing towards Top-Right corner*" Droplet is *Black*. |
| 228 | 2 | Missing Figure is • Outside box is "*Black*" • Inside box is "*White*" |

| QUESTION | ANSWER | REASONING |
|---|---|---|
| | | • Droplet is "*Pointing towards Bottom-Right corner*" |
| | | • Droplet is "*Black*" |
| **229** | 4 | Missing Figure is<br><br>• Outside box is "*Black*"<br>• Inside box pattern is "*Grid lines*"<br>• Droplet is "*Pointing towards Bottom-Right corner*"<br>  • Droplet is "*Black*" |
| **230** | 5 | Missing Figure is<br><br>• Outside box is "*Black*"<br>• Inside box is "*White*"<br>• Droplet is "*Pointing towards Top-Right corner*" |

| QUESTION | ANSWER | REASONING |
|---|---|---|
| | | • Droplet is "*Gray*" |
| 231 | 3 | Missing Figure is • Black Circle is on the "*Bottom-Left Corner*" • Rectangular prism is placed "*Vertically*" • Rectangular prism Pattern is "*Vertical lines*" Note: Answer choice 4 is incorrect. Pattern is incorrect |
| 232 | 5 | Missing Figure is • Black Circle is on the "*Top-Left Corner*" • Rectangular prism is placed "*Horizontally*" • Rectangular prism Pattern is "*Vertical lines*" |

289

| QUESTION | ANSWER | REASONING |
|----------|--------|-----------|
| | | Note: Answer choice 4 is incorrect. Prism is upside down. |
| | 3 | Missing Figure is <br><br>• Black Circle is on the "*Top-Left Corner*"<br>• Rectangular prism is placed "*Vertically*"<br>• Rectangular prism Pattern is "*Vertical lines*"<br><br>Note: Answer choice 1 is incorrect. Prism is upside down. |
| | 2 | Missing Figure is <br><br>• Black Circle is on the "*Bottom-Left Corner*"<br>• Rectangular prism is placed "*Horizontally*" |

| QUESTION | ANSWER | REASONING |
|---|---|---|
| | | • Rectangular prism Pattern is "*Vertical lines*"<br><br>Note: Answer choice 1 is incorrect. Prism is upside down. Pattern is incorrect in answer choice 3. |
| 235 | 4 | Missing Figure is<br><br>• SIZE is "*Small*"<br>• NUMBER is "*1*" |
| 236 | 3 | Missing Figure is<br><br>• SIZE is "*Big*"<br>• NUMBER is "*7*" |
| 237 | 2 | Missing Figure is<br><br>• SIZE is "*Small*"<br>• Number is "*7*" |

| QUESTION | ANSWER | REASONING |
|---|---|---|
| **238** | 5 | Missing Figure is <br>• Number of Hexagons is "*1*"<br>• Hexagon is "*Gray*" |
| **239** | 4 | Missing Figure is <br>• Number of Hexagons is "*2*"<br>• Big Hexagon is "*White*"<br>• Small Hexagon is "*Black*"<br>• Small Hexagon is on the "*Left side*" |
| **240** | 1 | Missing Figure is <br>• Number of Hexagons is "*1*"<br>• Hexagon is "*White*" |

| QUESTION | ANSWER | REASONING |
|---|---|---|
| **241** | 3 | Missing Figure is <br><br> • Number of Hexagons is "2" <br> • Big Hexagon is "Gray" <br> • Small Hexagon is "Black" |
| **242** | 4 | Missing Figure is |
| **243** | 5 | Missing Figure is |

293

| QUESTION | ANSWER | REASONING |
|---|---|---|
| **244** | 1 | Missing Figure is <br> • SIZE is "*Big*" <br> • Number is "*1*" |
| **245** | 1 | Missing Figure is <br> • Shape is "*Black*" <br> • Top arrow is "*Pointing towards Right*" |
| **246** | 3 | Missing Figure is <br> • Circles are decreasing by "*2*" <br> Note: Option 5 is incorrect, circles are on the top. <br> Option 5 is incorrect, Colors are not matching with first picture |

294

| QUESTION | ANSWER | REASONING |
|---|---|---|
| **247** 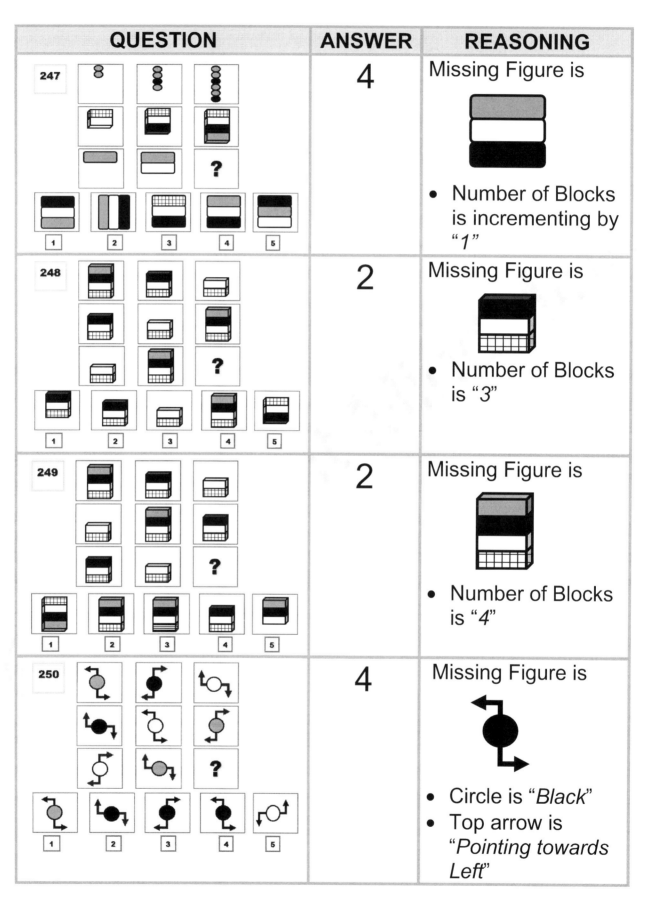 | 4 | Missing Figure is<br><br>• Number of Blocks is incrementing by "1" |
| **248** | 2 | Missing Figure is<br><br>• Number of Blocks is "3" |
| **249** | 2 | Missing Figure is<br><br>• Number of Blocks is "4" |
| **250** | 4 | Missing Figure is<br><br>• Circle is "Black"<br>• Top arrow is "Pointing towards Left" |

# ANSWERS

# to

# Practice

# Tests

# PRACTICE TEST-1

| QUESTION | ANSWER | REASONING |
|---|---|---|
| **1** | 2 | Missing Shape is <br>• Color is "*White*" |
| **2** | 1 | Missing Shape is <br>• Color is "Black" <br>• Size is "Big" |
| **3** | 3 | Missing Figure is <br>• Black Stripe is "Horizontal" <br>• Black Stripe is "in the back" |

| QUESTION | ANSWER | REASONING |
|---|---|---|
| 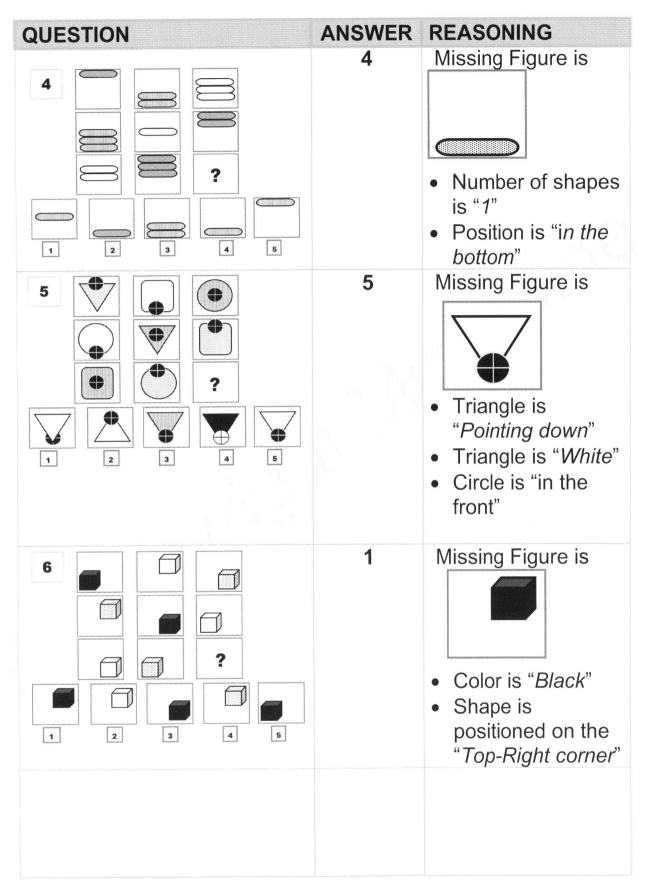 | 4 | Missing Figure is<br><br>• Number of shapes is "*1*"<br>• Position is "*in the bottom*" |
| | 5 | Missing Figure is<br><br>• Triangle is "*Pointing down*"<br>• Triangle is "*White*"<br>• Circle is "in the front" |
| | 1 | Missing Figure is<br><br>• Color is "*Black*"<br>• Shape is positioned on the "*Top-Right corner*" |

298

| QUESTION | ANSWER | REASONING |
|---|---|---|
| 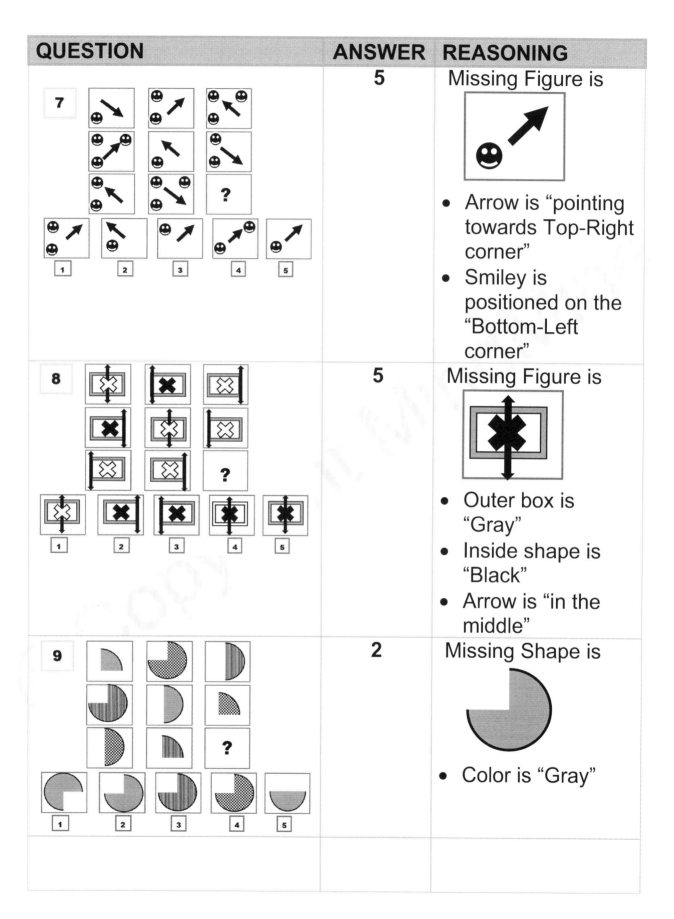 | 5 | Missing Figure is<br><br>• Arrow is "pointing towards Top-Right corner"<br>• Smiley is positioned on the "Bottom-Left corner" |
| | 5 | Missing Figure is<br><br>• Outer box is "Gray"<br>• Inside shape is "Black"<br>• Arrow is "in the middle" |
| | 2 | Missing Shape is<br><br>• Color is "Gray" |

299

| QUESTION | ANSWER | REASONING |
|---|---|---|
| **10** | 3 | Missing Figure is <br><br>• Number of shapes is "1"<br>• Color is "Gray" |
| **11** | 4 | Missing Figure is <br><br>• Outside shape size is "Big"<br>• Outside shape is "Gray"<br>• Inside shape is positioned on the "Top-Right corner" |
| **12** | 5 | Missing Figure is <br><br>• Number of shapes in the column is "2"<br>• Color is "Black" |

300

| QUESTION | ANSWER | REASONING |
|---|---|---|
| | | • Shapes are positioned on the "Left side" |
| **13** | 3 | Missing Figure is <br> • First shape is of size "Small" <br> • Arrow is of size "Small" <br> • Arrow is "Black" |
| **14** | 3 | Missing Figure is <br> • Number of shapes is "1" |
| **15** | 4 | Missing Figure is <br> • Number of horizontal lines is "2" <br> • Lines are in the "Back" |

| QUESTION | ANSWER | REASONING |
|---|---|---|
|  |  | • Number of vertical columns is "2" <br> • Vertical columns are "Gray" |

# PRACTICE TEST-2

| QUESTION | ANSWER | REASONING |
|---|---|---|
| **1** | 5 | Missing Figure is <br>• Outside shape is "Gray"<br>• Inside shape is <br>• Inside shape pattern is "Dots" |
| **2** | 1 | Missing Figure is <br>• Pattern is "*Dots*"<br>• Size is "*Big*"<br>• Letter inside is "A" |
| **3** | 5 | Missing Figure is <br>• Color is "*Gray*"<br>• Arrow is pointing "Up" |

| QUESTION | ANSWER | REASONING |
|---|---|---|

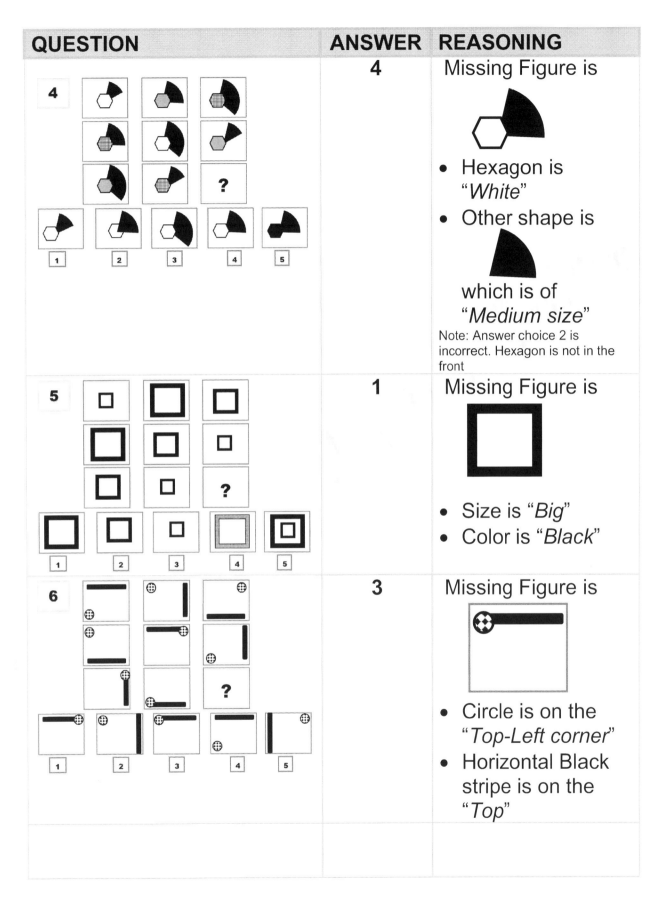

**4**

Missing Figure is

- Hexagon is "*White*"
- Other shape is

which is of "*Medium size*"

Note: Answer choice 2 is incorrect. Hexagon is not in the front

**1**

Missing Figure is

- Size is "*Big*"
- Color is "*Black*"

**3**

Missing Figure is

- Circle is on the "*Top-Left corner*"
- Horizontal Black stripe is on the "*Top*"

| QUESTION | ANSWER | REASONING |
|---|---|---|

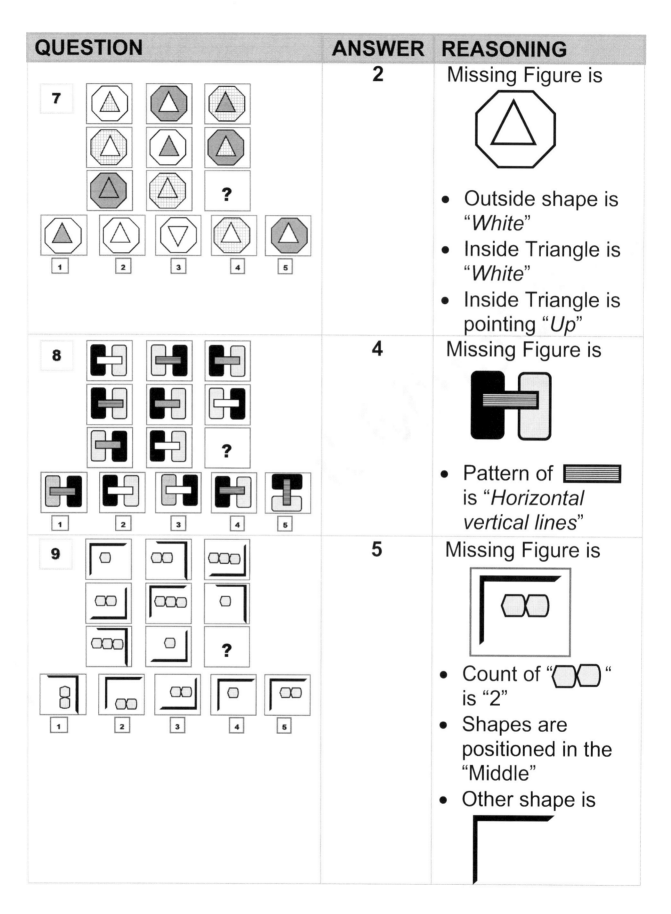

| | ANSWER | REASONING |
|---|---|---|
| 7 | 2 | Missing Figure is<br><br>• Outside shape is "*White*"<br>• Inside Triangle is "*White*"<br>• Inside Triangle is pointing "*Up*" |
| 8 | 4 | Missing Figure is<br><br>• Pattern of ▦ is "*Horizontal vertical lines*" |
| 9 | 5 | Missing Figure is<br><br>• Count of "⬡⬡" is "2"<br>• Shapes are positioned in the "Middle"<br>• Other shape is |

305

| QUESTION | ANSWER | REASONING |
|---|---|---|
| | | • Other shape is positioned on the "*Top-Left Corner*" |
| **10** | 4 | Missing Figure is • Count of Rectangles is "*1*" • Rectangle is "*Black*" |
| **11** | 3 | Missing Figure is • Size is "*Big*" • Shape is on the "*Top-Right corner*" |
| **12** | 3 | Missing Figure is • Shape is "Hexagon" • Color is "*White*" • Inside number is "*7*" |

306

| QUESTION | ANSWER | REASONING |
|---|---|---|
| 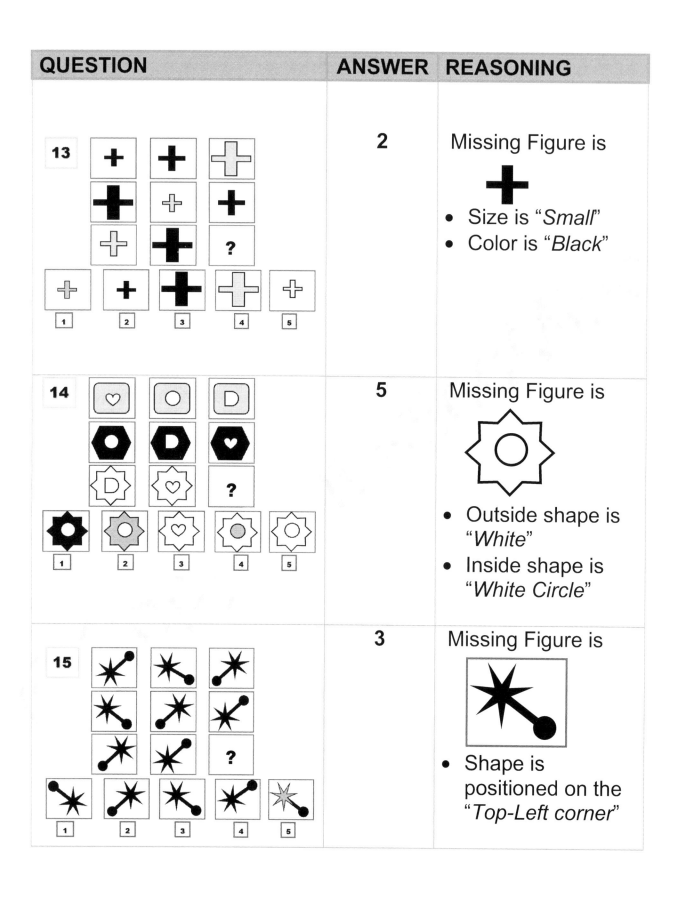 | 2 | Missing Figure is ➕ • Size is "*Small*" • Color is "*Black*" |
| | 5 | Missing Figure is • Outside shape is "*White*" • Inside shape is "*White Circle*" |
| | 3 | Missing Figure is • Shape is positioned on the "*Top-Left corner*" |

307

# Other ways to use this book

## 15 Mini Practice Tests

Questions are organized by each individual concept. Picking 15 questions randomly and solving them out of order serve as a mini practice test. **About 15 mini practice tests** can be generated.

## 500 Additional Questions

- After solving each question, Write down the answer in the box with **"?"**.

- Now cover first box on first row and solve question. This will generate 200 additional questions.

- Now cover 2nd box on first row and solve question. This will generate 200 additional questions.

- Now cover First box on 2nd row and solve question. This will generate 200 additional questions.

- Now cover 2nd box on 2nd row and solve question. This will generate 200 additional questions.

Note: Additional questions Do Not have answer choices.

89

118

154

220

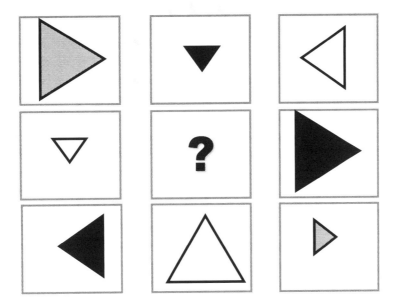

# Additional Help

Have a question? You can reach author directly at
**mindmineauthor@gmail.com**

Made in the USA
Monee, IL
02 May 2023

32833110R00175